# CHINA THREAT?

# CHINA THREAT?

## The Challenges, Myths, and Realities of China's Rise

**Lionel Vairon**

CN Times Books, Inc.
501 Fifth Avenue
New York, NY 10017
cntimesbooks.com

Ordering Information: Quantity sales. Special discounts are available on quantity purchases by corporations, associations, and others. For details, contact the publisher at the address above. Orders by US trade bookstores and wholesalers. Please contact Ingram Publisher Services: Tel: (866) 400-5351; Fax: (800) 838-1149; or customer.service@ingrampublisherservices.com.

| Translators: | Kenneth Barger |
| | Daniela Ginsburg |
| Copy Editors: | Judith Robey |
| | Joanne Gerber |
| Proofreader: | Carolyn Wendt |

Design and Composition: IGS

Printed in the United States of America

ISBN: 978-162774-089-0

# CONTENTS

# CHINA'S RISE: CHALLENGES, MYTHS, AND REALITIES

## INTRODUCTION

The May 2008 Sichuan earthquake, with its toll of over 80,000 dead and over 15 million displaced, could be "karma"—and well deserved—for crimes allegedly committed by the Chinese against the Tibetans. This parallel statement by American actress Sharon Stone, made at the Cannes International Film Festival in France that same month, illustrates perfectly the level of insensitivity, propaganda, and growing, gratuitous hostility that characterized the attitude of some of the Western public in the face of the successes achieved by the Chinese and their leaders after 30 years of hard work. The year 2008 marked the beginning of a new era in international relations. China's hosting of the Olympic Games in Beijing was the culmination of an intense anti-Chinese campaign that began in January 2005 with the expiration of textile quotas. Western media and politicians had seized upon what was portrayed as a major threat to many economies of developed and developing countries alike. Over the course of the year preceding the Olympics, one issue after another came up: charges of complicity in genocide due to China's relations with Sudan; daily reports in mid-2007 questioning the quality of Chinese products, especially toys; virulent denunciations of Chinese policy in Myanmar; persistent criticism of China's environmental policies; the European Union's April 2008 resolution to condemn China's foreign policy in Africa; and last but not least, the denunciation of Chinese policy toward minorities after the events in Tibet.

The campaign of denigration that China has faced, in our view, has ushered in a new era in contemporary international relations, although few observers, let alone the general public, have fully appreciated this change in attitude. The late French author Jean-François Revel, a supporter of liberalism and an unconditional admirer of the United States, said in his 2002 book, *Anti-Americanism*:

> *The European Right's anti-Americanism stems fundamentally from our continent's loss, during the twentieth century, of its six-hundred-year leadership role. Europe had been the powerhouse of enterprise and industry, innovator in arts and sciences, maker of empires—in practical terms, master of the planet. It was sometimes one European country, sometimes another, that took the lead in this process of globalization* avant la lettre, *but all more or less*

*participated, either in concert or by turns. Today, by contrast, not only has*
*Europe lost the ability to act alone on a global scale, but it is compelled in*
*some degree to follow in the footsteps of the United States and lend support.*[1]

Paradoxically, the anti-Chinese frenzy that gripped Western media and politicians at the time, in anticipation of the Olympic Games in Beijing, seems to
mark the beginning of a new era of Chinese emergence that follows to some
extent the lines of what Revel describes. This exploitation of the visible manifestations of Chinese power achieved its aim, first planting a seed of doubt
in public opinion regarding the true designs of Chinese leaders behind their
usually appeasing discourse before the international community, then transforming that doubt into a growing conviction that behind this façade of cooperation lurked solid hegemonic ambitions. In the United States, this approach
was well received in the most conservative, militaristic, and hawkish quarters.
In Europe, feelings were more mixed. After all, in the 20th century, to their
dismay, Europeans had seen their influence slip into American hands in the
wake of two world wars, the price of having succumbed to their own nationalist demons. The two world wars, apocalyptic events for Europe, had allowed
for the rise of a major player, albeit one that was European in its origins despite
being geographically non-European. Although the birth of this new world-
geopolitics was painful, at the beginning of the 21st century—with the proliferation in Europe of pro-American regimes (Nicolas Sarkozy's France, Silvio
Berlusconi's Italy, Václav Havel's Czech Republic, Angela Merkel's Germany,
and of course Great Britain, a staunch ally of the United States since 1945[2]),
France's return to NATO, and the pro–United States leanings of many new
states joining the European Union—the United States seems to be poised to
win a definitive victory within the Western camp. This was notwithstanding
some fierce resistance on the part of public opinion, however steeped in American cinema and anesthetized by the media's lenient treatment of American
transgressions it might have been. This persistent resistance on the part of some
sectors of European public opinion, intellectuals, and politicians has stood in
the way of America's complete domination. China's newfound power is a welcome rallying cry for the worn concept of the West.

The Olympic Games provided an excellent opportunity for forcing Chinese
leaders to make concessions, on threat of boycott, and for denouncing what
was framed as excessive spending meant to impress, or better yet intimidate,
the rest of the international community.[3] The objective, which was perhaps at
times unconscious, was to remind China—with its stunning growth rate in

---

[1] Jean-François Revel, *Anti-Americanism*, trans. Diarmid Cammell (Encounter Books, 2003), 4.
[2] In 1944, British Prime Minister Winston Churchill told General de Gaulle, "How can you ask us, the British, to take a
position separate from that of the United States?… Whenever we must decide between Europe and the open sea, it is always
the open sea that we shall choose. Every time I have to decide between you and Roosevelt, I shall always choose Roosevelt!"
Charles de Gaulle, *Memoires de Guerre, L'Unite*, Paris, Librairie Plon, 1956, 224.
[3] "The List: Five Ways Beijing Will Be the Biggest, Baddest Olympics Ever," *Foreign Policy*, July 26, 2008, http://www
.foreignpolicy.com/articles/2008/07/25/the_list_five_ways_beijing_will_be_the_biggest_baddest_olympics_ever.

light of the recession looming on the horizon in the United States (and therefore also in Europe—that its insolent good economic health would not get it
into the big league, that it was not up to withstanding Western pressures, and
that at the end of the day, the 19th century was not over yet. "Universal" values
were still Western values, and they could still be imposed on the entire planet.
In order to mount a continuous campaign against China, any excuse would
do. No smear was spared, from "China's genocide Games"[4] to remarks from
a CNN commentator referring to Chinese leaders as a "bunch of goons and
thugs,"[5] not to mention Franco-German Member of the European Parliament
Daniel Cohn-Bendit's comparison of the Games to the 1936 Berlin Olympics,
hosted by the Nazi regime.[6] In Europe, this kind of remark made against, for
instance, Jewish people or Israeli leaders would have led to criminal prosecu-
tions and convictions for "incitement to racial hatred." In China, no television
commentator would be authorized, even in the most virulent critiques, to use
this sort of racist language in reference to leaders from, say, the United States,
no matter how dishonorable some of the members of the George W. Bush
administration, in power at the time, might have been. Why was this language
tolerated by the powers that be and public opinion? Why were such expressions
of hatred and contempt directed at a country that never ceased to sing the virtues of a "harmonious international society" and the need for mutual respect,
the need for better distribution of world wealth, and the need to strengthen
aid to developing countries whose populations were at risk? The goal of this
book is to bring into view both the abstract causes—perceptions—and the
concrete motivations of this virulent campaign, and explain its underlying reasons, based on different aspects of current Chinese geopolitics, so that the
reader, armed with a better understanding of the forces behind these attacks,
may wisely, calmly, and patiently assess the fits and starts of a rapidly changing
world, based on an order—or disorder—created in the wake of World War II
and now obsolete.

Indeed, with the end of the Cold War and the dissolution of the Soviet
Union in December 1991, liberal democracies found themselves suddenly
thrust into a "world without meaning."[7] From 1945 on, the Soviet Union and
the socialist bloc had allowed liberal democracies to construct a positive identity, to give "meaning" to their struggle against autocratic or tyrannical Marxist-Leninist regimes. The constant evocation of this threat, real or supposed,
as the case may be, allowed the camouflaging or justification of actions often
more driven by economic greed than by real democratic ambitions in the face
of a socialist world portrayed as the very incarnation of evil. The disappearance

---

[4]Eric Reeves, "China's Genocide Games," *Boston Globe*, March 22, 2008.
[5]Remarks from Jack Cafferty made April 9, 2008, on CNN, where he referred to Chinese leaders as "a bunch of goons and thugs."
[6]"Cohn-Bendit fait le parallèle avec l'Allemagne de 1936," AFP, August 8, 2008.
[7]Zaki Laïdi, *A World Without Meaning: The Crisis of Meaning in International Politics*, trans. June Burnham and Jenny Coulon (London: Routledge, 1998).

of the Soviet threat in 1991 left a gaping ideological chasm that necessitated a profound rethinking of the foundations on which liberal societies were built. The world seemed to be approaching the "end of history"[8]—the definitive advent of a sole model for society, liberal democracy—and the prospect was deeply terrifying.

This search for meaning had come to naught until recently, notwithstanding Washington's efforts to make the phenomenon of Islamist terrorism—quite probably a fleeting one on a historical scale—into the object of this quest for a credible, long-term adversary. The fluidity of terrorist movements, which were usually transnational; their intangibility despite their use of violence; and the denunciation of the methods used to combat them (the prisons at Guantanamo or Abu Ghraib in Iraq and the use of legalized torture are particularly striking examples, running counter to the very principles on which the Western alliance has officially been founded for a half-century: democracy, transparency, and respect for civil liberties[9])—all have seriously compromised the credibility of American policy and led Washington to look for a new target.

The best choice, of course, to fulfill this role of potential bad guy, as had already been anticipated in George W. Bush's presidential campaign in 1999, was an actor who could evoke all of American society's bogeymen: an atheist regime controlled by a Communist party that authorized or encouraged abortion[10] and had enough power at its disposal to look like a credible, long-term threat. This perception allowed an American administration to strengthen an already-extravagant military program—despite the fact that the preference for a buildup of nuclear firepower would be useless in any Iraqi-style intervention (in this light, Cuba, Vietnam, or North Korea would not have made a good adversary). It was a matter not only of finding a credible enemy, but, above all, of finding an enemy whose likely longevity—notwithstanding some doomsday analyses—justified a hegemonic global policy for America based upon tightening transatlantic ties around its leadership, constantly increasing defense spending, and engaging in a moralistic discourse on human rights that allowed the United States to conceal its own failings, practices, and dominant economic interests. The current and potential economic power of China furthermore arouses latent fears in Western public opinion. This adversary must also stoke, by its religious differences, a theological and messianic discourse

---

[8] Francis Fukuyama, *The End of History and the Last Man* (Free Press, 1992). The fact that his predictions were shown to be totally erroneous in no way kept the author from pursuing these analyses and predicting the imminent explosion of China ("Francis Fukuyama: *quand la Chine explosera …*," interview quoted by the AFP, October 13, 2012).

[9] The Guantanamo prison camp, for instance, has allowed the United States to hold hundreds of prisoners totally arbitrarily, without due process or legal rights. The American practice of scattering prisoners accused of terrorism or complicity with terrorist organizations across the globe in order to allow for the use of interrogation techniques condemned on American soil led to criticism of the unacceptable practices of the Bush administration in 2005.

[10] "China's government is an enemy of religious freedom and a sponsor of forced abortion—policies without reason and without mercy." Speech by George W. Bush, November 19, 1999. https://www.mtholyoke.edu/acad/intrel/bush/wspeech.htm.

determined to put this world of sinners back on the right track, the road mapped out by voluntarism and American determination.[11]

Only one country in the international community was wonderfully, almost miraculously, qualified to play this role: China. Communist China, reviled as an atheist autocracy, would finally give new meaning to a Western bloc whose cohesion had seriously eroded in the absence of a shared goal under the domination of economic considerations over increasingly amorphous societies eagerly seeking a new faith (existing religions, millenarian sects, rampant consumerism, racism, etc.). The politicians in these societies seemed more and more helpless to open new horizons or to find solutions to ever-increasing economic and social challenges (unemployment, an aging population, industrial shifts, etc.) that cried out for profound transformations. The role that China would be definitively assigned, then, would be that of a *scapegoat*.

In recent years, an atmosphere of suspicion and denunciation of China's intentions has settled insidiously over the West, but particularly in the United States and France. To illustrate the situation in China, we heard again and again an alphabet soup of truncated news: half-truths about illegal organ transplants, convicts sentenced to death whose families were billed for the price of the bullet, deplorable working conditions for Chinese workers forced to work 15 hours a day, the ravages of unemployment on laid-off state workers, corruption of local officials, and the size of the Chinese military budget, a sure sign of a hidden agenda. The extrapolation of specific cases was held up as "analysis."

From the long-term threat of nuclear war between the United States and China to the disappearance of the African elephant due to Chinese demand for ivory, each week brings a new round of critique and denunciation of the risks this nascent superpower poses to the stability of the entire planet. Bookstores are filled with more and more evocative titles, from Richard Bernstein and Ross H. Munro's famous *The Coming Conflict with China*, published in 1998, to French journalist Philippe Cohen's more recent *La Chine sera-t-elle notre cauchemar?*, cowritten with Luc Richard; not to mention *La Chine en folie: l'heritage de Deng Xiaoping* by French AFP journalist Philippe Massonnet.

With the textile crisis of 2005, predictable though it was, the inevitable impact of China's economic rise on the world economy—in developed countries saddled with growing deficits as well as in developing countries whose economies are not complementary to, but competitive with, the Chinese economy—had stoked the fires of this atmosphere, which had now morphed into a campaign.

It should be noted that all these authors address a certain number of real issues facing China today, whether they concern unemployment or human rights, the weakness of the judicial system or corruption. These authors like-

---

[11]"The only way to protect our people, the only way to secure the peace, the only way to control our destiny is by our leadership. So the United States of America will continue to lead." President George W. Bush, State of the Union Address, January 2006.

wise raise a certain number of fundamental questions that bear asking (e.g., whether China seeks to modernize its military or pursue long-term strategic ambitions). But the answers we get are usually based on ideological considerations (the fact that the regime is communist) or on a view of international relations influenced by the American lens (the importance of economic and social liberalism, promotion—at least in form—of parliamentary democracy, overemphasis of human rights criteria as the basis of a determent strategy, etc.).

China boasts considerable assets that allow it to look to the future with some degree of confidence, but some of its weaknesses are just as considerable and may well compromise its success in the long term. Contrary to the claims of a growing number of Western analysts and media, China cannot represent a threat, even in the long term, for lack of one key asset controlled today and for the foreseeable future by the United States: mastery of the imagination. The uncontested domination, or supremacy in terms of worldwide distribution, of American film, of the imaginary lifestyle promoted by Hollywood, of the power attributed to the United States (as seen in high-tech war films), holds sway over the world's imagination, particularly among young people. Even if these very images also provoke violent reactions of rejection (the September 11 terrorists drank Coca-Cola and many of them were alumni of Western institutions of higher learning), America's superiority in promoting its image represents a firm down payment on economic and military superiority. Moreover, leaders and public opinion do not usually recognize the power of these images and offer no resistance to them. And so it is that Air China's long-haul flights often show only American films, whose hidden messages showcase American technological superiority, often to an exaggerated degree more resembling science fiction than American realities. China, for its part, does not yet have this ability to win over hearts and minds, and the campaigns waged against it go all out to prevent China's development and way of life from holding any attraction for Western public opinion or developing countries. When certain aspects of Chinese policy are tried in the court of public opinion, unilaterally and usually with great bias (its utterly negative effect on Africa, human rights violations portrayed as systematic, constant harping on the "Chinese military threat," etc.), the objective, conscious or not, is clearly to check China's growing influence over the international order. This is occurring precisely at a time when European public opinion is questioning more and more the meaning, not of globalization itself, but of overly liberal globalization that disregards human relationships and privileges individual excesses over the group; in developing countries public opinion has brought into question the relevance of a model portrayed since decolonization as superior and applicable to all in the same way: ultraliberalism.

What is doubtless most striking in today's context is Western public opinion's incapability of comparing what are portrayed as issues unique to China with what is happening in other regions of the world. It is clear that some of the attacks launched against China by certain Western leaders are meant to conceal their own current actions or distract from past transgressions. While some simplistically evoke the "cultural genocide" in Tibet, no one mentions in the same breath the forced exile from Iraq, since the American invasion, of Christians who have lived in those lands for two thousand years. Their disappearance was a direct result of radical Islamist movements as well as the policies of a government put in place by the American administration. Since 2003, dozens of civilians have been murdered daily, oftentimes by the US Army itself, which classifies these murders as "blunders," to the indifference of all. No angry demonstrations in front of American or Iraqi embassies, no media campaign demanding protection for the last survivors of this community. European governments, for their part, try to efface their mistakes, failures, and moral compromises in Africa by accusing China of not respecting the environment or workers' rights, and, still more astoundingly, of pillaging the continent's natural resources. This is how a short memory and misinformation allow European policy makers to turn public opinion against China and away from their own support of autocratic regimes—"the presidents for life"—whose main virtue lies in their having chosen—until now—to hand over part of their natural resources to European or American companies, or to systematically award public projects to them.

It was with an eye to understanding the motives behind this torrent of anti-Chinese sentiment that we felt it necessary to make an impartial assessment of the scope of the challenge that 21st-century China poses, not only to the international community, but also, or perhaps especially, to its own leaders. The economic rise of 20 percent of the world's population cannot occur without bumps in the road. Add to this the rise, albeit slower, of India, which represents another 17 percent of the world's population. This specter that haunts Western leaders cannot be banished with invective. We have entered a new historical period that will see a new balance in the relationships among the great civilizations, with China and India once again among the ranks of great nations that have something to say about the definition of the values and policies necessary to march down the road of peace and development. For hundreds of years, until the end of the 18th century, China's GDP surpassed that of Western European countries, and the Chinese saw the first mass industrial organization with the manufacture of porcelain starting in the 10th century. The industrial revolution in Europe set this situation on its ear. After over a century of stagnation, these ancient empires have begun to stir, and their potential is a source of anxiety. This introduction to China in the early 21st century raises the main issues facing the country today and, in light of the vastness of this field of research, deals with them in a non-exhaustive fashion.

## Chapter I

# *THE "CHINA THREAT": GENESIS OF A MYTH*

T he first 30 years of economic reforms in China have led to a totally unique situation in history, recognized even by the very international financial institutions least suspected of indulgence toward a country whose political regime they abhor. The pragmatic nature of the reforms, their micromanagement by central authorities, and their obvious determination not to be seduced by "models," but rather to progressively build a powerful economy on empirical foundations, were a far cry from the Western, liberal notion of the economic reforms indispensable for a country wishing to join the ranks of developed nations. Post-Soviet Russia, for its part, had placed its trust in the American "golden boys" who, after the dissolution of the USSR, rushed to Moscow to give the new Russian authorities lessons in liberal economics and assist in the process of transformation from a planned economy to an open one. The results were in quickly: ten years later, Russia was nearly bankrupt. The particular characteristics of Russian economics and society had been neglected, supposedly universal models had been applied, and Russia had lost its way.

Meanwhile, China, convinced of the value of experience, had opted to very progressively phase in certain principles of liberal economics, while at the same time carefully avoiding their brutal, careless implementation. And the formula had proven to work. Thirty years later, in 2012, China was the world's second economy in terms of GDP, with $8,250 billion, well ahead of Japan ($6,058 billion), and behind the United States ($15,653 billion).[1] During the first quarter of the decade of reforms, Americans and Europeans followed with interest this extraordinary economic growth, so promising in terms of markets for Western companies and investment funds. But the warm welcome based on hopes of economic and commercial expansion—China would finally begin to open its doors, in keeping with its progressive "Open Door Policy"—gradually gave way to growing concern over some of the unexpected effects of this growth. In economic terms, an excess of capital in China led the large Chinese companies, with the government's blessing, to turn around and invest abroad, first in the energy and natural resource sectors, and then more and more in a diverse range of industrial sectors, from information technology to appliances, from the auto industry to textiles, and especially in energy. The results of this strategy were soon shown to be rather encouraging. More and more each year, large Western companies faced their Chinese counterparts in traditionally captive markets, such as Africa for the Europeans or Latin America for the Americans, and these new competitors were winning a growing number of contracts.

Not satisfied with taking great bites from traditionally Western markets, China began to eye countries traditionally in the orbit of the West, including some developing countries that had undergone decades of liberal policies imposed and managed by the World Bank or the IMF, usually with devastating

---

[1] IMF, Data and Statistics, http://www.imf.org/external/pubs/ft/weo/2012/02/weodata/weoselgr.aspx.

results. These countries were now witnessing the rise of an atypical economy that was not based on models but was producing remarkable results. Considerable difficulties indeed arose over the years, but thus far, these had been overcome one by one with a pragmatic approach, and above all, without any interference from the West. The growing attraction of "Chinese-style" development came to represent a threat to Western powers that had ruled the world for nearly two centuries, handing out report cards to third-world states and leaders.

The first threat to appear to Western eyes was the prospect of what some term the emerging "Beijing consensus,"[2] which might take the place of the "Washington consensus" and thus deal a stiff blow to American global influence. This threat was all the more serious given that China's economic rise was taking place in a very different context from that of Japan a few decades prior. Indeed, the rise of Japan did not present a real global risk for Westerners for two main reasons. On the one hand, Tokyo showed no signs of political ambition or global diplomacy—its political alignment with the West was total and unconditional. On the other hand, and this point is naturally linked to the previous one, Japan completely lacked a national defense, its self-defense capabilities having been stripped to the bare minimum, and the United States took charge of the archipelago's defense. On several occasions Washington used its protection as leverage to make Japan accept American economic constraints. In 1997, for instance, during the Asian financial crisis, Japan, having considered aloud selling part of its reserves in dollars, was quickly put in its place by the American administration, which threatened to remove its defensive shield over Japan. The Japanese government did as it was told without further ado. Then, in September 1985, Tokyo was forced to accept the brutal devaluation of the dollar to the yen and the deutsche mark through the Plaza Accord, which led to a decadelong recession in Japan.[3] In the case of China, unlike that of Japan, it had become nearly impossible for Westerners to exert these kinds of pressures and force Chinese authorities to accept measures that went against their national interests (such as the sudden revaluation of the renminbi). Thanks to China's military modernization, which makes it indifferent to American military pressure; the influence its economy exerts over the world economy (with its GDP growth rate of 8.2 percent for 2013, according to IMF projections, China remains the engine for world growth, with India lagging behind at a projected 6 percent, and the United States at a mere 2 percent[4]); and its

---

[2] Joshua Cooper Ramo, *The Beijing Consensus: Notes on the New Physics of Chinese Power* (London: The Foreign Policy Centre, 2004); Stefan Halper, *The Beijing Consensus: How China's Authoritarian Model Will Dominate the Twenty-First Century* (Basic Books, NY, 2010).

[3] With the signing of the Plaza Accord on September 22, 1985, Japan agreed to the devaluation of the dollar, which reached 51 percent between 1985 and 1987 compared to the yen. American exports became more competitive, which lowered the American trade deficit with Europe, but not with Japan. This agreement led to a severe recession in Japan in the late 1980s.

[4] IMF, *World Economic Outlook*, October 2012.

growing influence in the management of major international crises (North Korea, the Iranian nuclear program, the situation in Darfur), China is up to the task of managing its emergence on its own as a future great power, although it of course behooves China to take into account the economic and political lay of the land elsewhere as well if it is to succeed in its development strategy.

This new set of circumstances—China's growing (national) world power (综合国力; *zōnghé guóli*)—was what led the West, particularly the United States, to take up again the concept, forgotten for some years, of a "Chinese threat," which had first come up in the context of Japan in the early 1980s. Indeed, while the disagreements caused by the growth of the Chinese economy still seem manageable by Westerners, notwithstanding the occasional conflict, if China continues on its present path of economic expansion, the emergence within a few decades of a non-Western major world power to contend with in foreign affairs, one that will be in a position to force Americans and Europeans to accept new rules not written by them, is disconcerting for all and unacceptable to most Western policy makers, and especially to Western public opinion. Since the early 19th century, a handful of Western powers (first Great Britain and France, and then the United States) have taken turns deciding the fate of the planet and have created a way of thinking about relationships among peoples heavily influenced (often unconsciously) by racist theories formulated by European minds (such as Arthur de Gobineau or Houston Chamberlain) and founded on the notion of the existence of a superior race. It must be noted that some voices in Europe denounced these theories,[5] but colonization and its attendant confrontation with peoples of different colors, religions, and customs helped cement the idea in Western minds of these different cultures' natural inferiority. Despite decolonization and the subsequent awareness of the absurdity of these racist theories, this feeling of superiority left its mark in the Western consciousness, which often sought confirmation in the world's varying degrees of economic or political development. And so it is that many Westerners cannot distinguish "development" from "civilization," as we witnessed in the images of young American soldiers, hopped-up on Coca-Cola and video games, landing in Iraq, convinced that they were bringing "civilization" to a land that had witnessed the birth of the Abrahamic religions and of history itself.

In the face of an independent and ever-more-self-assured China, Westerners are increasingly frustrated, due to several factors. Foremost among these is

---

[5]"Superior races! Inferior races! It is easy enough to say! For my part, I am not so proud since I saw German scholars demonstrate scientifically that France must be defeated in the Franco-German War because the French were a race inferior to the Germans. Ever since, I must confess, I take a second look before I look at a man or a civilization and utter, 'inferior man or civilization!'... Look at the history of the conquest of the peoples you call barbarians, and you will see violence, the most heinous crimes, oppression, rivers of blood, the weak oppressed, tyrannized by the victor! Here is the history of your civilization! ... How many abominable, atrocious crimes have been committed in the name of justice and civilization. To say nothing of the vices the European brings with him: alcohol, the opium he spreads about, or imposes if he wishes. This is the sort of system you seek to justify in France, the birthplace of human rights! ..." Speech by Georges Clemenceau on July 30, 1885, before the Chamber of Deputies, in response to Jules Ferry. http://gallica.bnf.fr/ark:/12148/bpt6k5462520q/f6.image.

their inability to apply in the case of China the "social engineering" strategy used elsewhere and founded on the sure infallibility of the so-called democratic model, based in turn on economic liberalism—or ultraliberalism—and parliamentary democracy. But this model is certainly capable of being adapted to suit the needs of the moment. Parliamentary democracy, then, is in name only when it comes to the support of local autocratic leaders. In many African or Asian countries, the United States lends unconditional support to regimes that have agreed to align themselves with Western or Israeli interests, as evidenced by the situation in Bahrain after the Arab revolts. In these cases, regularly scheduled elections are hailed as a "major step toward democracy," even as hundreds of opposition candidates are arrested and prevented from running for election. There are presidents who have been in power for decades with the blessing of Europeans and Americans, as long as they continue to do favors for Western oil companies or patronize the Western weapons industry. Western countries will use any means to reach their ends: military intervention (Iraq, Afghanistan, or Libya yesterday, Iran or Syria tomorrow; Vietnam or Granada yesterday), ultimatums legalized by Security Council resolutions (against Syria or Iran today), activism by so-called "nongovernmental organizations," greasing the palms of local political or financial players, and so on. Unlike these countries, which thus far have made up the vast majority of the West's "clients," China has shown itself to be perfectly capable of determining its own economic and political strategy and resisting external pressures to change its fundamental orientation.

The second factor contributing to Westerners' frustration lies in China's extraordinary ability to "sinicize" external phenomena. Just as Buddhism has been sinicized to the point where most Chinese now consider it a national religion, Western-style economic liberalism became, in the 1980s, the "socialist market economy," an idea that escaped Westerners' grasp, with which they were uncomfortable, and which they could not control. This begs the question, is it conceivable that the same might happen to the political landscape? Could China's very progressive political evolution, quite evident to any foreign observer willing to set aside ideological biases and take an objective look at movements on the political scene, eventually engender a Chinese-style democratic system that respects the Chinese people's cultural and historical background? It is difficult for Westerners to imagine what such a system would look like, given their certainty of the absolute validity of their own model. The strategy that Chinese leaders seem to have adopted, reforms that implant political democracy in a very progressive and pyramidal process of transformation from the bottom up (elections of village leaders, then district leaders, etc.) must, however, be viewed in the more restrictive context of globalization, particularly of the media—a consideration that Westerners did not face during the development of their democratic systems. Moreover, for European countries the spread of democratic thought occurred gradually, over more than a century after the

French Revolution, and during that time, democracy suffered serious setbacks in Europe (Nazism, fascism, Francoism, the Greek military junta, the Vichy government in France, etc.). And let us not forget that most of the European dictatorships that arose between the two world wars came to power thanks to the democratic system, through elections.

The eventual success of the process undertaken in China and the appearance of a Chinese "Third Way" would be a bitter blow to Western propaganda —which has claimed for decades that no alternative system can exist—and would cast new doubt on the political domination of developing countries. The Chinese experiment today is usually portrayed as the economic domination of a clearly autocratic or authoritarian system.[6] This model is said to pose a threat to the process of democratization aspired to by Westerners because the Chinese offer authoritarian regimes a path to economic development without political openness. These analyses fail to take into account the solid hypothesis of a phased-in evolution of China, a hypothesis supported by the political evolutions within the regime since 1978 as well as by the debates currently shaking up not only Chinese society, but the Party itself.

These factors go a long way toward explaining the coexistence today of two competing concepts: the "Chinese threat" (中国威胁; *Zhōngguó wēixié*) versus "China's peaceful rise" (和平崛起; *hépíng juéqǐ*). Those promoting the first of these concepts denounce the structural weaknesses that impede—some say cripple—Chinese development, and they attribute world-scale hegemonic ambitions to Chinese leaders. They hold up the term "Middle Kingdom" (中国; *Zhōngguó*), as the Chinese refer to their homeland, to prove their point that its only possible ambition can be world conquest. In the mind of China's critics, and for much of the public, this very term proves that China can only view the world through the lens of its geographical and cultural centrality. China bashing[7] is all the rage, with many adherents in Western media and among researchers, as we see clearly in the case of the anti-Chinese campaign set off by the run-up to the 2008 Olympics. For China's part, the term "China's peaceful rise" was coined in late 2003 and articulated the discourse of a Beijing that, fully aware if its partners' concerns, sought to reassure them. For Chinese leaders, China would be the first empire capable of such a rise without becoming embroiled in major conflicts and without displaying hegemonic ambitions. Naturally, many Westerners remain unconvinced. The potentially threatening connotations of the very term "rise" led Chinese strategists in 2004 to quickly amend this wording to "China's peaceful development" (中国和平发展; *Zhōngguó hépíng fāzhǎn*) in speeches and official documents.[8]

---

[6] Halper, *The Beijing Consensus*.

[7] In the 1980s in the United States, the term *Japan bashing* referred to the campaign orchestrated against Japan, which was blamed for the American economy's ills.

[8] President Hu Jintao used the expression for the first time in August 2004 during the 10th reunion of Chinese ambassadors posted abroad ("中国, 和平发展道路的战略抉择" ["The strategic choice of the path of peaceful development for China"]), *China Net*, March 25, 2008.

Any assessment of the prospects of development in China, the eventual evolution of its political system, and the effects that its emergence will eventually have on the world economy and on the strategic positioning of the major economic and military powers requires a realistic and dynamic approach to this country. Above all, this assessment should be free of the ideological charge that today generates so much anxiety and hostility. Today's China cannot be reduced to its officially Communist regime and its Maoist past. Nor can it be subjected to some sort of liberal frenzy that would lead it to adopt at any price an economic system imported from the West, the limits of which we are more and more aware, particularly since the 2008 financial crisis. China, first and foremost, is the product of its geographic centrality in Asia and of thousands of years of history marked by civil wars, constant invasions, and brutal humiliations, but also by amazing discoveries (from gunpowder to printing), extraordinary contributions to world heritage, and thinkers who have influenced the Chinese worldview and transmitted it throughout the Asian continent.

## *Historical factors*

Until the 19th century, Chinese sovereigns showed indifference tinged with condescension toward the world beyond their borders. For centuries, their only major concern was dealing with the tribes located within their immediate vicinity, particularly the nomadic tribes of the steppes, whose thirst for conquest frequently destabilized the dynasties in power. The Han's most implacable foes were the Xiongnu[9] and other nomadic peoples of the northern steppes. It was these fierce warriors whom the emperor Qin Shi Huang (259–210 BC) meant to keep out when he built the Great Wall.[10] Under the reign of Wudi of the Western Han dynasty (206 BC–23 AD), the Chinese empire quickly spread south, with the conquest of the two Guangs and Nan Yue, now North Vietnam; to the southwest, where the Yunnan and Sichuan barbarians submitted to the Han emperor's rule; to the north and the west, where the Xiongnu were repulsed, as the empire took control of inner Mongolia; to the Tian Shan in the northwest; to Liaodong; and to northeastern Korea. With this expansion of his empire, Emperor Wudi became the first Chinese sovereign to develop a regional strategy on a Central Asian scale. Constant skirmishes with the Xiongnu sapped the empire's strength and represented a constant threat to its power. Wudi had heard tell of the founding of a powerful nation in what is now Bukhara, born of the forced exile of a tribe related to the Xiongnu and banished from their homeland in Hexi. In 139 BC, Wudi sent a mission through the Tian Shan (now the Xinjiang Uyghur Autonomous Region) to forge an

---

[9]Nomadic people of ancient China who lived in what is now Mongolia, linked to the Huns by some authors.
[10]To be precise, Ying Zheng, also known as Shǐ Huángdì (始皇帝), or First Emperor, linked the sections of wall built by local lords to defend against barbarian invasions, then reinforced them in order to create an indestructible means of protection.

alliance with Bukhara against their enemies from the steppes. The strategy was a spectacular failure. The emperor's envoy reached his destination, but he was imprisoned for over 10 years and finally made it back 13 years later. On his quest, however, he was able to explore the routes of Central Asia and learn of the existence of robust trade with a country called *Sindhu*, or India. Within a few decades, Han China would conquer the tribes of the nomadic confederation of the steppes and create a stronghold in the western reaches of their land, with the aid of their southern Xiongnu allies, who fought with the Chinese against their northern brothers.

The constant struggle to keep the steppe tribes at bay went on for centuries, and China gradually expanded the limits of its empire and placed advanced military posts at the doors to Central Asia and at the borders of Turkestan. These colonies were populated by both soldiers and civilians. But at the same time, the emperors' rule forced the displacement of conquered tribes toward the interior of the empire. The very thing that these tribes had sought to do for centuries, enter China, was now granted to them as vanquished peoples! The Xiongnu settled in Shanxi, the Tibetans in Gansu and Sichuan, and the Tungus in Zhílì on the east coast. They retained their traditions and their forms of tribal administration. In exchange for their submission to the emperor, these peoples were allowed in with their cultures intact. With this policy, Chinese sovereigns laid the groundwork for a long tradition: the political assimilation of foreign populations, willingly or not, into Chinese territory, while allowing them to retain their cultural, linguistic, or religious traits. This policy, of course, carried with it certain risks, as evidenced by numerous internal revolts carried out by some tribes. Within a few centuries, dozens of peoples were integrated into Chinese civilization, such as the Toba Tatars, who abandoned their traditional dress and language under the Northern and Southern Dynasties and changed the name of their clan to *Yuan*.

The Tang dynasty (618–907), whose brilliant civilization and power were felt even in the most far-flung countries, including the Roman Empire, was doubtless the first dynasty to spread Chinese influence throughout Asia. Emperor Taizong's name, in particular, was heard in the four corners of Asia at the very moment when Asia Minor was seeing the rise of a new religion, Islam, whose rapid expansion would soon reach the borders of the Chinese empire. The last Sassanid[11] emperor, Yazdegerd III, took refuge in Chang An's court, and his son Firuz was named Chinese governor of Persia in exile. The first caliphs themselves, Omar and Othman, in their quest to conquer an Arab empire in the name of Allah, sought the Chinese emperor's friendship and sent missions laden with precious gifts from Medina. This first contact between China and Arabic followers of Islam turned out to be profitable for both parties, who undertook a burgeoning trade. Under the Tang, the Chinese empire stretched from the Yellow Sea to the Aral, from Siberia to India. No purely

---

[11]Sassanid Empire founded in AD 226 at Ctesiphon, in what is now Iraq. It collapsed in the 7th century with the Arab expansion and the spread of Islam.

Chinese empire had ever controlled so much territory, even without their hegemony over dependencies in Mongolia, Turkestan, Kashgar, and Tonkin.

The Chinese drew several key lessons from this first historical period, which lasted until the early 19th century. First, they are the heirs of a brilliant civilization that influenced for centuries the rest of Asia and to a certain extent Europe. Take, for example, Voltaire's fascination, and that of some other Enlightenment philosophers, with Chinese civilization.[12] Second, their strength lies in their uncanny ability to integrate and sinicize foreign influences and peoples who have come into contact with them over the centuries, even when those influences shake the very foundations of their culture. They sinicized the Mongols, the Manchus, Christian missionaries and Jews, Indian Buddhism, and more. Truly Chinese dynasties ruled China for barely six centuries, interrupted by a long succession of Turkish, Tatar, Mongol, or Manchu dynasties. Finally, the greatest threats to the empire always came from inland, from nomadic peoples, never from the coast. The sea was always a source of wealth brought by merchants from the four corners of the world.

The 19th century would bring China a rude awakening from some of the ideas so deeply rooted in the minds of its sovereigns and strategists. As the Tsarist Empire and Great Britain cast their eyes to the East, the Chinese empire finally realized, far too late, the weakness of their eastern seaboard and how ill prepared they were to face the powers of this world that they had ignored for too long. In the face of British pressures, the empire reacted in accordance with traditional norms, not taking into account the true scope of the threat or of the cultural differences that pitted Western norms against those of the Chinese. During the Anglo-Nepalese War (1814–1816), China refused to come to its tributary state's aid out of "impartial benevolence" (一视同仁; *yí shì tóng rén*), which required it to deal with all states as equals, be they tributary states or states outside of its sphere of influence. A year later, with the Treaty of Titalia, Sikkim was brought under Great Britain's protection. The Court of Beijing was following its own rules of international relations, but Western powers saw this as a sign of weakness, which encouraged them to pursue their expansionist strategies to China's detriment. In the East, beginning with the first Opium War (1839–1842), China never ceased to give way to the powers from the sea. American President John Quincy Adams made no bones about describing the Opium War in terms of "a battle between progress and Asian barbarity." It was perhaps during this period that the fundamental rift was born, which would form a deep divide between the West and China and engender a deep-seated feeling of humiliation for generations of Chinese. Well aware of the grandeur of their civilization, the Chinese suddenly found themselves labeled "barbarians," their historical relevance[13] denied, their traditional Asian hegemony

---

[12]René, Étiemble, *L'Europe chinoise* (Paris: Gallimard, 1989).
[13]Ibid.

brought to a halt, their territory carved up, and their wealth lost to the pillage and vandalism of vengeful troops. "No dogs or Chinese": this sign allegedly posted in the Shanghai French Concession was always considered as a sad testament to this unforgettable humiliation.

For a century, until Mao Zedong's rise to power in 1949, the Chinese suffered one humiliation, and one blow, after another. Tragic episodes such as the wars with the West, revolts of the millenarian sects, the Japanese invasion with its attendant massacres, and the civil war between nationalists and communists contributed to the Chinese People's gradual awareness of their own weaknesses and the urgent need to create conditions that would one day allow them to resist external pressures and freely choose their own way. When the time finally came, in 1949, the excessive ideological baggage that prevailed over state affairs, and one man's single-handed rule of the Party, and therefore of the whole country and its citizens, plunged China into a dramatic and lasting state of isolation and political and internal economic chaos from which it would not emerge until 35 years later, more battered and bruised than ever. This experimental ideology, which saw the Chinese undertaking rectification campaigns as part of the Cultural Revolution, from the Hundred Flowers to the Great Leap Forward, plunged the country into a state of ongoing turmoil that over a few decades eliminated the ancient regime's bourgeoisie, intellectuals, and landowners of all stripes. Even erstwhile revolutionaries suddenly morphed into supporters of international reaction: no one could escape the ongoing revolution. While China has certainly experienced periods of relative calm that have allowed it to lick its wounds for a while and not sink into permanent chaos, it had clearly fallen behind in economic, cultural, scientific, and technological terms, until reason and pragmatism finally prevailed under the leadership of Deng Xiaoping, doubtless the providential man the Chinese had so anxiously awaited since the 19th century. At one time, they thought that they had found this man in Sun Yat-sen, father of the republican revolution, but his desire to transform China could not overcome traditionalist resistance.

This century of Chinese history, stretching from the beginnings of imperialist interventions against the Chinese empire to the end of the Cultural Revolution in 1976, anchored within the Chinese psyche certain convictions and reinforced some (without a doubt preexisting) features:

• China has been a unified power since 221 BC, under the reign of the emperor Qin Shi Huang, and the preservation of this unity is fundamental. Territories lost to Western colonial pressures and to the Japanese must be brought back into the fold definitively (Hong Kong and Macao were reintegrated in 1997 and 1999, respectively, and regaining Taiwan remains a future goal). This reunification would relegate to the past the humiliations suffered by China and finally allow it to regain its rightful place among the great civilizations culturally, and among the great powers politically and economically. National unity, therefore, is the top priority of Chinese leaders. Any straying from this path, any measure likely to compromise the cohesion of the Chinese nation as a whole, is intolerable. Phenomena such as separatist movements (Xinjiang or Tibet), religious terrorism (Uyghur extremist organizations), sectarian movements manipulated from abroad (the Falun Gong sect or the evangelists) must be strictly controlled, or attacked if they become dangerous. In the 19th century, the Taiping Rebellion (1851–1864), led by Hong Xiuquan, a Chinese convert to evangelical Protestantism, nearly brought down the empire. Hong had managed to rally millions of supporters by creating an atmosphere that was deeply mystical and challenged the corrupt local Qing administration. The impoverishment and social polarization that Central China experienced in the mid-19th century did much to stoke the fires of this rebellion. These problems had already fueled a strong movement to resist the taxes levied by the imperial administration. In today's terms, the current economic and social situation of part of China, especially in certain rural areas, and the spread of Chinese evangelist groups in these same regions can only be alarming to central authorities, as is the current spread of corruption.

• If it is to be respected, a country must have at its disposal the same accoutrements of power as its partners or adversaries. And so China must closely watch their movements and keep up with them if it wishes to avoid falling behind economically or technologically. These accoutrements, such as nuclear capacity or a navy worth its salt, must also be up to the task of protecting its interests, not just regionally, but globally if necessary in the future. While the United States began work on its missile defense shield, the acceleration of the Chinese space program in recent years, with several manned spaceflights starting in October 2003 and the Tiangong 1 Space Station, placed in orbit September 29, 2011—the only one in operation today besides the International Space Station—was evidence of the priority Chinese leaders place on technology.

• For nearly 40 years, ideological excesses were a direct cause of China's troubles. Pragmatism and flexibility must now guide the decisions made by the Party and the State, even if it means flying in the face of the ideological party line of strict adherence to Marxism-Leninism and Mao Zedong Thought. China's economic and political development will no longer be based on ideologies—whether they are the application of Marxist theory, liberal dogmas in economics, or principles of parliamentary democracy in politics—but on empiricism. Its economic and social policies are the fruit of lessons drawn from: experiments conducted in other countries and from China's own recent past; a cautious approach that requires a clearly determined, long-term objective and plan of action; and the step-by-step experimentation with the solutions found, at the risk of backsliding in the event of failure, but avoiding at all costs straying from the path long enough to endanger the development process as a whole. China has excelled at this method since 1978, no matter what the doomsayers who have predicted China's imminent collapse every year for two decades may have to say about it.

## *Geographical factors*

China's surface area (3,706,581 square miles[2]) and its population (1,374,900,000 in 2013) make it a geographical giant, both a continental and maritime power, whose importance in Asia, and therefore in the world, can no longer be ignored. Unlike Japan, isolated to the east, and Russia, confined to the north, China enjoys a central position on the continent that grants it a decisive strategic position and allows it to influence, through proactive policy or simply through its economic clout, the attitudes of countries everywhere in Asia, from Japan to Iran, from Russia to Bangladesh. But its central position makes it vulnerable too, as we can plainly see if we compare it to the geographical position of, say, the United States. China shares land or maritime borders with 18 countries. Three of these are nuclear powers, and a fourth, North Korea, has just joined the club, albeit on a small scale thus far. This direct contact with so many states, of course, plays a central role in how current Chinese leaders perceive the world and its threats. When the region is stable, its exceptional geographical position offers China several political, economic, and strategic advantages. It allows China to stand out politically by carrying on good-neighbor relations, and to develop its trade relations by taking advantage of a communications network dating from the days of the Silk Road. This network has continued to develop since the start of reforms.

After 1949, the country's relative isolation from the rest of Asia, due as much to the nature of its political regime as to the fears it aroused in its neighbors, has led Beijing to settle for tumultuous relations with countries such as the USSR, India, and Vietnam. The geopolitical context and the effects of the Cold War made it impossible to envision the prospect of a peaceable and calm world stage. Chinese leaders instead prioritized maintaining some measure of strategic balance (战略稳定; *zhànlüè wěndìng*) that could assure an armed defensive peace. But the implementation of economic reforms in 1978 set this strategic vision on its ear. Now the priority was economic development, no matter what the ideological cost, as in Deng Xiaoping's famous phrase "It doesn't matter whether a cat is white or black, as long as it catches mice."[14] But carrying out economic reforms on a scale that could eventually place China among the ranks of the developed countries would require political and economic openness with the rest of Asia and the easing of tensions with its neighbors.

---

[14]Deng Xiaoping appears to have used this phrase for the first time in March 1961 in reference to the famine caused by the Great Leap Forward and the need to revitalize agricultural production.

This geographical position is uncomfortable in the extreme in strategic terms, and it represents a major handicap for Beijing's foreign policy when it comes to political or economic alliances. The long list of neighboring states, many of which have grappled for years with domestic guerrillas (India, Russia, Pakistan, and Laos), or more disturbing still, with chronic instability caused by the activities of transnational Islamist movements (Russia, Kazakhstan, Kyrgyzstan, Pakistan, and India), is one of the factors that led China to launch its program of military modernization in the 1980s and to strengthen its military capacities in order to keep up with the growing threats on its unity and security. But this military modernization, framed by Beijing as a defensive move, is viewed by some of China's neighbors as a threat to their own security, particularly those countries that have been involved in armed conflicts with China in the past (India or Vietnam). Other countries, also within China's natural sphere of influence, have their own concerns about this burgeoning military power, concerns provoked or encouraged by Washington's discourse of denunciation aimed at China's hypothetical hegemonic ambitions.

China's geographic centrality also represents a natural challenge to American hegemony on the Asian continent. The division of Asia into ideologically antagonistic states, naturally suspicious of their neighbors' aspirations to power, ever ready to associate with other Asian states or with external powers to keep any one of them from becoming dangerously strong on its own, has served the United States' Asia strategy well for decades. Its main objective, in Asia as well as on the other continents, was to prevent the rise of a regional power that could not only endanger its own domination, but also eventually rally the other states to a position hostile to the United States. The Cold War with the Soviet Union and the ideological conflict between the latter and China supplied an endless range of possible alliances of convenience that could be discarded abruptly according to the geopolitical movements of the given moment. The dissolution of the USSR in December 1991 put an end to this very comfortable configuration and left the United States as the sole

| Country | Border length |
|---------|---------------|
| Afghanistan | 47 mi/76 km |
| Bhutan | 292 mi/470 km |
| North Korea | 880 mi/1,416 km |
| India | 2,100 mi/3,380 km |
| Kazakhstan | 953 mi/1,533 km |
| Kyrgyzstan | 533 mi/858 km |
| Laos | 26 mi/423 km |
| Mongolia | 2,906 mi/4,677 km |
| Myanmar | 1,358 mi/2,185 km |
| Nepal | 768 mi/1,236 km |
| Pakistan | 325 mi/523 km |
| Russia | 2,240 mi/3,605 km |
| Tajikistan | 257 mi/414 km |
| Vietnam | 796 mi/1,281 km |

*Land borders with China*

unilateral hyperpower capable of representing a threat to the security of other members of the international communty in the pursuit of its own national interest. In the early 1980s, given overwhelming American technological and economic superiority, the United States would have had a hard time convincing its Asian partners of an imminent threat from the Chinese. The attacks of September 11, 2001, very timely in strategic terms, gave American foreign policy the conquering impulse that had been a bit lacking under the Clinton administration and allowed for the temporary identification of a new enemy, Islamist terrorism. This new enemy would justify American military deployments worldwide and astronomical military spending. But the specter of a Chinese "threat" still lurked in the background. China's extraordinarily rapid economic development made it an ideal target for the Republican administration, which could at last identify a new enemy state, and one ruled by a Communist party besides. In taking up anew a Cold War frame of reference, some commentators in the United States have made no bones about claiming that in the face of China's efforts to counter this strategy in Asia, Sino-American hostilities would "force all the other countries to choose up sides," bringing the world back to a state of latent hostility that would justify the deployment of troops, the swelling of military budgets, and shady tactics within the framework of an "asymmetrical" war.

But the strategic landscape has undergone major shakeups in Asia since September 2001. In the wake of the US show of force in Afghanistan as well as Iraq, doubtless reassuring for its allies such as Japan, but by the same token worrisome for other US partners such as India, Pakistan, or Korea, many Asian leaders began to question the relevance and durability of an alliance with Washington. The simultaneous arms sales to Pakistan and India in 2004 contributed to a feeling on the part of these countries' leaders that they were being manipulated by the United States, whose interests could suddenly diverge from theirs. In this context, China seized upon the opportunity to progressively create a regional dynamic, in security matters as well as economic ones, with those Asian countries likely to be receptive to a discourse of integration unhampered by ideological considerations. Geography, not to mention history, certainly lends China the legitimacy to dialogue with its neighbors in order to attempt to bring about, in a progressive manner, common approaches to economic, energy, and security issues. These agreements, however, elude Western law-based reasoning and come about based rather on informal social mechanisms and methods of negotiation and influence more in line with the traditions of solidarity and patronage, or vassalage, as some would call it, that have driven the creation of relationships of power in the region for centuries. It is actually not so much a matter of institutionalizing these relationships as reinforcing interpersonal and group networks, a process whose results are quite visible in the very strong decentralized ties that have been created ("growth triangles," partnerships between provinces in different national territories, the role of diasporas in the development of trade) and the growing trend of denationalization of regional dynamics, even in China. In China, this can be seen in the close relationships between the southern province of Fujian and Taiwan, the province of Canton and Hong Kong even before the transfer of sovereignty, or Xinjiang and Kazakhstan. Unlike in Europe, regional integration appears to occur from the bottom up, not just from the establishment of bilateral frameworks from the top down.

In Central Asia, China has won undeniable successes, in close collaboration with Russia, whose interests in the region are largely the same. The American intervention in Afghanistan, which meant the presence of American bases in Uzbekistan (Karshi-Khanabad) and Kyrgyzstan (Manas), followed by American and British troops' invasion of Iraq, gave new impetus not only to Washington's energy strategy, but also to its *containment* policy toward China and Russia. These moves were meant to allow the United States to reinforce its positions in a strategically vital region while it waited for its chance to leap the hurdle of Iran and draw ever closer to the Chinese and Russian borders. But the American military breakthrough, reinforced by the *color revolutions*, was met with the disapproval of major regional players and the establishment of a bloc of resistance that Moscow and Beijing are looking to draw new partners into, such as India, Iran, or Pakistan.

Since 2001, China, India, and Russia have shown a clear willingness for cooperation and dialogue that appears to point to the possibility of a shake-up in relationships of power, something that Zbigniew Brzezinski in 1997 considered unimaginable in the foreseeable future: "...being technologically much more backward than America, they [Russia and China] do not have the means to exercise—nor soon attain—sustained political clout worldwide."[15] Eurasia's place in world political, strategic, and economic balances, for Brzezinski, fully justifies the eternal domination of the region by the United States, the sole guardians of "the future of freedom, democracy, open economies, and international order in the world."[16] As evidenced by American support for some nondemocratic regimes in the region and the indulgence often shown by Washington for some of these regimes' human rights violations, freedom and democracy are not really the two determining criteria for American strategy, whose priorities are based more on the alignment of regimes based on American economic and strategic interests.

China and Russia take issue with analyses like Brzezinski's and would like to free the Eurasian continent of such rhetoric. As far as Beijing is concerned, China historically played a decisive role in Asian stability until the arrival of colonial powers in the 19th century, and the American strategy in recent years, officially focused on the struggles against so-called global threats (particularly terrorism and the spread of weapons of mass destruction), has become instead

---

[15] Zbigniew Brzezinski, *The Grand Chessboard: American Primacy and Its Geostrategic Imperatives* (Basic Books, 1997), 24.
[16] Samuel P. Huntington, "Why International Primacy Matters," in *International Security* (Spring 1993), 83.

the cause of growing disorder and the destruction of certain delicate balances that had been the result of more pragmatic policies. Aware of the role its geographic centrality lends it, China today feels entitled to keep American power in check in continental Asia, wary of American errors of judgment—such as its support of anti-Soviet guerrilla forces in Afghanistan, which then later contributed to the Islamist revival in the 1980s—and deliberate actions against China from bases and networks installed at its periphery for many years, but considerably strengthened after October 2001. On November 19, 1999, in his first speech on foreign policy as a presidential candidate, George W. Bush laid out the framework of an American strategy in Eurasia that Beijing has never since lost sight of:

> *Right now, America has many important bilateral alliances in Asia. We should work toward a day when the fellowship of free Pacific nations is as strong and united as our Atlantic Partnership. If I am president, China will find itself respected as a great power, but in a region of strong democratic alliances. It will be unthreatened, but not unchecked.*[17]

This warning banked on the weakness represented by China's proximity to a great number of countries relatively easily manipulated by Washington through a clever combination of economic seduction, political pressures, and military operations. It was clearly with this threat in mind that Chinese leaders during the Bush administration pursued with great perseverance a policy of diplomacy of proximity meant to defuse potential crises, manage latent conflicts, especially border disputes, and reassure its neighbors and partners regarding their intentions. China's most important partner was now Russia, which became its main supplier of military equipment after the sanctions imposed on weapons sales to China in 1989. On July 16, 2001, the two countries signed the Treaty of Good-Neighborliness and Friendly Cooperation, laying the groundwork for a new relationship between Moscow and Beijing, adversaries for four decades. In May 2002, China signed border delimitation agreements with Tajikistan and Kazakhstan, the two Central Asian former Soviet republics it shares a border with, in order to stabilize the border regions and implement "confidence-building measures" in the military arena.

Moscow and Beijing were able, through the Shanghai Cooperation Organization, to secure the closure in November 2005 of the American base Karshi-Khanabad in Uzbekistan. They also got India, Pakistan, Iran, Afghanistan, and Mongolia to join the organization, as observers for the time being. Also in 2005, Russia reestablished its influence in Kazakhstan, particularly in the

---

[17]Governor George W. Bush, "A Distinctly American Internationalism," Ronald Reagan Presidential Library, Simi Valley, California, November 19, 1999.

defense sector.[18] The strengthening of energy cooperation relations among Iran, India, and Pakistan, but with China as well, at a time when most major consumers are concerned about the repercussions of the spike in oil prices, has become a major factor in diplomatic and political decision-making in the region's capitals, even as American pressure remains strong in order to mitigate the risks of the weakness of these countries vis-à-vis Iran's nuclear program. This is at bottom an alliance of convenience headed up by Moscow and Beijing, progressively put in place, which could eventually lead to the United States' regional isolation within an Afghanistan that proves harder and harder to control.

India, meanwhile, has had major disputes with China since 1949. Several issues were involved: Chinese sovereignty over Tibet, the ravages of the 1962 Sino-Indian War, border disputes over several parts of the McMahon Line,[19] the level of relations between New Delhi and Moscow in the era of the Soviet Union, and more. Mutual suspicion weighed heavily on relations between the two Asian giants, stymieing any attempt at rapprochement. In 2003, the situation changed quickly with Beijing's encouragement. Before Indian Prime Minister Vajpayee's June 2003 visit to China, Prime Minister Wen Jiabao announced that Beijing was willing to accelerate negotiations for a "fair" and "mutually acceptable" solution to the Sino-Indian border issue, emphasizing the need to keep the peace in the border region. This was the first visit by an Indian head of state in 10 years. Wen Jiabao added that the border issue was "a historical legacy inherited by both countries from the colonialists." In 2004, Vajpayee's successor, Manmohan Singh, committed to finding a solution to the territorial dispute with Beijing, even as he announced that he meant to strengthen "strategic relations" with the United States and Russia. In December 2004, India and China decided to renew high-level military relations, and the Chinese defense minister announced Beijing's willingness to develop close ties of cooperation with New Delhi in the areas of defense and security. The ambiguity of American policy vis-à-vis India and Pakistan at the time naturally contributed to this Sino-Indian rapprochement, as India objected to Washington's weapons sales to Pakistan, a project announced by the Bush administration in November 2004 and carried out in March 2005. China now found itself in a more favorable position to step up its rapprochement with India, but it ran up against a worldview held by the Indian elite, educated in American or British universities, that deems the cultural and strategic chasm between the Chinese and Indians insurmountable, and instead prefers a policy of political and strategic alignment with the United States.

In recent years, however, in the wake of Beijing's maladroit actions in the South China Sea and its repeated incursions into Indian maritime territory

---

[18] Richard Weitz, "Kazakhstan-China Military Exchanges Continue," The Jamestown Foundation, November 9, 2012.
[19] The McMahon Line, named after chief negotiator Sir Henry McMahon, separated British India from Tibet. It was established by the Simla Accord on April 27, 1914, and although ratified by the Chinese delegation, it was immediately denounced by China, which claims the state of Arunachal Pradesh, located to the south of the line.

to conduct naval exercises with neighboring countries, Washington's policy of seduction of India, and disputes over the construction of new civil and military infrastructure, such as the Three Gorges Dam project, relations between the two largest Asian powers have once again cooled, and mutual suspicion has returned, particularly in the Indian military. However, in economic terms, a greater integration of the two economies is underway, as evidenced by the November 2012 signing in New Delhi of multibillion-dollar agreements between Chinese and Indian companies.

The first East Asia Summit, held in December 2005 in Kuala Lumpur, from which the United States, to its great displeasure, was excluded, seemed to signal a new phase in China's containment strategy toward American power in Asia. After successes achieved in Central and South Asia, China seems determined to work toward still broader economic and security integration including all Asian countries. The summit was the first chance for a meeting of the four major Asian powers, China, India, Russia, and Japan, although the latter was at the time relatively isolated due to Prime Minister Koizumi's policy of full alignment with the United States. The pro-American policy adopted by the new Japanese Prime Minister Abe and the new American dynamic in Asia call into question this Chinese strategy, particularly after the United States joined the organization in 2011.

This sort of structure in Asia, however, would be capable of reducing existing tensions and would likewise be favorable to economic development and the construction of an Asian security architecture able to take on major threats, particularly the specter of the alarming spread of Islamist terrorism in Southeast Asia.

## *Cultural factors*

Notwithstanding the widespread notion, China was not fundamentally transformed by the revolution and its four decades of a fusion of Marxism-Leninism and Maoism. Its principles and customs were certainly temporarily disrupted, but ancient traditions cannot be eradicated in a fortnight. The Cultural Revolution did, however, attempt to obliterate whatever remained of traditions labeled "feudal" or "reactionary" after 17 years of Communist rule and political campaigns. For centuries, a Confucian worldview had dominated Chinese society and governed relationships between leaders and followers, the center and the periphery, Heaven and Earth. The advent of Communist rule could not elude this timeless order. After all, was not the very term "revolution" (革命; *géming*) a direct allusion to imperial tradition, since it literally meant "to change the mandate (of Heaven)" (革; *change and* 命; *the mandate*)? Did not the July 1976 earthquake likewise announce the loss of "Heaven's mandate" for the Cultural Revolution? The death in September of that year of Chairman Mao Zedong, on the heels of Prime Minister Zhou Enlai's death, and then the arrest of the Gang of Four and the rise of a new regime, one that would quickly launch major reforms that would change the face of China, seemed to confirm the traditional cycles of Chinese political succession.

The weight of tradition is today one of the fundamental parameters that explain Chinese economic growth and the attitude of the Chinese people toward the daily struggle of the underclasses. Confucian values are gradually regaining their place in Chinese society after having been officially repressed for three decades by the government. But they have been noticeably watered down to better suit the needs of late-20th-century China. In Confucian society, the merchant caste was the most reviled of all, because the quest for material wealth must be renounced in favor of a nobler ideal. Confucian economic thought instead privileged agriculture, and man must learn to appreciate poverty in order to follow the Way. But Confucianism was not at bottom a political theory but a spiritual system; this fact diminished somewhat the effect of its teachings on economic development. The economic successes achieved in the 20th century by countries heavily influenced by Confucianism, such as Taiwan, South Korea, and Singapore, demonstrate how little influence Confucian economic principles exert over Confucian societies. The philosopher placed special emphasis on the role of the State in the enrichment of the people. Government officials were also charged with allowing the people to strive to enjoy a comfortable life, but it was up to the individual to seek a spiritual path. The enrichment that Deng Xiaoping extolled in 1978, then, was merely a return to tradition, after the break with the Maoist era. Moreover, Confucius held that the State was responsible first and foremost for education, the highest value of Confucian society. Confucians ceaselessly built schools for centuries, and the level of education in pre-modern China was considerably higher than in the West. The family, another pillar of society according to Confucian thought, also survived the revolutionary period and has since regained its central place in post–Cultural Revolution China. Though the size of the family unit has been reduced by the one-child policy, family solidarity has slowly regained not only its social role, but its role within the family as well. The massive investments in continental China made by the Chinese diaspora starting in 1979, a major driver of economic development in the 1980s, were concentrated in the provinces of the east coast, where immigrants had come from for centuries. These investments went to their villages of origin and then moved through family channels. This family relationship was for Confucius the very origin of morality, and it should govern not only human relationships but government policy as well. As in many other countries, misappropriation on the part of some local government officials in China and rampant greed fly in the face of Confucian morality, but the anti-corruption campaign undertaken for the last few years aims to reestablish discipline among State and Party officials. What some observers have termed "neo-Confucianism" is slowly on the rise in a China in a state of perpetual movement.[20] It is characterized by a stable political system (only one political party, for example), constant state involvement in economic life, a fairly high educational level for the society as a whole, strong collective awareness in entrepreneurial terms, strong predominance of the family and clan, real concern for workers' well-being and harmony in interpersonal relationships, a protected society with a low crime rate, and a high priority placed on education. These principles can be seen, on the one hand, in the current evolution of Chinese society, and on the other hand, in the discourse of Chinese leaders who describe the ends that these collective efforts should lead to. China seems to be moving toward a model society that might be described, at the risk of audacity, as *Confucian socialism*, for the two philosophies do after all have certain features in common.

## China looks inward

The history of the 19th and 20th centuries has made the Chinese aware of the obsolescence of their millenarian political system, their technological weaknesses, the anachronism of an imperial conception of relations between China and the rest of the world—the need, in short, to rethink itself. Attempts to do so have ranged from total, violent rejection of the outside world, with the Boxer Rebellion of September 1901, to the no less radical rejection of traditional Chinese culture, with the overthrow of the empire, the May Fourth Movement in 1919, and the Communist revolution. With the foundation of the People's Republic of China in October 1949, the revolutionaries, supported by much of the Chinese population, especially the peasantry, sought to bring an end to these tragic episodes and establish anew a strong central power, the first since the mid-19th century. Mao Zedong referred to the United States and its allies as "paper tigers" at the time, a term that to his mind expressed the strategic approach of the Communist Party of China. Pointing to the collapse of Nazi Germany, the tsarist empire, and Japan, he predicted the fall of American imperialism, notwithstanding its nuclear supremacy.[21] This analysis rested on the struggle of "the peoples of the whole world" and the victory of "socialist forces" pitted against the "forces of imperialism," but it never alluded to a direct armed struggle between China and the United States, except in the case of the Korean Peninsula.

Chinese military intervention alongside the North Korean Communists did in fact, for the first and last time, officially pit American and Chinese forces against one another. The 700,000 Chinese troops were officially termed "volunteers," in order to keep the Sino-American conflict from coming to a head. On February 7, 1953, in remarks to the 4th Session of the National

---

[20]Daniel A. Bell, *China's New Confucianism: Politics and Everyday Life in a Changing Society* (Princeton Univ. Press, 2008).
[21]"Remarks before the Wuchang meeting of the Central Politburo of the CPC," December 1, 1958, in *Œuvres choisies de Mao Tsé-toung*, Tome IV.

Committee of the First Chinese People's Political Consultative Conference, Mao Zedong expressed China's wish for peace, and at the same time, its determination to "go on fighting side by side with the Korean people" as long as the United States refused to give up its "arrogant and unreasonable demands and its scheme to extend aggression." Beijing was convinced that by establishing a massive, long-term presence in the Korean Peninsula and marching its troops to the Chinese border, the United States was posing a direct threat to the vital interests of the fledgling People's Republic. China clearly entered this conflict grudgingly, at a moment when the Party was considering demobilizing some of the five million troops that had allowed it to take power, and whose upkeep was a serious burden on the country's budget. Direct confrontation with the United States meant a long-term rupture with the West that Beijing in fact wished to avoid at any price.[22] Despite the support lent by China to the Democratic Republic of Vietnam until 1973, the Chinese military was never in direct contact with American forces. Chinese leaders instead sought an accord with Washington in the context of their disagreements with the USSR, which at the time represented a more direct threat, given its geographic proximity. This process led to President Richard Nixon's historical trip to Beijing in February 1972, and finally to the renewal of diplomatic relations between the two countries on January 1, 1979.

Aware of its military, economic, and strategic shortcomings, China sought to forge alliances of convenience from 1949 to 1979, first with the USSR and the socialist bloc against the United States, whose technological and military superiority directly threatened its vital interests in Asia; then with the United States against the USSR, whose strategy of encirclement in the late 1970s, after the Vietnamese-Soviet rapprochement, had become a major source of concern. Nonetheless, for a decade, between the break with Moscow and the rapprochement with Washington, the lack of a dependable ally placed China in a delicate position. For this reason Beijing stepped up its nuclear program during this period, carrying out its first nuclear test on October 16, 1964. China had thus chosen to respond to its international isolation and whatever threats might arise against it with a strategy of deterrence.

With the implementation of economic reforms in 1978, a new vision of international power relationships and of China's status emerged. Ideology gave way to economic development, and China took a Maoist tack with an eye to assuring its eventual economic independence and the mastery of its own security. Deng Xiaoping intended to use the reforms to transform China into "a rich country with a powerful army" (富国强兵; *Fùguó qiángbīng*), an ideal that Chinese writers usually date to the first Opium War and the subsequent disintegration of the empire.[23]

---

[22]Marie-Claire Bergère, *La République populaire de Chine de 1949 à nos jours* (Paris: Armand Colin, 1987), 16.

[23]王小东 [Wang Xiadong], "全球化背景下的中国民族主义" ["Chinese nationalism in the context of globalization"], October 21, 2005, http://blog.voc.com.cn/blog_showone_type_blog_id_51808_p_1.html.

The Deng Xiaoping years assured the triumph of this pragmatist vision over the ideological approach. The Chinese leadership that came to power with the elimination of the authors of the Cultural Revolution (the "Gang of Four") was deeply convinced that China had fallen seriously behind its partners and adversaries in the West and Japan over the previous three decades. China in 1977 was no more than a wasteland wracked with the throes of a dying radical ideology, haunted by the despair of millions of men and women who had devoted their entire lives to an ideal and then discovered to their shock that this overly rigid ideology had taken them down a dead end. Millions of intellectuals were still banished to the countryside or had spent years dedicating most of their energy to learning, at the Party's demand, the skills that hundreds of millions of peasants and workers had possessed for millennia, forsaking their own knowledge. China must rise again, get back to work, and forget the color of the cat.… The torments suffered by the Chinese people starting in the late 1950s, having reached their peak between 1966 and 1976, were a thing of the past, and economic development was the new long-term national priority. Deng Xiaoping's famous slogan "To get rich is glorious" provided the impetus China needed to banish its old ideological demons and set out on the road to development that could allow its population to attain the standard of living that South Korea or Portugal enjoyed within a reasonable time frame. Though China's (nominal) GDP indeed surpassed by far the GDPs of these two countries long ago ($7,298 billion for China versus $237 billion for Portugal and $1,116 billion for South Korea), China remains, of course, well short of this objective due to the size of its population (Chinese GDP per capita is three times lower than in Portugal and almost four times lower than in South Korea). The national-scale redistribution of the strong results achieved since the implementation of reforms on a macroeconomic level thanks to this pragmatic approach, then, still remains to be carried out at the microeconomic level.

## The return of Chinese nationalism?

Is Chinese nationalism making a comeback, as the Western media seem to claim with increasing regularity? Max Boot writes of "the fervor with which the Communist Party oligarchy adopted a xenophobic nationalism to justify the perpetuation of its reign."[24] Any attempt to understand nationalism's place in China and the role it may end up playing in coming years requires viewing it within the proper historical context and in light of its specific characteristics. First, the emergence of the very concept of *Chinese* nationalism is recent. Traditionally, most Chinese refer to themselves not by the term "Chinese," 中国人; *zhōngguó rén*, but as 汉人; *hànrén*, or "descendants of the Han." The Han dynasty (206 BC–220 AD) built on the founder of the empire's achievements and extended its power well beyond the original realm of Chinese civilization. Its military and

---

[24]Max Boot, "Beijing's Plans for National Greatness," *The Weekly Standard*, October 5, 2005.

diplomatic expansion allowed it to stimulate, in turn, the economic expansion of the empire and establish relationships of suzerainty, if not direct administration, of its immediate neighbors (Korea, Vietnam, Manchuria, etc.). But its glory lay not only in conquest. Under the Han dynasty, the educated became influential. This period saw the development of a legal system set up by the First Emperor (Qin Shi Huang), based on a real administrative and military organization that controlled the entire territory and governed the peasantry. And so the Chinese considered themselves direct descendants of this dynasty until the end of the 19th century. But while the Chinese empire was based on a cultural identity that had remained intact since unification under Qin Shi Huang, made up of a "confluence of common notions and an already formalized way of thinking,"[25] it was not immune to major outside influences, such as the spread of Buddhism in the first century. For centuries, philosophers reflected upon the relationship between Man and Heaven for their frame of reference, but they never saw China as a nation-state. The idea of nation in China did not appear until rather late in comparison to Europe, where it only really spread after the French Revolution of 1789. In 1924, Sun Yat-sen himself, the father of the Chinese revolution, lamented this state of affairs:

> *The Chinese people have shown the greatest loyalty to family and clan with the result that in China there have been family-ism and clan-ism but no real nationalism. Foreign observers say that the Chinese are like a sheet of loose sand.... The unity of the Chinese people has stopped short at the clan and has not extended to the nation.*[26]

The genius of this Cantonese politician raised in Hawaii was what allowed the crystallization of Chinese *nationalism* (民族主义; *mínzú zhǔyi*), a term borrowed from the Japanese (*minzoku shugi*), a language Sun Yat-sen learned in his long stay in Japan after a failed coup in 1895. Japan was in a period of rapid expansion, encouraged by modernist reformers who admired Western achievements and took inspiration from them in order to extricate themselves from the bonds of Confucianism and Shintoism, which they saw as obstacles to modernity. In a way, Japanese nationalism was the main impetus to modernity. In fact, the reforms of the Meiji era had been orchestrated starting in 1868 by the Japanese government and admiralty, anxious to respond to Western military pressures.[27] As Alain Dieckhoff writes, "Nationalism is a central feature of modernity, though it sometimes takes on hateful forms."[28] As modernity took hold, the late 19th century and early 20th century saw a move from what one

---

[25]Anne Cheng, *Histoire de la pensée chinoise* (Seuil, 1997), 26.
[26]Sun Yat-sen, 1924, quoted by Dru C. Gladney, *Ethnic Identity in China* (Harcourt Brace, 1998), 17.
[27]Edwin O. Reischauer, *Histoire du Japon et des Japonais* (Paris: Editions du Seuil, 1973), 209.
[28]Alain Dieckhoff, *La nation dans tous ses États* (Flammarion, 2000), 14.

writer describes as "antiquated, narrow-mindedly nationalist dogmatism"[29] to a modernist, republican nationalism extended to all of China's peoples. Sun Yat-sen even introduced the idea of the existence of a Chinese nation made up of five peoples: the Han, the Man (满族, Manchus), the Meng (蒙族, Mongols), the Zang (藏族, Tibetans), and the Hui (回族, a term used at the time to refer to all of China's Muslim peoples, whatever their ethnicity or language), with the Han comprising the vast majority. This approach allowed him not only to rally the nationalist sentiments of the Han against the Manchu dynasty, which had been in place for almost four centuries, but also to grant status to non-Han populations, who had thus far been considered peripheral to the Chinese nation. In his seminal work *Three Principles of the People* (三民主义; *sānmín zhǔyì*), Sun Yat-sen emphasized the importance of the first principle, national-ism, the paramount requirement if the process of modernization of China was to be carried out. After the division of the country in 1949, this work became the bible of the Taiwanese government, which used it to keep the flame of na-tionalism burning in the hopes of reconquering the continent. Though many Western writers concur that the birth of modern Chinese nationalism dates from the first Opium War, it seems instead that resistance to Western powers led to the rise of intense xenophobia among the Han population, but that the concept of *Chinese* nationalism per se did not truly emerge until Sun Yat-sen.

With the overthrow of the Manchu dynasty in 1911, the Chinese were cer-tainly liberated from foreign domination, but they still had to deal with their weaknesses in the face of Western powers and Japan. For all of their traditional pride in their culture, some among the intelligentsia now sharply questioned traditional values, and this movement culminated in the events of May 4, 1919, set in motion by Germany's transfer of concessions in Shandong Prov-ince to Japan according to the Treaty of Versailles. The nationalist reactions that then broke out were nothing more than the expression of a sea change among Chinese intellectuals receptive to the theories of Kang Youwei, Yan Fu, and Liang Qichao. These three scholars believed that attachment to Confu-cian values could lead to the eventual total disintegration of China as a socio-political entity. Only historical progress, seen as harmonization with cosmic evolution, which according to them was what had allowed the West to develop more quickly than the East, could bring the answer to their woes. This nascent Chinese nationalism did not fare well in this analysis, which questioned the very foundations of traditional Chinese thought.

Finally, the idea of nation in China skipped the phase of coopting by the bourgeoisie and the ruling class and instead went from an original revolution-ary concept to one of proletarian internationalism, becoming the leitmotif of the workers' movement. In the People's Republic of China, in fact, national-ism was largely eradicated by the adoption of two fundamental principles of

---

[29]Vadime and Danielle Elisseeff, *La civilisation japonaise* (Arthaud, 1987), 219.

Marxism-Leninism: "solidarity between peoples" and "proletarian internation-alism." True, Mao Zedong had called on Chinese patriotism, until final victory, in order to dismantle the Kuomintang and its American ally, but he insisted on the need to oppose the "narrow-minded patriotism" [30] that he attributed to Nazi Germany or imperialist Japan. After the founding of the People's Repub-lic, he never tired of repeating that China absolutely must "eradicate the chau-vinism of the great powers, resolutely, radically, completely, totally." [31] He like-wise pointed out that "whether large or small, every nation has its strengths and weaknesses."[32] The concept of nation in China has always remained immanent to the people who acquired sovereignty by incarnating the national idea, par-ticularly when faced with foreign occupiers from the West or Japan, or when rallying "minority nationalities" (少数民族; shǎoshù mínzú), populations inhabiting the territories of the empire, to stand with the Han majority. But that the nation never attained a transcendent status in China, the sort of *divine* entity "to which every citizen owes his devotion, his taxes, and in the event of war, his life, notwithstanding whatever inequalities or injustices he may see."[33]

The nationalist spirit in China has never gone beyond the stage of *national-ism of liberation* (in the face of Western imperialism and Japanese occupation). It never became expansionist nationalism as in the case of Japan, a nationalism that likely sprang from territorial greed based on a contrived discourse, and above all, based on a messianic vision of a political, cultural, or religious nature. Mao Zedong often reminded the Chinese population of the risks of "great Han chauvinism" (大汉沙文主义; Dàhàn shāwénzhǔyì), a strong tendency that had to be resolutely opposed in the interest of the paramount concern of strengthening national unity, which meant the sacred union between the Han majority and the minority nationalities. This tendency is born of a deep-seated feeling of cultural superiority on the part of the Han population, which usu-ally manifests as great indifference toward the other peoples who make up the empire. Since 1949, the central authorities, aware of this weakness, sought to eliminate this antagonism, but the persecutions that minorities, particularly religious minorities, have suffered during the Cultural Revolution have instead further alienated them from the Han majority in power in Beijing. Things have improved since 1978, but strong identity conflicts remain and continue to threaten the great national unity aspired to by Chinese revolutionaries.

The relationship between the Chinese and the Japanese is in fact the main outlet for Chinese nationalism, which finds expression when confronted with a much more violent and outward-looking sort of nationalism whose consequences have been devastating for Asia for decades: Japanese nationalism. For more than a century, Japanese politics have been the main driver behind manifestations of Chinese nationalism. With the 1895 Treaty of Shimonoseki,

[30]"A la mémoire de Norman Béthune (21 décembre 1939)," *Œuvres choisies de Mao Tsé-toung*, Tome II.
[31]"A la mémoire du Dr Sun Yat-sen (novembre 1956)," *Œuvres choisies de Mao Tsé-toung*.
[32]"Opening address to the 8th Conference of the CPC," September 15, 1956.
[33] Dieckhoff, *La nation dans tous ses États*, 23.

Tokyo had a hand in carving up the Chinese empire with its annexation of Taiwan, which it was not forced to surrender back to China until its defeat in 1945. In May 1919, the provisions of the Treaty of Versailles regarding Shandong Province, part of which was to come under Japanese occupation, led to the explosion of nationalist sentiment cited above. After the Manchurian Incident of September 18, 1931, Japanese aggression lit a fire under nationalist resistance, and even made it possible, for a time, to rally Communist forces and Kuomintang troops around a common goal: getting Japan out of China. The Japanese defeat in 1945 and the archipelago's status as a protectorate of the United States eliminated for several decades the risk of serious deterioration of Sino-Japanese relations. During Prime Minister Junichiro Koizumi's administration (2001–2006), however, the two countries' relations did indeed deteriorate, and manifestations of nationalism reappeared in China, tinged with hostility toward Japan, which it accused of still harboring hegemonic and aggressive designs on Asia. Some writers have even attributed the Chinese demonstrations after NATO's bombing of the Chinese embassy in Belgrade during the war in Kosovo to nationalist excess. This is a rather spurious idea, for after all, Chinese public opinion saw this is a protest against a violation, albeit officially an accidental one, of the rules of international relations and respect of diplomatic missions. The anti-Japanese demonstrations held in major Chinese cities in 2005 and 2012, on the other hand, were indeed nationalist in nature.[34] Chinese sensibilities are particularly raw toward the Japanese, who most Chinese feel never truly learned the lessons of the past or owned up to their imperialist and criminal past. Sino-Japanese relations are probably the area in which Chinese nationalism may be most fiercely expressed, especially since the joint American-Japanese statement on February 16, 2005, calling the situation in the Taiwan Strait a "common strategic objective." The intervention of Japan, the former colonial power, in the Taiwan issue could only exacerbate Chinese nationalist sentiment and tensions between the two countries.

Outside of the context of this relationship with Japan, one rarely detects a resurgence of nationalism in any form that could represent a threat to the international community as a whole in official Chinese discourse, actions, or meaningful reactions of public opinion, with the exception of a few ultranationalist blogs. Beijing's determination to protect its interests when they are directly threatened, from strategic moves related to hydrocarbons to economic trade disagreements, cannot seriously be described as a nationalist stance. It is all the more untenable to accuse China of a nationalist resurgence when American leaders' speeches are peppered with political-religious language often of a virulently and overtly nationalist bent. This American nationalism is

---

[34]Major Chinese media criticized the violent demonstrations against Japanese interests in China and called for calm and reason ("Irrational, violent anti-Japanese protests should be avoided," *Global Times*, September 16, 2012). However, relations with Japan continue to be a sore point for Chinese public opinion, and authorities must on the one hand show firmness toward Tokyo on the sovereignty issue, and on the other hand prevent any public demonstration that is likely to escalate.

further characterized by messianic overtones, for according to American political philosophy, this "indispensable nation"[35] is called upon to bring light, liberty, and democracy to the world. The hardline nationalism of many American citizens, coupled with their xenophobia, often religious in nature, reached a fever pitch after the attacks of September 11, 2001, when dozens of Muslims, both American and foreign, were assaulted in the United States for their religion or skin color, regular American citizens interviewed by the media called for the extermination of Muslims in the Near East and Middle East, but also during presidential campaign season, as American journalists and politicians, including the Republican candidate, deliberately associated Democratic candidate Barack Obama with radical Islam because of his origins. When European politicians and government officials call for "economic patriotism," on the other hand, the Western media are careful to point out the reemergence of aggressive nationalism implicit in these appeals. When Kosovo claimed independence on February 17, 2008, unilaterally and along strict ethnic lines, the Europeans and Americans decided immediately to recognize the fait accompli, unconcerned with the risks posed to the region by this new Kosovan "nationalism." Western media and governments do not denounce the nationalist demon until they need it to increase political pressures on a country or throw uncooperative governments to the lions of public opinion, too often unaware of local realities, and above all, unable to separate lies from truth.

## A new Chinese geopolitics

With the 9/11 attacks, and the triumph—doubtless temporary, fortunately— of neoconservative approaches to foreign policy in Washington, China found itself facing new strategic challenges that would require profound modifications to its vision of international relations. Indeed, it appeared that the American administration was suddenly implementing the sentiment espoused by George W. Bush in his aforementioned November 1999 speech:

> *If I am president, China will find itself respected as a great power, but in a region of strong democratic alliances. It will be unthreatened, but not unchecked.*

American control over Central Asia seemed poised to drastically increase, directly threatening Chinese as well as Russian interests. This meant not only the prospect of long-term deployment of American troops and military bases in the region, at the very borders of China but, eventually, American control of the hydrocarbon resources of Central Asia and the Caspian Sea, also highly

---

[35]Statement of Secretary of State Madeleine Albright, February 19, 1998, to NBC: "We are the indispensable nation. We stand tall and we see further than other countries into the future, and we see the danger here to all of us." The phrase was taken up again by Barack Obama in May 2012: "The United States is exceptional, and will always be the one indispensable nation in world affairs," (White House, May 23, 2012).

coveted by Beijing. After the specter of encirclement by the Soviet Union vanished in 1991, China found itself once again squarely in the sights of another hostile superpower applying the very same strategy. In April 2003, with the fall of Saddam Hussein's regime, the taking of Baghdad by American and British forces, and the deployment, initially intended to be long-term, of over 150,000 American troops in the region, the Middle East's stock of hydrocarbon resources was suddenly within striking distance of American military forces, and therefore fell under American control in a sense. China, dependent upon this region for over 60 percent of its energy supply, found itself more and more beholden to the United States' will in the event of tensions, or open conflict, with Washington or its allies.

Within this new context, China set about revising its approach to international politics and the balance of power, creating something closely akin to a global strategy, one to be applied to the whole planet, to counteract American plans. In order to assure its pursuit of economic development and its eventual place among the great powers, China must no longer think of itself as a merely regional power whose strategy was based only on the traditional idea of "market pacification." Rather, it was now a full-fledged world power whose interests could be defended not only in Asia, but in the other continents as well, even at the very doors of the United States if need be, in Latin America.

This new strategy, of course, gave rise to questions and caused concern about long-term Chinese ambitions, adding to the already destabilizing economic effects of China's newfound power. In an effort to allay these fears, Chinese theorists introduced a new concept around which they could construct a reassuring discourse: "the peaceful rise." In November 2003, during Prime Minister Wen Jiabao's visit to the United States, this phrase was used officially for the first time. In remarks at Harvard, he said in essence, "China today is a country in reform and opening up, and a rising power dedicated to peace.... China's development and emergence represent a peaceful rise, we wish to follow a different path than that taken by some great powers, that of a peaceful rise."[36] He drove home the message that China remained a "developing country" destined to remain so for "a rather long time," a phrase also meant to reassure China's neighbors and partners. Wen Jiabao went on to say that China would "never have hegemonic ambitions, would never be expansionist."[37] That same month, CPC Chairman and Secretary General Hu Jintao reiterated this position and added that this peaceful rise policy was still based on the Five Principles for Peaceful Coexistence agreed to in 1954 by China, India, and Burma (mutual respect for each other's territorial integrity and sovereignty, mutual non-aggression, mutual noninterference in each other's internal affairs, equality and mutual benefit, and peaceful coexistence). The notion of a peaceful

---

[36] 郭万超 [Guo Wanchao], 中国崛起－一个东方大国的成长之道 [China's rise, the path of growth for a great Eastern power], (Jiangsu Popular Ed., 2004, 9).
[37] Ibid.

rise was meant to refute experts in the history of international relations who held that no great power had ever emerged on a world scale without having expansionist ambitions and therefore provoking major conflicts. Hu Jintao, on the other hand, held that in the case of China, this risk would be abated by its "5,000-year civilization, glorious past, but also by its past humiliations," a position he expounded on at length in March 2004 before the 10th National People's Conference. China aspired rather to take advantage of world peace to strengthen itself, but also to "use its own development to contribute to peace in the world." Its rise would essentially be based on its own strengths and would in no way seek to dominate other peoples. This reassuring take on China's development and its consequences on a regional or world scale is not, of course, shared by the other major players of the international community, particularly the United States.

# China seen from outside

China's recent emergence as a growing global power has led in the United States and Europe to unexpected and disproportionate reactions. Particularly since the period preceding the Beijing Olympic Games in August 2008, we have seen Western governments and politicians give in to the temptation to stigmatize China, accusing it of every sort of transgression, taking it to task for everything from strategic errors, to their own countries' economic shortfalls, to those of the international financial system, charges that have been broadly echoed by Western media. China gets the blame for all the planet's ills, from the "threatening" conquest of hydrocarbon resources (the abortive takeover attempt of the American group Unocal in summer 2005) to the "manipulation" of its exchange rates, not to mention the disappearance of the great African elephant. The campaign was taken up anew as the Olympic Games approached, with a wave of anti-Chinese hysteria, less in terms of public opinion than among Western media and politicians. The quest for a scoop, the lure of increased sales for the media (the demonization of China sells papers), political anti-communist manipulation, governments' need to distract public opinion in their countries from ongoing problems or prevailing gloom-and-doom sentiments, complete ignorance on the part of most journalists, naïveté on the part of most non-governmental organizations and the complicity of others with certain hidden powers were all factors that stoked the fires of this campaign. China's extraordinary economic growth and its growing influence in the world likewise provide fuel for the now-dominant discourse of a "Chinese threat," while public opinion, lacking access to objective information and facing a virulently anti-Chinese dominant ideology, is unable to judge for itself the relevance of this discourse.

The remarks of some politicians and the writings of some authors issue forth from the torrents of a past that had seemed to be buried since the end of the Second World War. Though the terms used have perhaps been somewhat updated to fit the realities of the early 21st century, the same general idea can easily be glimpsed behind the ironic catchphrases ("unbridled growth," "cannibalistic expansion,"[38] "employee or worker wages averaging 500 yuan allowing some to survive but not to enjoy the new, enticing society of consumption"[39]). It is almost enough to make us forget those left behind by Western societies— the homeless or minimum-wage earners—and look down on these Chinese, overcome with "general hysteria in the quest for money" that leads them to an extraordinary circumstance: "Department stores become the favorite destination of the masses. Sometimes just for window shopping, often for extravagant purchases out of proportion with the shoppers' incomes."[40] Clearly, any move to match the consumption of Western "masses" can only be evidence of bad faith.

## A historical constant: the perception of a yellow menace and the myth of awakening

The apocryphal Napoleon Bonaparte quote that became the shock title of a bestseller by Alain Peyrefitte, "When China wakes, the world will tremble," is repeated *ad nauseam* in Europe today to denounce the Chinese threat. This image is now joined by the old refrain of a "yellow menace," a catchphrase used with great success after the late 19th century in countries holding Asian colonies, particularly in Germany, where the expression *gelbe Gefahr* first appeared to designate *die Bedrohung der weissen durch die gelbe Rasse* (the threat to whites from the yellow race).[41] The phrase "yellow menace" was often uttered in close succession with other expressions charged with strong racist connotations, frequently based on entomological metaphors likening Asians to hordes of insects because of the population density already weighing on the large East Asian states. It is difficult to use this sort of language in a direct sense nowadays, but it pops up more and more frequently to illustrate, with a wink, observations on the economic development of China and its emergence on the international scene. This is a culturalist approach to China built on an assortment of political and historical approximations, ideological considerations, and irrevocable judgments. Popular clichés die hard, and they feed the debate about China's impressive development. The Chinese are described as having intrinsic virtues and flaws that make them different as a people. They are industrious, submissive, able to reproduce nearly perfectly what others have invented, but devoid

---

[38] Philippe Cohen and Luc Richard, *La Chine sera-t-elle notre cauchemar?* (Paris: Mille et Une Nuits, 2005), 141.
[39] Philippe Massonnet, *La Chine en folie: l'héritage de Deng Xiaoping* (Éditions Philippe Picquier, 1997).
[40] Ibid., 14.
[41] F. A. Brockhaus, *Brockhaus Enzyklopädie* (Wiesbaden, 1969), Band 7, 50.

of imagination. The adjectives used to describe their activities would not be out of place in Joseph Arthur Comte de Gobineau or Ernest Renan's[42] best work, even if they are couched in gentler terms. And so malls built in China are "pretentious"; a popular author published in China is nothing more than a "clever hack";[43] cultural exhibitions are "a poor excuse for a show" that "can in no way sustain a permanent installation"; cellular telephone users "play" with their devices, "preferably in public and to talk about nothing if possible" (any resemblance to phenomena seen in other latitudes is pure coincidence); growing Chinese consumption is a "stunning display of consumerism by hundreds of millions of people"; security regulations are violated in entertainment venues such as movie theaters and karaoke bars "as long as there is enough glitz to catch the eye of the ignorant, fun-seeking clientele"; and the list goes on. For the icing on the cake, Mo Yan, winner of the Nobel Prize in Literature, was merely a "Nobel-consecrated apparatchik,"[44] according to another Chinese writer living in France who chastised him for not choosing the comfortable life of a dissident in Europe. This recent, increasingly prevalent wave of writings denigrating Chinese development and its excesses usually ascribes to China—as if pointing out features of this country alone—phenomena or behavior that can be seen not only in developing countries, but in industrialized countries as well.

Are corrupt bureaucrats a symptom particular to the Chinese economic and political system? In Asia, the most recent survey done in 2012 by *Transparency International* placed India in 94th place in terms of Asian corruption, which puts it 14 places below China. It was tied with Greece, while Italy held 72nd place, a poor record for European Union member states. Prostitution, homelessness, workers contending with highly dangerous working conditions, lack of health coverage for millions of workers, and the environmental impact of industrialization are all issues that certainly must be tackled by Chinese authorities, but they are not unique to post-reform China. Though ethnic minorities such as the Uyghurs are certainly struggling in terms of employment compared to the Han majority, unemployment figures for blacks in the United States in 2011 were double those of whites (10.4 percent versus 5.2 percent). While China has brought 300 million people out of poverty since the beginning of the reforms in 1978, American workers have seen their annual earnings fall by about $4,500 between 1973 and 1999 for non-college-educated wage-earners. In the United States, a hyperpower that spent over $80 billion on military

---

[42]Nineteenth-century French writers and cultural racism theorists.

[43]Cohen and Richard, *La Chine sera-t-elle ...* , 192. The author mentioned here, Wang Shuo, seeks "success at any price" and "prefers quantity over quality." Is this not precisely what many observers frequently criticize in Europe? The same book refers to "mental ordeals" to evoke the difficulties faced by writers in China, a generalized and categorical label that can only be surprising when considering the current profusion of "social" literature on the continent, literature describing daily life and the challenges faced by marginalized populations in a hybrid economic system, with writers such as Yu Hua, Zhang Xianlang, Han Han, and Ye Mang.

[44]Liao Yiwu, "Mo Yan, un apparatchik nobélisé," *Le Monde*, December 10, 2012.

programs in 2011, 48.6 million Americans lack any kind of health coverage due to increased unemployment and skyrocketing premiums, and 46.2 million live below the poverty line.[45] According to UNICEF, the United States and Great Britain have the greatest numbers of child laborers (around two million) among developed countries. The American organization Human Rights Watch (HRW) estimates that several hundred thousand children work in American agriculture, usually putting in an average of 14 hours per day and earning less than minimum wage.[46] Is the situation described by Philippe Cohen, who writes that doctors he spoke with near a Chinese waste treatment facility "confess their fears that a spike in cancers in workers will be the logical outcome of the waste treatment,"[47] fundamentally different from the situation observed by HRW in the United States?

*An estimated 100,000 children suffer agriculture-related injuries annually in the United States. The long-term effects of pesticide exposure are not yet completely known, but have been linked to cancer, brain tumors, brain damage and birth defects. Child farm workers interviewed by Human Rights Watch for a recent study described working in fields still wet with poison and being exposed to pesticide drift from spraying in nearby fields.*[48]

By no means should the gravity of Chinese social or economic issues be denied; rather, it should be remembered that China entered a stage of economic modernity only 30 years ago, more than a century after the United States, a country that still tolerates abuses and social and economic woes that its level of development should have eradicated long ago—or is its healthy economy perhaps partly thanks to the continued existence of this very instability and these same social vulnerabilities? When the United States underwent the Industrial Revolution around the turn of the 19th century, the country's population was under six million, reaching only 76 million a century later. The economic results achieved in a quarter-century of reforms in China have already surpassed anything seen before. This development should not be cause for alarm; rather, we should seek to understand its strengths and weaknesses. Other countries have undergone this rise before China, and the impact was resounding, as in the case of Japan or the new industrial Asian countries, but these countries now make a major contribution to the health of the world economy, and at the end of the day, their rise was very beneficial for the West.

But China, so often described as the greatest threat of the 21st century, was not always seen as such in the West. In fact, Deng Xiaoping's China offered extraordinarily promising opportunities for profit for Western liberalism, setting off a feverish rush to set up partnerships that discreetly looked the other way

---

[45]"Income, Poverty, and Health Insurance Coverage in the United States: 2011," *United States Census Bureau.*
[46]http://www.hrw.org/support-care.
[47]Cohen and Richard, *La Chine sera-t-elle …*, 152.
[48]Victoria Riskin and Mike Farrell, "Profiting on the Backs of Child Laborers," *Los Angeles Times,* October 12, 2000.

when it came to Chinese workers' conditions. Indeed, these very conditions were what allowed Western investors to give free rein to a capitalist frenzy on a par with the Western Industrial Revolutions of the 18th and 19th centuries. After all, because the Chinese fell into the category that Gobineau, in his *Essay on the Inequality of the Human Races*, described as that of eternal laborers, hardworking but lacking in imagination, they fulfilled an international division of labor that privileged developing countries and their industries, not unlike in colonial times, and permitted these demographically important states to be kept in a subordinate position. Naturally, the political excesses of the first 30 years of existence of the People's Republic of China did not go unnoticed, but there were high hopes that it would eventually completely abandon this ideology—and all signs seemed to point in that direction in the 1980s—in favor of a liberal economic model beholden to the interests of Western economies. No one could have predicted such a high rate of growth. The myth of China's "awakening" once again took the stage.

In the face of this extraordinary economic metamorphosis and its impact on the world economy, the West began to cast a new gaze on China, remember the warnings of a "yellow peril," and realize their error in judgment. China, willing to go along with growing economic openness to the world and to foreign capital and companies, intended to benefit quickly from its development and claim its place as a nascent superpower. Its economic emergence and its ever greater involvement in the *globalized* international community seemed to merit this recognition, whatever its weaknesses at the time, no matter how long the road that lay ahead, as China was the first to admit. This international recognition, which had already materialized in terms of China's admittance, in two decades, to all major international economic and diplomatic organizations and bodies, passed for dialogue on an equal footing with the United States and European Union and the enforcement of the same rules that were applied to other countries. But for the West, especially the United States, the Communist status of the Chinese regime continued to be an insurmountable obstacle to true normalization, a process that would have meant, among other things, lifting the sanctions on weapons sales to China that had been in place since the June 1989 events at Tiananmen Square. In the view of many American officials, especially neoconservatives, there is a clear link between the officially Marxist status of the Chinese political system and its fundamental atheism. Such a regime can be nothing other than expansionist and a threat to world peace. The simplistic, messianic tendencies of neoconservative American ideology preclude the idea of a partnership with China, an ideological position that played out in the change in China's status from that of *strategic partner* during the Clinton years to that of *strategic competitor* under the Bush administration.

In the hardline "preemptive strike" doctrine adopted by the Republican administration, Chinese leaders were suspected of harboring hostile designs toward the United States and its allies, and the only possible response was a return to a strategy of containment rather similar to that which was used against the Soviet Union during the Cold War years. American policy toward Beijing has often been faltering, given the very contradictory pressures and influences brought to bear on the administration. American industry is directly affected by Washington's waffling and demands a clearer and more open approach to China, a country on which their profits depend more and more every day. Part of public opinion, on the other hand, is concerned with the impact of China's economic rise on employment in the United States, while in parts of America that currently welcome Chinese investors, the infusion of Chinese capital, which prevents job loss in threatened sectors, is enthusiastically welcomed. In politics, the anti-Chinese lobby, made up of a mix of neoconservatives and the far right, strives to pass ever-tougher laws regarding Beijing on every issue (human rights, pollution, etc.[49]), while others attempt to make realism and pragmatism prevail. The media, for their part, never cease to report bad news (industrial accidents, crackdowns on demonstrators, unemployment figures). In the United States and Europe, it is difficult to find a clear vision of the challenge of China in the flood of contradictory information, but whatever the analysis, it is clearer than ever that it is impossible to ignore this new power that is shaking the foundations of 21st-century international relations.

---

[49] In the previously cited *Weekly Standard*, Max Boot, a conservative considered one of the 50 most influential personalities in the United States on foreign affairs issues, naïvely revealed the American strategy: "Besides containment, determent, and economic integration, there is a strategy that the British never used against Germany or Japan—internal subversion. Sorry, the polite euphemisms are 'promotion of democracy' and 'protection of human rights.'"

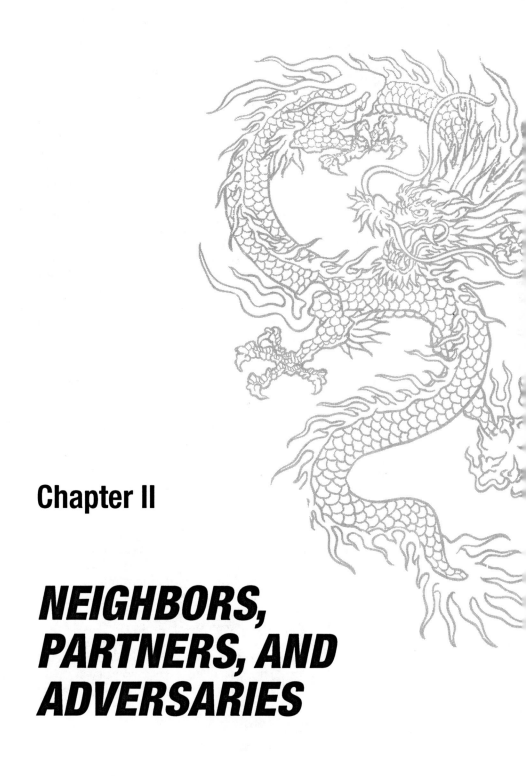

# Chapter II

# NEIGHBORS, PARTNERS, AND ADVERSARIES

Intense debates are raging all around the world today about the meaning of China's formidable economic development, its policy of military modernization, and its moves on the energy geopolitics chessboard. The challenge is to decipher the official discourse of Chinese leaders and place it in perspective in light of their actions and strategic choices. In the United States and Europe, this analysis too often rests on overly ideological criteria, either demonizing China or framing it in terms of Marxism-Leninism and Maoism for those who are nostalgic for the old days. These analyses pay little heed to the policy choices of the current Chinese leadership, which, despite the survival of slogans and references to the founding documents, are largely pragmatic and devoid of ideological considerations. In China's immediate vicinity, particularly in Southeast Asia, these debates are heavily influenced by the American discourse that depicts China as a threat with perhaps no historical precedent other than the Mongols in continental Asia. Also tingeing these debates is an inevitable feeling of vulnerability on the part of smaller, if not miniscule, states facing the giant of the planet. Naturally, whenever Beijing takes too aggressive a position on the South China Sea territorial disputes, as has been the case several times in recent years, this lends credence to the American discourse and reinforces the fears of China's neighbors.

In India, the memory of the 1962 war for Tibet still lingers, casting suspicion on Beijing's attempts at rapprochement since 2003. Russia, whose relations with China have always been complicated by rivalries for influence in Central Asia and territorial disputes in the border regions, has opted for an alliance of convenience with Beijing in order to stand up to American incursions in Central Asia, but without abandoning a certain mistrust of China's true intentions. Japan, for its part, constantly seesaws between sudden overtures to its neighbors and an unapologetic and arrogant nationalism (during the Koizumi years and now again under Prime Minister Shinzo Abe), when Japan has shown open hostility toward China and participated in its demonization alongside Washington.

Among Chinese leaders, a reassuring discourse prevails as they endeavor to defuse their partners' fears, but the very nature of the one-party system and the natural impact of China's economic growth on the economies of developed or developing countries everywhere blur the message and tend to discredit it in the eyes of Western democracies. Furthermore, the new international environment created by the aggressive politics of Washington (unilateralism, repeated violations of international law, promotion of the concept of the "preemptive strike") does not foster a discourse of consensus. How then can one speak, as Beijing does, of negotiations based on dialogue to resolve conflicts between countries, noninterference in the affairs of other states, or renouncement of the use of military force for the hegemonic purposes of any one country in the international community,[1] when the theory of "preemptive strike" is back on

---

[1] 中国国际战略 [*China's international strategy*]，倪建民-陈子舜，人民出版社 [People's Ed.], Beijing, 2003, 438.

the table and the struggle against terrorism justifies any and all state lies and the reduction to cinders of recalcitrant states? Where is the truth among the shadows of Chinese strategy in the early 21st century? What are the parameters that can confirm or discredit China's professions of good faith? It is more critical than ever to decipher these riddles in order to look to the future of China, and therefore the future of the planet and those of us who live on it. If China continues its rise in the coming decades, the current international order, already shaken up by the Bush administration's revisionist bent and its determination to impose an undisputed *Pax Americana*, supposedly democratic and probably heavily influenced by religious considerations, will be profoundly transformed, and Western powers as well as developing countries will be required to adapt to the new lay of the land, lest they risk an armed conflict whose consequences would obviously be devastating for the planet. China's major international strategic priorities, some of which we will describe in greater detail below, seem to us to fall into the following order: economic development, pacification of the periphery, securing the energy supply, recognition of China's status as a great power, and resolution of the Taiwan issue. These priorities naturally raise a question: Is conflict with the United States inevitable?

China's strategy rests on two major concerns: economics and security. Unlike the United States or the Soviet Union of yesteryear, China does not have a political agenda. Its ideological dimension has disappeared in domestic policy as well as foreign policy, notwithstanding its professed adherence to Marxism-Leninism and "Mao Zedong Thought." With the dissolution of the USSR in 1991, the socialist camp is gone, and only a few shreds of the old "socialist bloc" remain: Cuba, Vietnam, and North Korea. Immersed in reforms that have reexamined the socialist model for development and chosen to free it of its main weaknesses and extract a new concept of "socialist market economics," China has modernized socialism after the countless failures of the former Soviet socialist bloc as a whole. Finally, China does not traffic in any religious or philosophical dogma made for exportation. The cultural proselytism that is so ubiquitous in the foreign policies of European countries is conspicuously absent from the Chinese strategy, which naturally benefits from the Chinese diaspora as it pursues its aims, but does not seek to promote one culture destined to dominate all others. However, Chinese leaders have rather recently undertaken a timid policy of developing a so-called soft power through major efforts to promote Chinese culture abroad, with the creation of the Confucius Institutes, for instance, and especially through the implementation of a media network designed to influence perceptions of China abroad (through television, newspapers, etc.). The methods chosen so far, extremely controlled and centralized, betray a poor understanding of the idea of *soft power* and will doubtless have a negligible effect on the perceptions of China from abroad.

# *International impact of China's economic rise*

In the late 1970s, Deng Xiaoping decided to renounce Marxist-Leninist dogma, which privileges theory over practice, and instead place economic development front and center. This strategic decision allowed China to envisage full reintegration into the fold of the international community and to hope for its eventual admission into the private club of great powers. In economic terms, reality would slowly erase all taboos, and the reforms implemented starting in 1979 would dismantle the traditional socialist system in favor of a hybrid brand of socialism. This hybrid socialism was characterized by its pragmatism: rather than follow a particular model, it would draw inspiration from experiments carried out in other countries as well as challenges particular to China.

The impact of the reforms on Chinese foreign policy was considerable. Existing relations with the United States on the one hand, and the socialist bloc on the other, were dramatically influenced by this radical change in course after an era of revolutionary excesses, which contributed to greater isolation for China but at the same time led to its rapprochement with Washington and Tokyo in order to counter the Soviet threat. With the collapse of the Soviet empire in the early 1990s, the strategic context was suddenly transformed, and the United States became the principal threat. However, the powerful American economy forced Beijing to follow a pragmatic policy of appeasement with Washington in order to ensure the continuation of the reforms. During the 1990s, US attention to Russia, combined with the consensual policies of the Clinton administration, gave the Chinese leadership some respite. Advancement of the reforms depended largely on regional stability, and the White House appeared willing to pursue a policy of economic engagement, even if it meant putting on hold for the time being its criticisms of China's poor record on human rights and freedom of speech. In this less tense context, China was officially accorded "strategic partner" status by the United States and was even recognized as a *most-favored nation,* much to the dismay of the American anti-Chinese lobby. When George W. Bush took office in 2000, China had already become an indispensable economic partner for Washington. With the hostile stance of the new American administration, Sino-American relations entered a new phase, more threatening to Chinese economic development. Maintaining the growth rate, which had hovered around 10 percent annually for three decades with a peak of 15.2 percent in 1984, was imperative for Beijing, which had set its sights very high for the coming decades. This was a matter not only of economic rise, but of the future of the Communist Party, whose legitimacy as sole decider of the country's affairs also depended on its ability to assure continuous improvement of the population's quality of life.

In this context of mutual mistrust between China and the United States, it was indispensable for Beijing to adopt a new strategy based on alliances of convenience with the main players of the international community and on economic expansion. The latter must be characterized by continuous growth in GDP as well as increasing participation in international finance (takeover of foreign companies, purchase of US Treasury bonds, creation of free-trade zones, etc.) to take advantage of globalization and to develop strong interdependencies. This economic strategy has been so successful that it now threatens to alter profoundly not only the international economic order built by the West, but also the very concept of economic liberalism founded on the Open Door Policy, so dear to American strategists and intended to secure American economic domination and the expansion of their own *open door empire.* [2] It is a strategy that allows China to limit external political pressures and the actions of an asymmetrical war waged by its adversaries to destabilize it.

In the Western camp, the other major economic player was of course the European Union, from which Beijing hoped to see not only important economic benefits, but also a willingness to have a hand in rebalancing a world that had become unipolar. China would have an ally to be reckoned with in international affairs in order to promote the emergence of a "new international order" founded on dialogue and cooperation. This greater European autonomy vis-à-vis Washington would have also, perhaps especially, strengthened China's position within the international community by weakening the American "camp." France's strong opposition to the American and British intervention in Iraq, as well as opposition by other European countries who followed France's lead, offered a glimpse of a real ability on the part of the European Union to distance itself from American policies. China by itself is not in a position to stand up to the United States at the United Nations, but as we have seen repeatedly, particularly on the issue of Iraq during the period of the sanctions, it is able to form a united front with France and Russia in the Security Council to block American initiatives of which it disapproves. Whatever credibility France enjoyed as a force for appeasement and reason in an international order menaced by American unilateralism was seriously bruised when it adopted a conciliatory stance at the United Nations in the months following the fall of Baghdad to American and British forces and voted for the resolutions recognizing the intervention and granting the United States and Great Britain authority to administer Iraq during a transitional phase that lasted in fact eight long years. The confusion that reigned within the European Union during the Iraqi crisis and European impotence due to the lack of a shared foreign policy approach—combined with divergences regarding relations with the United States—made Beijing aware of the considerable weakening of the European Union in the wake of this challenge. This impression was underlined by the failure in France and the Netherlands of the referenda on the future of Europe, and it led Beijing to take a lower profile in its relations with Washington.

[2] William Appleman Williams, *The Tragedy of American Diplomacy* (Norton Paperback, 1972), 70.

Beijing today considers the European Union an important and relatively captive economic partner. In fact, with the rather gloomy economic outlook of the historic core countries of the European Union and the collapse of its newer member states since 2008 (Greece, Spain, and Portugal), the Chinese market, with its potential for development, is increasingly coveted. In 2004, the European Union was tied with the United States as China's main trade partner (147.73 billion euros for the United States, 146.12 billion for the European Union). The European Union finds itself increasingly beholden to this relationship. China is also its second-largest trade partner after the United States, with an annual trade deficit of 156 billion euros in 2011. This deficit was only 48.6 billion in 2000. In Chinese global strategy, the European Union has gone from the status of "potential diplomatic and strategic partner" to one of "privileged economic partner." In 2011, the stock of foreign direct investments (FDI) in China reached $711 billion, while Brazil and India saw only $607 billion and $202 billion in FDI, respectively.[3] With the financial crisis that battered the United States and Europe, China became the most attractive country for FDI, and in 2012, it surpassed the United States in FDI.

In order to assure its long-term economic development, it is imperative for China to be actively involved in promoting international stability and managing crises. China's statements on foreign policy persistently reiterate the priority it places on stability and express a reality that the other great powers should doubtless integrate into their own strategies. This stance is identical on all points to that of American leaders before the First World War, who considered peace and stability two dynamic elements indispensable to American economic expansion and well-being.[4] China's opening to the world over the last 30 years has allowed it to attract foreign capital and find a market for its massive exports in an increasingly favorable trade environment (thanks to China's accession to the World Trade Organization [WTO] in December 2001). It is the economies of other countries, particularly Western ones, that must now agree to open up to Chinese capital, and this new phase will be particularly delicate. Naturally, this process started only timidly a few years ago, but it is now booming. Resistance in this area will be particularly fierce, as we saw in 2005, when a public Chinese group attempted to purchase the American energy giant Unocal, or more recently with the failed takeover bid of the American group 3Com by Huawei.[5] In a general sense, protectionism has again reared its head in Western politicians' discourse, and China is its first target. The tariff barriers erected by George W. Bush to protect the American steel industry; the massive increase in farm subsidies; stumbles in the management of the Danone issue in France in 2005; and also the withdrawal in 2006 of European efforts to block the

[3]Ken Davies, "Inward FDI in China and Its Policy Context, 2012," *Columbia FDI Profiles*, Vale Columbia Center on Sustainable International Investment, October 24, 2012, 1.
[4]Ibid, 128.
[5]Steven R. Weisman, "U.S. Security Concerns Block China's 3Com Deal," *New York Times*, February 21, 2008.

ments were often an excuse to settle other political or strategic differences. In the 1960s and 1970s, Beijing settled its border conflicts with its most receptive neighbors (Burma, Nepal, North Korea, Mongolia, Pakistan, and Afghanistan). After the collapse of the USSR, normalization was achieved with the new Central Asian republics (Kazakhstan, Kyrgyzstan, and Tajikistan), and then with Laos and Vietnam. Russia, which had been a difficult partner at best, finally agreed in May 1991 to settle the dispute that had poisoned its relations with Beijing since 1949. In this agreement, Beijing got only 52 percent of the territory it claimed, but it considered stabilization of its relations with Moscow a higher priority. In October 2004, a complementary accord completed the delimitation of the eastern section of this shared border, removing one of the major causes of tension weighing on the strategic alliance established between the two countries.

The conflict with Vietnam was a particularly tough episode. After settling the dispute on December 30, 1999, with the signing of a border treaty in Hanoi, the two countries signed an agreement on December 25, 2000, regarding border delimitation in the Gulf of Tonkin, a highly contested area due to the hydrocarbon reserves it may hold. But the agreement was not ratified by Vietnam until June 25, 2004. In December 2008, the two countries completed the full and final delimitation of their land border after 10 years of work, an event that both parties hailed as a historic landmark in their relations.[8] But 2009 brought a setback in this new appeasement between the two countries with the dispute over the Spratly Islands (南沙群岛; *Nánshā qúndǎo* in Chinese and *Quần đảo Trường Sa* in Vietnamese) and the Paracel Islands (西沙群岛; *Xīshā Qúndǎo* or *Quần đảo Hoàng Sa*) in the South China Sea. This issue weighs heavily on Sino-Vietnamese relations, and Vietnam has sought support from the ASEAN membership and the United States in the face of an increasingly assertive Chinese approach to this highly strategic region since 2009. The noticeable rise in anti-Chinese sentiment in Vietnamese public opinion, further stoked by a series of incidents in the area, has encouraged the Hanoi leadership to adopt an intransigent position toward Chinese claims. Washington's direct intervention in the conflict, particularly with Hillary Clinton's speech in July 2010 in Hanoi, in which she stated that the conflicts in the South China Sea were in the "national interest" of the United States,[9] reassured Vietnam in its resistance to Chinese pressures while simultaneously confirming China's conviction that Washington harbors hostile intentions toward it and is determined to implement a strategy of encirclement and *containment* not unlike the Cold War years.

---

[8] "Sự kiện có ý nghĩa lịch sử trọng đại trong quan hệ Việt Nam - Trung Quốc [An event of historical importance for relations between Vietnam and China]," *Nhân Dân*, January 1, 2009; "中越陆地边界云南段完成竖界碑665个 勘定边界线" ["665 markers placed on the Yunnan stretch of the Sino-Vietnamese border to demarcate the border"], *Huanqiu shibao*, January, 3, 2009.

[9] "Clinton wades into South China Sea territorial dispute," *Washington Post*, July 23, 2010.

## Settling border disputes

China still has border disputes to resolve with India, some ASEAN member states in the South China Sea, and Japan.

The settlement of the border conflict with India in recent years has been a priority for the same reasons as the rapprochement with Moscow. In June 2003, during Indian Prime Minister Vajpayee's visit to China, the two countries took a major step toward settlement. India recognized China's sovereignty over the Tibet Autonomous Region,[10] but China's public position on the status of Sikkim, annexed in 1975 by New Delhi, remained ambiguous. The spokesperson for the Chinese Ministry of Foreign Affairs (MOFA) stated in a press briefing during the visit that "Sikkim is 'an enduring issue left over from history' and cannot be resolved overnight.... We have to respect history. We have to take into consideration realistic factors." Despite the agreement to open border trade between Sikkim and Tibet, which looked to certain observers like a recognition on the part of China of Indian sovereignty over the small state, Beijing has not recognized this formally. However, the issue appears to have been dropped with the 2004 publication by the Chinese MOFA *World Affairs Year Book 2003–2004*, which for the first time since the 1975 annexation of Sikkim does not list this territory as an independent state. It still remains, however, for the two countries to proceed to the formal political delimitation of this border.

Nonetheless, there are still two border disputes that continue to block this Sino-Indian rapprochement: sovereignty over certain parts of the territory of Arunachal Pradesh (China claims 35,000 square miles of it and refers to it as the Prefecture of Southern Tibet [藏南地, Zàngnán dìqū]) and Kashmir (India accuses China of illegally occupying 15,000 square miles and contests the 1963 handover from Pakistan to China of 2,000 square miles in the area of Kashmir). Beijing and New Delhi, however, have committed to settling these disputes as quickly as possible based on a "reality-based arrangement" (as Chinese Prime Minister Wen Jiabao put it in March 2005). In April 2003, the two countries signed an agreement outlining the broad principles to be followed and specifying that the border would be established "along well-defined natural geographic features, easily identifiable in order to be acceptable to both India and China." The prime minister clearly laid out Chinese ambitions with his statement, "We will build a bridge of friendship linking the two countries, a bridge that will lead us together into the future." To Beijing's eyes, these claims for a few thousand square miles in the far reaches of the country are of relatively little concern compared to the importance for China of a rapprochement with India, a major partner in Asian strategy, but the pressures of nationalist

---

[10] Statement of the Indian prime minister after the visit: "I would only like to say there is no ambiguity or inconsistency in our position on the Tibet Autonomous Region of the People's Republic of China. We were therefore happy to reiterate our position in the Joint Declaration." Prime minister describes China visit as fruitful," Press Trust of India, June 27, 2003.

public opinion opposed to any "handover of territories" are a major stumbling block for both parties. However, Beijing's renunciation of part of its claims would be a token of goodwill in order to establish a relationship of trust indispensable to the opening of new trade routes to the Indian subcontinent, extend the strategic alliance already created with Russia to include India as well, and counter American overtures toward New Delhi. For decades, American-Indian relations were characterized by mutual suspicion and the refusal on the part of India to ally itself with any great power, in accordance with the nonalignment principles that Indian leaders helped create. But relations with Washington began to warm with President Bill Clinton's March 2000 visit to India. This rapprochement picked up speed in 2004 with American encouragement. In January 2004, the two countries signed a first agreement titled "Next Steps in Strategic Partnership with India," which contemplated greater cooperation in civil nuclear power, civil space programs, and high-tech trade. The agreement was implemented quickly, with Washington's decision in September of that same year to lift the export controls on equipment destined for Indian nuclear facilities in exchange for New Delhi's commitment to respect American concerns about nuclear nonproliferation. In June 2005, the signing of a "Defense Framework Agreement" was hailed as "historic" by India. This was followed by the July 18th joint statement published after the Indian-American summit, which set the areas and conditions for development of cooperation between the two countries on nuclear power, space programs, and trade issues. The Bush administration confirmed this partnership for civil nuclear energy during the American president's March 2006 visit to India, with his signature on an agreement in which New Delhi was to dedicate most of its nuclear stock to civil usage currently and in the future, under the control of the International Atomic Energy Agency, in consideration for American assistance. The April 2010 agreement with the United States authorizing India to reprocess its fuel, within the framework of the nuclear cooperation agreement signed in 2008, clearly went against the spirit of nonproliferation, which Washington shows such a strong attachment to under other circumstances. As a result, tensions increased in South Asia.[11] In September 2008, thanks to American support, India became the only country to be granted an exemption by the Nuclear Suppliers Group (NSG) allowing it to participate in international trade of nuclear fuel although it refused to adhere to the Non-Proliferation Treaty (NPT), to which it should be noted that Iran has continued to adhere after the Islamic revolution. The reason cited by the American administration was India's democratic system. No mention was made of the December 2001–July 2002 crisis during which India and Pakistan were on the brink of war, both wielding nuclear weapons.

---

[11]Mark Hibbs, "Moving Forward on the U.S.-India Nuclear Deal," Carnegie Endowment for Peace, April 5, 2010.

For China, this Indian-American rapprochement represents a long-term threat. China is not really in a position to counter this American influence in Indian political circles. On the one hand, many current Indian leaders, particularly within the National Congress, attended American schools and are culturally very Western. They see Chinese overtures as nothing more than an attempt to draw them away from their Western allies, and the Chinese culture and political system inspire no sympathy in them. On the other hand, the United States continues to be an important partner on several important issues facing the region (terrorism, nuclear proliferation, energy, technological cooperation), and though Russia is an important arms supplier for India, no other country today can take the place of the United States in this regard. Finally, despite a remarkable improvement in the atmosphere of the region, particularly in terms of relations with Pakistan and China, India remains very cautious in its alliances. The prospect of a true, lasting détente and close cooperation between Beijing and New Delhi is certainly one of the United States' major concerns in Asia, and Washington is following very closely the developments of this normalization process. China's military modernization and its desire to take a position in the Indian Ocean may block this Sino-Indian rapprochement and discourage Indian leaders for years to come from forming too close a relationship with Beijing, beyond a greater economic openness. The two countries' status as rivals could likewise hobble this rapprochement, even if the energy cooperation agreement signed in January 2006 aimed to mitigate the effects of this very rivalry through closer cooperation regionally as well as in international markets. (At the time of the agreement the Indian minister for petroleum and natural gas stated, "We look upon China not as a strategic competitor but as a strategic partner.")[12]

But India is also aware of the limits of an alliance with the United States, which is perfectly capable of suddenly turning its back on India, as in the case of the 1998 nuclear crisis with Pakistan. The simultaneous sales to Pakistan and India in March 2005 of F-16 fighter jets, despite New Delhi's opposition, were symptomatic of the constant tension with Washington and the impact of American policy on the arms race in the region. Indeed, when the Bush administration announced the sales, it cynically added that it was authorizing American companies to supply India with the latest generation of sophisticated warplanes (including F-16s and F-18s) and to develop expanded military cooperation, particularly for missile defense systems. In practice, the United States would supply India with sophisticated military equipment that would allow it to blast the previous-generation Pakistani planes out of the sky. Such a policy could only lend further credence to the Chinese discourse charging the United States with perpetuating or even accentuating existing tensions for its own commercial and hegemonic ends.

---

[12] "China, India sign energy agreement," *China Daily*, January 13, 2006.

In the South China Sea, China must deal with ancient territorial disputes involving claims by a long list of countries. The area is of economic interest to all regional players because of its hydrocarbon reserves, but it represents a major strategic interest for China as well. More than half of the world's merchant marine fleet (in tonnage) sails the region annually, carrying most of East Asia's energy supply. More than 80 percent of Japan, South Korea, and Taiwan's supply of crude oil follows this route, as well as the supply of liquefied natural gas headed for such countries as Indonesia, Malaysia, and Vietnam. Thus, two-thirds of South Korea's energy supply and 60 percent of that of Japan and Taiwan depends on the navigational security of these waters.

Armed incidents have broken out repeatedly between the countries in the region, with particularly violent confrontations between the Chinese and the (South) Vietnamese in 1974 and in 1988. These territorial disputes pitted not only China against its southern neighbors, but also Malaysia against Brunei or Cambodia against Thailand. In February 1992, the adoption by the Chinese People's Conference of a "Law on territorial waters and contiguous zones of the PRC (中华人民共和国领海及毗连区法)" raised new concerns among ASEAN member states involved in the disputes. But all the parties manifested for over a decade their wishes to resolve the disputes via negotiation. In November 2002, China signed a *Declaration on the Conduct of Parties* with ASEAN member states, committing to resolving territorial disputes by peaceful means and renouncing the use of "threats and force." The incidents that have since taken place (with Vietnam[13] in January 2005 and Indonesia[14] in September of the same year, for instance) were in fact settled politically and without broad media coverage. In recent years, there has been a considerable toughening of Chinese positions regarding Beijing's claims, and this has led to more serious incidents, particularly with Vietnam and Indonesia. The launch of China's first aircraft carrier in August 2011 reinforced the fears of the countries on the South China Sea; their concern is that China might use its newfound military might to impose its sovereignty in the contested areas. Washington's intervention in the conflict with the previously cited statement by Hillary Clinton contributed to a very volatile environment.

This region is highly strategic for China for two reasons. On the one hand, the safe passage of tankers through this maritime route is essential to Chinese economic stability. The South China Sea is infested with pirates who regularly attack vessels and represent a real threat, so much so that it is the maritime region most affected by large-scale piracy. Moreover, in the event of conflict with Taiwan or Japan, Chinese military presence in its waters would allow Beijing

---

[13]Eight Vietnamese fishermen were killed by units of the China Coast Guard. Vietnamese authorities acknowledged that they were in Chinese territorial waters. They were sailing off the coast of Thanh Hoa, 124 miles south of Hanoi.

[14]A Chinese fisherman was killed by the Indonesian Navy in the Arufa Sea, off the coast of Irian Jaya. The four Chinese boats had been accused of illegal fishing, and the Indonesian Navy claimed to have given standard warnings before opening fire. A boat was seized and the crew was taken into custody.

to seriously disrupt those countries' energy supplies, despite the presence of the United States Seventh Fleet, based in Japan. China will therefore continue to pursue its territorial claims over the Paracel and Spratly Islands. Although Beijing seeks a negotiated settlement of these disputes, it contemplates no other settlement than one favorable to its claims.

The most delicate border dispute facing China, and doubtless the most explosive, is its disagreement with Japan regarding sovereignty over a number of islets in the East China Sea. For decades, both countries had kept a low profile on this issue. In March 2004, the alert was sounded over the Diaoyu Islands (Senkaku in Japanese[15]), when the "China Federation for Defending the Diaoyu Islands" announced its wishes to establish a regular maritime link between Xiamen, in the Chinese province of Fujian, and the islands. In August of the same year, the Taiwanese prime minister unleashed a storm by accusing Beijing of "threatening regional stability." Chinese surveillance boats had allegedly been sighted off the coasts of Japan some 20 times between 2004 and 2005. He claimed that "they intend to break the island chain linking Japan, Okinawa, Taiwan, and the Philippines and confront the United States." Likewise, the November 2004 incursion of a Chinese submarine in Japanese territorial waters south of Okinawa was fiercely denounced by Tokyo and broadly reported in the media. This virulent reaction came two days after Kyodo News reported on scenarios developed by Chinese strategists that envisioned attacks on Japan or Taiwan in the event of conflict over the Taiwan issue or energy rivalries. Tensions over the border dispute intensified in 2005, soon followed by a major political crisis between the two countries. The crisis was set in motion by the bellicose discourse of the Japanese prime minister regarding his Asian neighbors when commenting on his visits to the Yasukuni Shrine. This shrine guards the souls of Japanese who died for Japan during different wars, including 1,068 war criminals, 14 of them Class A war criminals.[16]

Japan cited the area's energy resources as justification of their firm position in the conflict. Koizumi even very theatrically stated his determination to defend Japan's energy resources and promised the National Diet to "do his best to assure its maritime resources rights." In February, Tokyo announced that it had now taken control of the lighthouse built by far-right activists on the island of Uotsuri-shima, the largest of the Diaoyu/Senkaku Islands. The builders of the lighthouse were no longer able to manage it, so Tokyo decided to have it administered by the state. Meanwhile, Japan initiated another conflict with South Korea by permitting a local assembly to adopt a decree claiming Japanese sovereignty over the Takeshima Islands (Dokdo for the

[15] These islands form part of the Prefecture of Okinawa, turned over to Japan by the United States in 1972 and claimed by both the People's Republic of China and Taiwan. They had been annexed in 1985 by Tokyo at the same time as Taiwan.
[16] The shrine's Web site in the mid 2000s used to read "1068 'Martyrs of the Shōwa period' were cruelly and unjustly tried as war criminals by a shameful criminal court of the Allies (the United States, England, the Netherlands, China, and others). These martyrs, too, are the Kami of the Yasukuni Shrine."

Koreans), currently under Korean control, to which former Korean President Roh Moo-hyun responded with an unusually virulent communiqué calling on Koreans to prepare for a "diplomatic war" with Japan and to prepare to make economic sacrifices. Thus, Japanese policy toward its immediate Asian neighbors, encouraged by unflagging American support, has only increased regional tensions and fueled China's denunciation of Tokyo's renewed hegemonic overtones. With Japan's decision in summer 2012 to purchase these islands from their owners, the Kurihara family, who had leased them to the Japanese government for decades, with the declared goal of avoiding their purchase by Tokyo, which was led by the ultranationalist and anti-Chinese Governor Shintaro Ishihara, the two countries plunged into the worst crisis yet over this issue. For China, which admittedly took advantage of the conflict in the context of preparations for the Eighteenth Congress of the Communist Party of China, this issue threatens to lurk permanently in the background of Sino-Japanese relations, as an October 25, 2012, editorial in the official Chinese newspaper *Global Times* predicted: "The Diaoyu Islands issue will never become what it used to be in the past. Japan should face reality, correct itself, and reach a new consensus with China. Only by doing so can the Sino-Japanese relations go back to normal."[17]

This territorial dispute will not likely be put to rest in the short or medium term. In fact, it could well degenerate into low-intensity armed conflicts between Japan and China if such a confrontation serves the political or strategic purposes of either party. After a period of relative appeasement on the Japanese side during the very short term of Prime Minister Yasuo Fukuda (September 2007–September 2008),[18] which was marked by a willingness on both sides to tone down bilateral relations, focus efforts on their points in common, and reduce tensions, the December 2012 reelection of Shinzo Abe will likely lead to renewed Sino-Japanese tensions. The reelected prime minister has in fact placed relations with the United States front and center among his concerns and reiterated his wishes to revise the constitution, giving the Japan Self-Defense Forces conventional army status and significantly increasing the defense budget. His position on territorial disputes is very firm toward China as well as Korea. His clearly stated objective during his official visit to the United States in February 2013 is to "restore Japan's strong foreign policy capability" and "[regain] the trust with Asian nations," particularly in the face of China, whose need for overt territorial conflicts with its neighbors he considers "deeply ingrained" due to the very nature of the regime.[19] His clearly excessive remarks were immediately attenuated by Tokyo, whose spokesman was quick

---

[17]Zhong Sheng, "No return to previous status quo on issue of Diaoyu sovereignty," *Global Times*, October 25, 2012.

[18]Yasuo Fukuda was elected on a political platform that emphasized rapprochement with China and South Korea, with an eye to easing Japan's isolation within its Asian environment.

[19]Chico Harlan, "Japan's Prime Minister Shinzo Abe: Chinese need for conflict is 'deeply ingrained,'" *Washington Post*, February 20, 2013; "Transcript of interview with Japanese Prime Minister Shinzo Abe," *Washington Post*, February 20, 2013.

to state that Abe's remarks on China in his interview with the *Washington Post* were "misleading" and that Japan values "mutually beneficial relations with China based on strategic interests."[20]

Accusations leveled by Shinzo Abe against China that it supposedly encourages the teaching of patriotism in order to lend the Party a new political legitimacy are all the more ironic given that in his first term as prime minister (September 2006–September 2007), Abe himself passed a revision of the Fundamental Law of Education to emphasize patriotism's place in secondary education.[21] The strengthening of ties with Washington declared during Abe's February 2013 visit to Washington can only add to the dismay felt in Beijing, about which Abe had this to say: "It is important for us to have them recognize that it is impossible to try to get their way by coercion or intimidation…. In that regard, the Japan-U.S. alliance, as well as the U.S. presence, would be critical."[22]

## Interdependence and regional cooperation

China has always maintained close relations with Southeast Asia. After China held a hegemonic position for centuries, the appetites of the colonial powers and their progressive conquest of the region starting in the 18th century, shared among the French, British, Dutch, and Spanish, deeply transformed the power relationships in the region. The slow whittling away of territories previously held by the Chinese emperor considerably weakened China's image and influence in Southeast Asia. The Qing court never really reacted until the threat was at its gates, in Tonkin, in the form of French conquerors. The Sino-French War for sovereignty over Tonkin (1884–1885) ended in a painful military defeat for China and its definitive abandonment of any designs on the Indochinese Peninsula.

While decolonization certainly transformed the geopolitical landscape, it led to an overall configuration that was no less disadvantageous for China. The colonial powers had essentially stepped aside for two new players, the United States and the Soviet Union, who would implement intrusive policies in the region. The Vietnam War, which saw the involvement of up to 536,000 American troops in 1968, kept tensions alive in the region and put pressure on China, which called for the departure of American troops from its periphery. Five regional countries (Thailand, Indonesia, the Philippines, Malaysia, and Singapore) decided to found on August 8, 1967, the Association

---

[20] Chico Harlan and David Nakamura, "Japan says Abe's quotes about China in Post interview were 'misleading,'" *Washington Post*, February 23, 2013.

[21] "Japan's Prime Minister Shinzo Abe: Chinese need for conflict is 'deeply ingrained'"; Passed on December 22, 2006, Article 5 of the new Fundamental Law of Education reads "… to foster an attitude to respect our traditions and culture, love the country and region that nurtured them."

[22] Fred Hiatt, "Shinzo Abe's new agenda: Better ties with U.S.," *Washington Post*, February 20, 2013.

of Southeast Asian Nations (ASEAN), whose purpose, as Thai Minister of Foreign Affairs Thanat Koman stated at the time, was to protect the region against both increasing incursions by great powers and confrontations with Southeast Asian countries. When ASEAN was founded, China was embroiled in its worst crisis since the 1949 Cultural Revolution, and Chinese leaders attempted to use the Chinese diaspora to destabilize governments in power. Suspicions that have persisted for decades of the Chinese diaspora's allegiance to Beijing have led to serious crises in the region, particularly with Indonesia (1965–66) and Vietnam (1978–79), and trust was never really reestablished, as evidenced by events in Indonesia in 1998 or in the Philippines during tensions over China's designs on the South China Sea.

| | Population (millions) | GNP (billions of dollars) | GDP per capita (dollars) |
|---|---|---|---|
| Brunei | 0.423 | 16.36 | 38,703 |
| Singapore | 5.18 | 259.85 | 50,530 |
| Laos | 6.38 | 8.16 | 1,279 |
| Cambodia | 14.52 | 12.76 | 879 |
| Malaysia | 28.96 | 287.92 | 9,941 |
| Myanmar | 60.38 | 52.84 | 875 |
| Thailand | 67.59 | 345.81 | 5,116 |
| Vietnam | 87.84 | 123.26 | 1,403 |
| Philippines | 95.83 | 224.33 | 2,341 |
| Indonesia | 237.67 | 846.82 | 3,563 |
| CHINA | 1,344.13 | 7,318.49 | 2,634 |

ASEAN Secretariat, 2011 – World Bank, 2011

With Deng Xiaoping's rise to power and the materialization of Sino-Vietnamese hostilities, provoked by the Hanoi government's alignment with the USSR, China finally approached ASEAN. Even if the parties did not have friendly sentiments toward one another, they at least had a common enemy in Vietnam, which they saw as a vector of Soviet expansionism in Southeast Asia. This shared hostility toward Vietnam strengthened their relations until the events of Tiananmen Square in June 1989, the brutality of which engendered a defiant reaction in Southeast Asia and the desire for renewed US involvement in the region. In a sign of the region's strategic importance, China reassessed its policy in Southeast Asia almost immediately. The normalization process took a decade, during which Beijing patiently set about regaining the trust of Southeast Asian leaders. China displayed great deftness in settling the Cambodian conflict of 1991, a first phase in its return to the region as a responsible power. It lent support to the institutional strengthening of ASEAN, which it could have opposed, by backing the formation in 1993 of the *ASEAN Regional Forum*[23] and engaging in exclusive talks in 1997 via the ASEAN Plus Three format (with China, Japan, and South Korea). After the *Joint Declaration on the Conduct of Parties,* signed by China and ASEAN in November 2002, the process led to China joining the ASEAN Treaty of Amity in October 2003. This treaty provided for a regional security mechanism based on dialogue, cooperation, and negotiation to "promote regional peace and stability and the key role of the United Nations." And now within a decade, China has become a privileged ASEAN partner, a position naturally bolstered by its economic prowess.

China's economic emergence on the regional and world stages has encouraged ASEAN states to seek a lasting relationship from which they can draw real benefits despite the nature of their economies, which are more competitive than complementary. The stunning growth in Chinese GDP over the last two decades, along with China's economic openness within the region, has led to growing interdependence. In 1994, China represented 2.1 percent of ASEAN exports and 1.9 percent of its imports, compared with 10.55 percent and 12.21 percent, respectively, in 2010. With its $234 billion in trade in 2010, or 11.34 percent of the total, China has become ASEAN's largest trading partner ahead of the 27-member European Union ($208 billion), Japan ($206 billion), and the United States ($186 billion), while ASEAN in turn became China's third-largest trade partner in 2011, particularly thanks to the ASEAN Free Trade Agreement taking effect in January 2010.[24] After Beijing's decision in November 2000 to encourage foreign investments, China alone invested over $6 billion in ASEAN in 2011, leaving it in third place behind the European Union—the largest investor with $18 billion—and Japan, with $15 billion. Meanwhile, US foreign direct investments ($5.87 billion) dropped by more than half between 2010 and 2011.[25] The Chinese diaspora in Southeast Asia, which at 30 million people represents half of the Chinese community abroad, naturally played a role in this rapprochement process.

China and ASEAN constitute major potential economic partners for each other, though both are currently more oriented toward faraway partners such

---

[23] In 1977, ASEAN opened partnership dialogues with several countries involved in the region, particularly the United States, meeting annually with their foreign affairs ministers. The ASEAN Regional Forum (ARF), created in 1993, became Southeast Asia's first multilateral forum on security issues in the Asia-Pacific region. It includes 22 members: Australia, Brunei, Myanmar, Cambodia, Canada, the People's Republic of China, India, Indonesia, Japan, South Korea, Laos, Malaysia, Mongolia, New Zealand, Papua New Guinea, the Philippines, Russia, Singapore, Thailand, the United States, the European Union, and Vietnam.

[24] *Asian Community in Figures 2011*, ASEAN Secretariat, 2011. Official Chinese sources set Chinese FDI in ASEAN at $3.5 billion and ASEAN's FDI in China at $6.3 billion for the same year.

[25] *Asian Community in Figures 2011*; ASEAN Secretariat, FDI Statistics.

as the United States or the European Union. This realization formed the basis for negotiations that led to the creation of the ASEAN–China Free Trade Area (ACFTA). As a result, the *Framework Agreement on Comprehensive Economic Cooperation between ASEAN and China,* signed in Phnom-Penh on November 4, 2002, went into effect on July 1, 2003. This agreement provided for the progressive suspension of tariff and non-tariff barriers to goods, progressive liberalization of trade in the service and investment sectors, implementation of the Early Harvest Program,[26] and strengthened economic cooperation in the priority sectors of agriculture, information and communications technology, human resources development, and investment in the development of the Mekong Basin. ACFTA opens the door to a market of 1.7 billion consumers, the largest free-trade area in the world with an estimated GDP of $2 trillion. It went into effect on January 1, 2010, for the six founding states of ASEAN (Thailand, Singapore, the Philippines, Indonesia, Malaysia, and Brunei) and will do so in 2015 for the remaining four (Myanmar, Vietnam, Cambodia, and Laos). At Bali on October 8, 2003, Japan and India each signed a document of intent with ASEAN. A final agreement was signed with India on August 13, 2009, completing the free-trade area, which went into effect on January 1, 2010. After the signing on October 8, 2003, of the *Framework for Comprehensive Economic Partnership between Japan and the ASEAN* and its entry into force on December 1, 2008, both parties likewise implemented liberalization of trade, albeit with a number of conditions relating to the differential development among ASEAN states.

In a decade, China had conquered a privileged place in Southeast Asia, which it sought to bolster at the first East Asia Summit held at Kuala Lumpur in December 2005. Much was at stake, because it brought ASEAN states together not only with Japan and South Korea, which were already members of the ASEAN Plus Three dialogue, but also with India, a growing power in the region, Russia, and above all, Australia and New Zealand. The latter two countries were invited at the express request of ASEAN, which was anxious to get partners outside the region on board, particularly those that the United States (whose request to be included had been declined) felt were likely to counter Chinese and Russian influence within this new multilateral structure. These two powers' declared intention to reduce US influence on the Asian strategic landscape is very uncomfortable for Washington, which has watched with some concern China's rising power in the region. In the process of normalization with ASEAN member states carried out by Beijing for over 10 years, there have been many challenges to China, whose superiority in terms of power raises natural concerns and suspicions among its immediate neighbors. China must consistently prove its goodwill and desire for peace to regional leaders,

---

[26] This program was intended to speed up the process of reducing tariff barriers for certain high-priority products: live animals, meat and offal, fish, dairy, other animal products, unfinished lumber, vegetables, fruits, and nuts.

among whom Washington, on the other hand, strives to foster and perpetuate the notion of a threatening China. This privileged relationship between China and ASEAN may suffer the destabilizing effects of greater challenges, such as international terrorism or the American policy of containment, as clearly evidenced by the first relative successes of the new American *Pivot to Asia* strategy.

## Marginalizing Japan in Asia

The relationship between China and Japan is much more complex and delicate. The 2005 crisis over Japanese textbooks only served to underline the depth of the chasm between not only the Chinese and the Japanese, but also between the Japanese and the Koreans, a rift they have been unable to close since the end of the Second World War. The Chinese and Koreans, as well as the peoples of Southeast Asia, harbor the painful memory, immortalized in history textbooks, of the period when Japan set out to conquer Asia. From the colonization of Taiwan in 1895 in the wake of the Sino-Japanese War to the massacres of the Second World War, the grievances are numerous. Japanese nationalism and militarism unleashed one of the bloodiest conflicts in Asian history, and the wounds have not entirely healed. It is true that unlike Germany, which the Americans and Europeans went to great lengths to denazify, Imperial Japan kept its emperor, though he could legitimately have been tried as a war criminal, and the labor of introspection was not imposed on Japan by the victors as it was in Germany. The recasting of institutions in postwar Japan under American supervision did not profoundly alter the nationalist sentiments of a country that had been so long isolated due to its insularity, then galvanized for decades by an imperialist discourse hostile to the West.

Notwithstanding the prevailing pacifist discourse, essentially brought on by the horrors of the atomic bomb and the feeling of victimization the Japanese drew from it, the labor of penitence that the Germans courageously and honestly undertook after 1945 was never truly accomplished in Japan, as evidenced by the series of "excuses" proffered by certain Japanese prime ministers and the questioning of their country's guilt by others. Aware of the restrictions the international community imposed on them in light of the magnitude of the crimes committed, the Japanese dedicated their efforts to reconstruction, and then to economic development, with well-known results. American protection allowed Japanese leaders not to concern themselves with security matters and instead to carry out their economic efforts. In 1985, this Japanese policy ran head-on into demands by its American protector, whose economic hegemony was threatened by this newfound Japanese economic power. This resulted in a painful period of Japan bashing in the United States and the imposition of constraints upon Tokyo for the purpose of preserving American interests.

Chief among these restrictions was the forced revaluation of the yen under the Plaza Accord. In light of this economic containment strategy, Japan began to recognize the limitations of its alliance with the United States and the need to turn to Asia, which they had been fully ignoring. Still keeping the American security umbrella, Japan focused more on both financial assistance to developing countries on the continent and trade development. As the only economic power capable of such a policy, Japan was received with interest in Asia, particularly Southeast Asia, whose economic emergence required ever-greater foreign investments. Japan's financial and economic power clearly lent it a certain influence over Asia, but its strategy of power devoid of hegemonic ambitions, which was based on the importance of networks of influence or the political ascendency that a clear and determined strategic vision brings (although American domination of the archipelago gave it some ambiguity), could not stand up to the rise of new regional players.

China's rapid rise was thus a real challenge for Japan because both powers, historically antagonistic, were now rivals in Korea and Southeast Asia, in economic terms as well as in terms of political influence. The differential in economic power in Asia looked to continue favoring Japan for a long time yet, but the gap continued to shrink. In 1980, trade with China represented a mere 1.8 percent of ASEAN's total world trade (26 percent for Japan), a figure that had risen to 2.4 percent 20 years later (16.1 percent for Japan). Although China's economic expansion outside its borders is relatively slow compared with great economic powers such as the United States and Japan, it makes up for this with its potential power, which piques the imagination of its partners and makes it a nascent soft power. Japanese economic power collided with its great rival's hegemonic momentum. This confrontation led Japan to reassess and fall back on a more overtly nationalist position based on a redefinition of its relationship with the United States.

Events came to a head in 2001. On April 26, Junichiro Koizumi, president of the Liberal Democratic Party, was named prime minister. On September 11 of the same year, the terrible events in New York allowed American neoconservatives to take power and launch a global offensive not so much intended to combat Islamic terrorism as to strengthen American hard power in the wake of this tragedy that inspired a unanimous outpouring of international solidarity, and to assume an apparently decisive advantage over their main partners or adversaries. Seizing the opportunity, the Japanese prime minister opted for a policy of total alignment with the Bush administration. Japanese participation in the American war effort in Iraq allowed him to enjoy the status of unconditional ally, a comfortable position after two decades of economic and commercial friction. Japanese troops were deployed to Iraq, and notably, the Japanese Navy reappeared in the Indian Ocean in November 2001 to lend logistical support to American operations in Afghanistan. By agreeing to participate in the missile shield, Tokyo launched a policy that Beijing looked upon as a real provocation.

Tokyo's determined alignment with American strategy in the Far East constitutes a major strategic challenge for Beijing. In fact, Japan's overt hostility toward China is a key parameter in China's management if its two greatest priorities: the Taiwan issue and access to the Pacific Ocean. In both cases, Beijing's priority must be to create a credible determent strategy vis-à-vis Tokyo in order to prevent direct Japanese intervention in any eventual regional conflict over Taiwan. Japanese leaders must realize the risks they would face in the event that the United States were to conduct operations against China from their facilities on the Japanese archipelago. Lacking an effective missile shield, this would be a major risk for Japan, particularly if Congress, under pressure from an American public still stinging from the failure of the Iranian and Afghan missions, were to refuse the American president authorization to defend Taiwan militarily in case of crisis. Tokyo would find itself very isolated in the face of China, in a regional and likely international environment in which, despite the inevitable protestations and threats, no one would dare enter into a conflict with a power like China in defense of 23 million Taiwanese.

In this context, Beijing's strategy is to place as much pressure as possible on Japan by taking advantage of Japan's mistakes, thereby further isolating it in the Asian environment. An ever-stronger alliance with Washington, associated with a more openly nationalist discourse (particularly under Junichiro Koizumi's administration), contributes to suspicions in East Asia regarding Japan's long-term intentions and places Tokyo in the Western camp, separate from this emerging Asia that seeks to forge an Asian identity. The difficulty Japanese leaders seem to have in owning up to their expansionist, imperial past, as well as the visits to the Yasukuni Shrine by former Prime Minister Koizumi and other Japanese politicians, has worsened the malaise. Japan's growing marginalization in the Asian environment seems to have increased apace with China's emergence in Asia. The economic challenges facing Beijing, Tokyo, and Seoul should nonetheless mitigate the scope of political crises and encourage continued dialogue, with occasional bumps in the road but nothing that would lead to irreversible deterioration. However, Japan's efforts to secure its archipelago thanks to the American missile shield and Tokyo's development of autonomous defense capabilities constitute a major challenge to China. China may find itself pressed to respond to this challenge by developing security dialogues with its neighbors, dialogues from which it would doubtless seek to exclude the United States.

## Toward a regional security architecture?

Concerned with regional security and the American strategy of establishing bases or logistical facilities on its periphery, China sought to develop multilateral and bilateral alliances. The 1996 creation of the Shanghai Five group was a first step. Facing a rise in radical Islamist movements in Central Asia, Beijing and Moscow agreed to cooperate on terrorism issues and encourage the adoption of confidence measures among the countries of the region.

Indeed, since the late 1980s China had been suffering an unprecedented wave of terrorism orchestrated by Uyghur Islamist movements, especially the East Turkestan Islamic Movement (ETIM), to which over 200 attacks were attributed between 1990 and 2001. The dissolution of the Soviet Union and the simultaneous birth of new republics with strong Muslim majorities had stimulated the region's Islamist movements, which saw the marked decline of Russian interests in Central Asia as a historic opportunity for creating an Islamic caliphate to unite all the Sunni Muslim peoples of the region. This threat, bolstered by the progress of the *jihad*[27] in Afghanistan and its extension to Islamist movements of Central Asia, produced a violent defensive reaction from the new republics and their Chinese and Russian neighbors.

Russia, embroiled in the war in Chechnya, where its troops had been deployed since December 1994, and China, deeply concerned by the rapid development of separatist activities, joined up in April 1996 to create a regional organization whose official mission was to guarantee Central Asian stability through good-neighbor policies and cooperation. They brought Kazakhstan, Tajikistan, and Kyrgyzstan on board with the new organization, initially called the Shanghai Five group (上海五国), after the city where its first meeting was held, and then the Shanghai Cooperation Organization (SCO) starting in 2001. The emphasis was now placed first and foremost on joint measures intended to create mutual trust on military issues in the border regions. Several agreements along these lines were signed. But with the rapid progression of radical Islamist movements in Central Asia, their concerns shifted to the risks of regional destabilization. In Chechnya, fundamentalist movements had developed essentially between 1997 and 1999, born of the population's resentment toward the Russians, notwithstanding some resistance by the population to the more radical movements. Chechen national resistance was likewise reinforced by an influx of foreign jihadist combatants, fresh from Taliban Afghanistan, further muddling the nature of hostilities in the former Soviet republic.

In China, the crisis between the central government and the Uyghur separatist movement came to a head in 1997 with the serious incidents in Yining that left dozens dead and helped solidify the antagonism between the Muslim populations and the local authorities. In Xinjiang, attacks on civilians and Muslims resistant to the pressures to adopt a Wahhabi version of Islam had increased sharply and had achieved their aim of alarming the authorities and provoking a violent crackdown. The Islamists seized on the crackdown to garner growing sympathy for their cause from a Uyghur population caught

---

[27] War waged by Islamist Afghan combatants against the Soviet occupation forces. The term *jihad* originally referred to the personal combat waged by a Muslim "on the path of God." The term has been extended to refer to the fight against infidels, defensive combat (against crusaders or colonizers), or offensive combat (against non-Muslims who must be converted, or within Muslim societies against those who do not abide by the principles of Islam).

between young radicals, whose modus operandi and religious discourse were entirely new to them, and the forces of law and order, largely dominated by ethnically Han Chinese, whose police tactics were rather lacking in subtlety. The Chinese authorities, who had at first sought through the Shanghai Five group to pacify the periphery and lessen military presence in the border regions, suddenly found themselves with a veritable civil war on their hands in a highly strategic region. Therefore, Beijing, in concert with Moscow, turned the focus of this partnership with Central Asia to the fight against Islamist terrorism and separatism, but also took care to make the necessary overtures to the Muslim minorities of Xinjiang to appease sentiments and regain an advantage over the clandestine preachers. Chinese policy in West China [西部 大开发; *xībùdàkāifā*] has met with undeniable successes in terms of economic development and the reduction of violent incidents. Along with it has come increasingly close cooperation on Islamic terrorism among Shanghai Cooperation Organization member states, as evidenced by the autumn 2005 decision to create a regional antiterrorist center in Xinjiang.

This experience is unique for China, which for the first time since the founding of the People's Republic finds itself participating in a regional security organization. It underlines both the importance Chinese leaders now place on regional stability and their determination to develop whatever structures and partnerships may be necessary for national security. Indeed, after September 11, 2001, Beijing took stock of the limits of the American conception of the "international war on terror." After having been extremely active in its support of the antiterrorist campaign led by Washington in the wake of September 11,[28] China had hoped in return to elicit greater sensitivity to its own plight with internal terrorism. It was particularly interested in seeing some Uyghur organizations accused of having carried out attacks on Chinese soil for several years added to the list of terrorist movements. Until May 2002, Beijing called in vain for the inclusion on this list of the organization known as the East Turkestan Islamic Movement (ETIM). But in May 2002, members of this movement were arrested in Bishkek, Kyrgyzstan, where they had been plotting an attack on the US embassy. The following September 11, the movement was finally listed by the UN Security Council, under paragraphs 1 and 2 of Resolution 1390 (2002), alongside organizations linked to Al-Qaeda, Osama bin Laden, or the Taliban.[29]

China's efforts to show that the terrorism it grapples with in its own territory is real have not been well received. It is always accused of trying to exploit the fight against terrorism in order to launch its own attacks against the Uyghur separatists. On the American side, the discourse on terrorism clearly goes after only those movements and organizations that attack American tar-

---

[28] "China's Post 9/11 Terrorism Strategy," *China Brief*, Vol. 4 Issue 8, 2004.
[29] http://www.un.org/sc/committees/1267/NSQE08802E.shtml.

gets, as George W. Bush made clear repeatedly over his two terms. If the "war on terror" launched by the United States in late 2001 authorizes Washington and its allies to employ any means to reach their ends, including patently illegal or immoral means such as the "outsourcing" of the torture of presumed Islamists to countries where police tactics are less subject to public scrutiny, China's struggle against Islamist terrorism is always the subject of sharp criticism and denunciations by Western governments and nongovernmental organizations. The line of demarcation between the two strategies is based on simplistic ideological considerations related to the "alliance of democracies" that the American administration never tires of mentioning in order to justify its own actions and condemn those of its adversaries. The definition given of *good and evil*, left entirely up to the discretion of Westerners, presents a major difficulty in this sense. The values framed as *universal* are those of Western countries, with no room given to other values that different cultures might hold. This situation, which engenders numerous growing tensions, has not ceased to deteriorate since 2001 due to the unilateralist policies of Washington and their devastating consequences for certain countries, of which Iraq is the most tragic example.

Faced with Western indifference to the terrorist issue in China, the Shanghai Cooperation Organization has gradually set about transforming itself into a real regional security organization, bringing a growing number of countries on board. Along with this strategy comes the establishment of bilateral strategic partnerships that allow for an increasingly dense network of defense relationships around China based on an increasing number of trust-building measures. Bilateral or multilateral joint military exercises are held regularly. In the August 2005 Sino-Russian exercises off the Shandong coast, the three service branches of the two countries collaborated for the first time in naval exercises, to which not only SCO member states were invited as observers, but also India, Pakistan, and Iran. Washington, whose request to participate was politely denied, had to settle for observing the exercises from afar. A strategic partnership between China and India has also been established, but the rapprochement of the two Asian giants goes against the interests of the United States, which would like to see India become its privileged strategic partner in South Asia in order to eventually delegate—or outsource—regional security to it, particularly in the Indian Ocean. For India, this convergence of interests with Washington and the "policeman" role it could play in South Asia would represent the long-awaited consecration of its global role. The rapprochement between the United States and India, however, runs up against the latter's stubborn independence, as seen repeatedly in the Iranian nuclear issue or the troubles in Myanmar with the recent political shakeups there. New Delhi therefore maintains its privileged military relations with Russia, which supplies it with military equipment, especially warships (such as the *Admiral Gorshkov*, a Kiev class aircraft carrier, in 2004). In September 2004, Prime Minister Manmohan Singh announced

India's wishes to strengthen its strategic ties with the United States—and Russia.[30] However, the repeated cancellation of joint exercises in April and then June 2011 revealed the friction between India and Russia. Nevertheless, during President Putin's visit to India in December 2012, the two parties signed military contracts for $2.9 billion, in an apparent signal that this partnership will continue at a high level.[31]

The great powers covet a strategic alliance with India because its emergence on the international scene, though slower than that of China, is doubtless just as long-lasting. The configuration of such an alliance could be decisive for the future of Asia. India has thus become a major factor in the hegemonic rivalry pitting Washington against Beijing in Asia.

One of the issues that may still provoke tension in the medium and long terms between China and India is energy supply, a sector in which the two countries may be increasingly competitive in coming years. The January 12, 2006, signing at Beijing of an energy cooperation agreement meant to reduce competition between the two countries shows, however, a shared desire to defuse potential conflicts that could arise between them. The Indian minister for petroleum, a signatory to the agreement, stated to the press that it was not "necessary for India or China to purchase energy security to the other's detriment."

The first East Asia Summit, held at Kuala Lumpur in December 2005, marked the pursuit of this Chinese security engagement strategy. Debates centered especially on maritime security issues and international terrorism, in a sign of converging interests between the region and the United States. This summit presented itself as a potential "driving force" for the development of a regional architecture. However, because of the privileged ties between Tokyo and Washington, Japan's presence within this new structure represented a potential roadblock for China's regional strategy. Russia, for its part, has shown its interest in the region by signing a "Comprehensive Program of Action to Promote Cooperation between the Association of Southeast Asian Nations and the Russian Federation 2005–2015," the first two articles of which outline both parties' security concerns. Russia finally joined the Summit in 2001 along with the United States, once China's objection was withdrawn. Despite the declarations of willingness to create a regional security organization through this summit, recent meetings have been marked by tensions between China and several ASEAN member states over the South China Sea.

This double Chinese and Russian offensive on ASEAN on regional security issues, which runs counter to the new American strategy in the region, could bear fruit in the medium term and encourage the countries of the region to commit to greater autonomy by rebalancing their strategic relations with Washington and Beijing in the direction of greater empowerment for Asian

[30] AFP, September 4, 2004.
[31] "India, Russia sign defence deals worth Rs 25,000 crore," *The Times of India*, December 25, 2012.

countries on security and defense issues. Although the United States clearly cannot be sidelined from the strategic landscape of Southeast Asia, Beijing may hope to encourage ASEAN to distance itself somewhat from Washington in this area by appeasing certain countries' fears regarding American power. Appeasing current tensions in a lasting way and participating directly in security measures will prove essential in allaying these fears.

## Energy diplomacy: a high priority

Two converging factors have jolted Chinese leaders into an appreciation of energy's importance: rapid growth in Chinese consumption and the hegemonic strategy of the United States in this sector. The explosion in consumption brought on by China's rapid economic development has surprised all the analysts and surpassed all predictions. This economic growth is largely conditioned on the long-term viability of the hydrocarbon supply, and keeping up the current rate of growth requires enough energy security to guard against market fluctuations and external pressures. Defense, too, depends heavily on this energy supply, for China's own reserves would not allow it to sustain an armed conflict for more than a few weeks. It is seriously vulnerable to an interruption or even a temporary disruption of its imports. Partly as a result of the Bush administration's aggressive discourse and operations in the Middle East, China has come to realize the importance of energy security and taken rapid steps to secure its energy supply.

China turned first to Central Asia and Russia in an effort to establish or strengthen its projects for cooperation with Moscow and the former Soviet republics. When the Americans entered Afghanistan in 2001, they drew closer to the resources of the Caspian Sea and Central Asia. In 2003, the occupation of Iraq gave them control over the second-largest oil reserves in the world—at least they hoped so at the time. And so China needed to work toward diversification of its supply in order to avoid entanglement in the Middle East, a region under American influence, and Central Asia. China's counteroffensive took it to well-known but underexploited territory, Africa, and then above all to entirely new ground: Latin America. Setting up shop in what had been exclusively America's domain and almost the private property of big American companies was a way to give Washington a taste of its own medicine by taking advantage of the fissures developing between certain South American countries and their North American guardian. The rapid increase in exchanges of official delegations, along with the signing of trade contracts and development aid agreements, shows the success of these Chinese overtures. For example, the day after his December 2005 election, Bolivian President Evo Morales addressed Beijing, calling for Chinese oil companies to invest in his country, after his announcement of the review of all the hydrocarbon exploitation contracts signed with the multinationals.

In Africa too, rivalries are increasingly fierce. China has made inroads in recent years, particularly in Angola and Nigeria, where it has scored points against its Western competitors. China's entry into the continent is accompanied by a major financial effort in the form of development aid. As in Latin America, these efforts are directed especially at countries stigmatized by the West for their authoritarian regimes. In January 2004, the Chinese president went on an "oil tour" that took him to Egypt, where he signed joint oil and gas exploration and exploitation contracts; to Gabon, where he signed a framework contract for the sale of Gabonese crude to China for the first time; and to Algeria, where he signed cooperation agreements for the construction of a refinery, development of an oil deposit in the Hassi Messaoud region, and the importation of Algerian oil to China. In January 2006, the purchase by China National Offshore Oil Corporation (CNOOC) of a 45 percent stake in South Atlantic Petroleum Limited's mining license in the Nigerian OML 130 zone, a region of very promising oil and gas fields, confirmed Beijing's marked interest in African resources, including those found in regions traditionally dominated by big Western companies. Africa's oil reserves, which represent 8 percent of global reserves, allow China to reduce drastically its dependence on the Gulf States and thus limit its geostrategic liabilities related to the massive American military presence in the Middle East. Beijing is already the second-largest importer of African oil after the United States, but these imports represent 30 percent of China's total, versus 20 percent for the United States. On January 12, 2006, China clarified its Africa policy with the publication of an official document outlining the general framework of these relations and emphasizing their economic significance. The document also underlined the Chinese authorities' desire to use various means of encouraging and promoting investments by Chinese companies.[32] China's promises of economic development hold an attraction for these African countries that undoubtedly creates favorable conditions for China's entry into Africa, allowing it a stronger presence in strategic sectors such as oil and ores. The November 2006 China-Africa Summit largely consecrated the success of the Chinese approach. The participation of 35 African heads of state in this summit held in Beijing showed the importance Africa now places on this partnership with China. The first India-Africa Summit, held in April 2008 at New Delhi, attended by only 14 African countries and four heads of state, further underlined China's strategic advantage over India, despite the historical advantage of India due to the presence of its diaspora on the African continent for centuries.

The competition to secure hydrocarbon reserves for the coming decades is not limited to those reserves located in developing countries; the race is also on to gain control of concerns partially or completely held by Western

---

[32] *China's Africa Policy*, Ministry of Foreign Affairs of the P.R.C. http://www.china.org.cn/english/features/China-Africa/82055.htm.

capital. The most striking example is the attempted takeover of the American group Unocal by CNOOC in summer 2005. With an offer of $18.5 billion, this was the largest investment abroad ever made by a Chinese group. It was much larger than the offer made by its main competitor, the American Chevron company, which eventually landed the deal after CNOOC withdrew its offer. The mass mobilization of American politicians against placing a company framed as "strategic" in Chinese hands, notwithstanding the indignation of some American economists who saw this stance as a flagrant violation of the basic rules of free trade as promised by the Americans for two centuries,[33] persuaded Beijing to err on the side of caution and avoid the conflict. Immediately after CNOOC's failed attempt, China National Petroleum Corporation (CNPC) scored a stunning success with its October 2005 acquisition of the Canadian oil company PetroKazakhstan for $4.2 billion. In a sign of the times, the CNPC offer won out over the rather lower offer of an Indian competitor, the Oil and Natural Gas Corporation. This company mainly exploits the Kumkol oil field in Kazakhstan, which was linked to Western China in 2005 by an oil pipeline with a capacity of 200,000 barrels per day. This oil is refined in Xinjiang before being shipped to industrialized eastern China. These moves reveal the long-term strategy of Chinese leaders regarding Central Asian hydrocarbon resources and their wishes to control, as much as possible, the exploration-exploitation-refining-consumption cycle in its entirety in order to reduce the risks of disruption to the energy supply.

China also looks to leverage the contradictions that plague American foreign policy and use them to make moves on the Asian chessboard, drawing its neighbors away from Washington's policies. The gas pipeline project between Iran and India, through Pakistan, is a particularly striking case, for it underlines the geopolitical transformations underway in the region. The demonization of Iran and the ban on American investments and trade relations with the Islamic Republic imposed by the 1996 Iran and Libya Sanctions Act are naturally favorable to the main Asian oil and gas consumers, from Japan, still a privileged US ally, to India or China. The idea of a great energy market, including China, Central Asia, Russia, India, Pakistan, and Iran, has begun to gain traction in recent years. The rapid rapprochement between India and Pakistan has opened the door to the possibility of building infrastructure to link the Iranian oil fields to the main consumers, India and China, through Pakistan, which used to be unreceptive to any cooperation with India. The strategic importance to India of this project explains New Delhi's cautious stance on the dispute between Iran and the International Atomic Energy Agency (IAEA). The September 24, 2005, vote by India against Iran at the IAEA had incurred

---

[33] The president of the New York–based Petroleum Industry Research Foundation stated in July 2005 that "this is not a company making military planes or missiles. At the end of the day, it's only energy." An oil analyst for Oppenheimer & Co. of New York likewise denounced the blocking of the acquisition as "the heights of hypocrisy" on the part of the United States, which regularly accuses Russia of not opening its oil market enough to American companies (*Washington Post*, June 24, 2005).

the ire of Tehran. The Iranians had immediately threatened New Delhi with the cancellation of the gas contract that was to supply India beginning in 2009 with 5 million tons of liquefied natural gas. When the Security Council took up the Iranian nuclear issue in 2006, New Delhi found itself on the horns of a nasty dilemma: should it seek energy security, reinforced by a partnership with Iran, or defer to American interests (and, more broadly, Western ones) in the region? But it is unlikely that India will be willing to support an Iran isolated from the international community in light of heavy lobbying from the American administration and certain European countries. The European embargo on Iranian oil that went into effect on July 1, 2012, has also significantly affected Iran's exports to India, China, and Japan, allowing these countries to exert pressure on Tehran to lower the price per barrel.

The Chinese energy strategy in developing countries is not unlike that of Western countries after decolonization. The means of wooing these countries are essentially identical, consisting of offering economic and financial assistance to these enormously needy countries. China finds itself in a situation comparable to that of the former colonial powers and the United States, which for decades lent support to autocratic regimes with an eye to maintaining privileged relations with countries that held the hydrocarbon reserves or ores indispensable to their economic growth. Interference in the affairs of these states was the rule, but no one seemed to mind, least of all the African leaders who in exchange for their submission enjoyed a tidy income and could act with impunity. With its noninterference in local politics and its no-strings-attached aid, China now holds a considerable advantage over its Western competitors, who are under increasing pressure by European and American lobby groups to use caution. The only political condition China imposes has to do with Chinese issues: Beijing requires its partners to recognize the One-China policy in order to carry on normal relations. The document outlining China's Africa policies, released in January 2006, states clearly that "the one China principle is the political foundation for the establishment and development of China's relations with African countries and regional organizations." Foreign Minister Li Zhaoxing's first visit to Dakar in January 2006 came on the heels of Senegal's severance of diplomatic relations with Taiwan. China's entry into Africa has been well received thus far, even if it threatens to shake up certain economic sectors, such as textiles, a sector in direct and ill-matched competition with Chinese exports. Yet the energy sector remains the priority of the Chinese authorities, who may rein in the aggressive spirit of their companies if they fear a backlash from local governments that could jeopardize the process of getting Chinese oil companies into Africa.

## Settling the Taiwan issue, Chinese style

The issue of Taiwan remains China's indisputable political priority and governs all of Beijing's relations with the international community. When it comes to Beijing's strategic and political relations with Washington, its partnership with the European Union, tensions with Japan, global diplomacy, and military modernization, the island's status and future constantly loom in the background. Any face-off between Beijing and Taipei would pose a major threat for the region and have considerable repercussions worldwide. Generally framed by the Chinese in historical and political terms—defense of national sovereignty—and by the Americans in terms of the Taiwanese population's *right to democracy and self-determination,* this is above all a highly strategic issue, as all parties are well aware.

A mere glance at the map of the Asia-Pacific region confirms that the Chinese coastline, neglected for centuries by the central authorities and now a major strategic issue for the defense of Chinese national territory, is seriously compromised by geographical factors. From the Japanese archipelago in the north to the Philippines in the south, the Chinese coast is separated from the Pacific Ocean by myriad islands that, due to the configuration of territorial waters, reduce to a set of rather narrow passages the Chinese Navy's access to the sea. As long as the status of Taiwan remains unresolved, China retains the prospect of securing direct access to the Pacific with reunification. This possibility would vanish immediately in the event of independence for the island. The possible presence in an independent Taiwan of sophisticated American surveillance systems would considerably compromise China's strategic position and deterrent capacity.

For the time being, Beijing can settle for the status quo, for the current level of Chinese military modernization lends no urgency to this access to the Pacific. This situation will change over the next 15 years, and the two sides will likely need to arrive at an acceptable solution for reunification by then.

Moreover, a proclamation of independence by Taiwan would formalize the appearance on the Chinese coast of a sovereign state allied with Washington, rounding out the American-Japanese alliance. Such a move would constitute a considerable strategic setback for China's security and could hobble its emergence as a great regional power for the long term. In a strategic context in which nuclear deterrence is as relevant as ever and the technological superiority of the US space program gives the Americans a decisive advantage over launch sites on the continent, rapid access to the deep waters of the Pacific for ballistic missile submarines becomes crucial for the credibility of the Chinese deterrence strategy. Beijing must possess not only technology sophisticated enough to minimize the chances of detecting its submarines, but also direct access to the sea. The need for this access precludes the possibility of Taiwanese territorial sovereignty in the waters of the East China Sea.

With the March 11, 2005, adoption of the Anti-Secession Law by the People's Conference, Chinese leaders set the terms for discussions between the two parties over the status of the island. There are no real signs of a desire on the part of Beijing to recover formal sovereignty over Taiwan by force in the short term, while the Taiwanese leaders, for their part, will not rule out entirely the possibility of engaging in negotiations on the issue. The May 2008 election in Taiwan of Ma Ying-jeou as the successor to Chen Shui-bian, who had shown great hostility toward the People's Republic of China and wanted to hold a referendum on independence, has changed things considerably. In fact, the Kuomintang, which Ma Ying-jeou chaired from 2005 to 2007, has clearly expressed its desire to appease relations across the strait and establish cooperative relations with Beijing. And so things moved forward quickly with cross-strait flights and exchanges of delegations, including visits to Beijing by the Kuomintang. Economic integration between the two territories is now reaching a point that will eventually make a turnaround impossible, lest Taiwanese interests be seriously compromised. Trade with the continent now represents over 30 percent of Taiwanese foreign trade, with a trade surplus that always favors the island.[34]

This rapid improvement in relations between continental China and Taiwan is emblematic of a *Chinese-style* approach to contentious issues, with both sides opting for patience, constructive engagement, and cooperation to eventually settle the dispute, but both maintaining the military capacity to discourage each other from making any hasty decisions that might rush rapprochement. This is why Chinese leaders, through military modernization and especially the development of projection capacity and access denial, try to discourage Washington from any direct intervention in the issue, whether through excessive strengthening of Taiwan's military capacity or direct involvement in the event of open conflict across the strait. Chinese leadership could opt for a more comprehensive strategy, particularly on economic issues, to swing Taiwanese public opinion in favor of reunification. The system of government that would be proposed for the island, currently a true parliamentary democracy, remains an unanswered question that will require plenty of imagination on both sides.

## *Is conflict with the United States really inevitable?*

There are widely differing schools of thought in the United States regarding the right strategy to adopt toward China. The most ideological of these, particularly among the neoconservatives who had their heyday during George W. Bush's first term, are obsessed with the nature of the regime and the challenge this country poses to American hegemony, which seemed poised to win a definitive victory in the wake of the September 11, 2001, attacks. More realistic quarters, who also express concern over Chinese economic and strategic competition, nonetheless still tend to favor strengthening the economic and political partnership with China in the expectation of an evolution of the regime. China, for its part, has opted to alternate between firmness and flexibility.

---

[34] "The Bilateral Trade between Taiwan and Mainland China," Ministry of Economic Affairs, R.O.C., September 9, 2011.

Whether in respect to its policies in Central Asia or Southeast Asia or hot-button issues facing the international community today (Iranian nuclear capability, oil prices, the American trade deficit, or the renminbi exchange rate), China is not prepared to confront the United States, nor does it want to. But it has no intention of sacrificing its economic growth on the altar of American or European economic and political interests, as evidenced by its resistance to pressures to revalue its currency. The only issue on which Beijing will remain entirely inflexible is Taiwanese independence. On other issues, Chinese leaders know when to grit their teeth and mitigate the risks of tension while at the same time striving to circumvent Washington's containment strategy. There are several reasons for China's cautious, nonconfrontational approach to Washington:

- In traditional Chinese thought, which is increasingly referred to in the People's Republic of China, life unfolds on the principle of alternating currents preserved by yin and yang and based on the "interrelated nature of every organic reality: coexistence, coherence, correlation, complementarity.... This results in a vision of the world not as a set of discrete, independent entities, each constituting an essence in itself, but as a continuous web of relationships between the whole and its parts, without any one transcending the others."[35] In the multipolar world envisioned by China's leaders, the United States is China's indispensable and complementary partner; it is not China's antithesis, but rather the other element that allows the real world to remain in balance. Naturally, seen from the outside, China seems so *communist* and so far from *traditional* that these concepts become irrelevant for defining Chinese strategy. But the weight of ancient tradition is greater than that of an ideology introduced less than a century ago. Chinese leaders' repeated statements that the Chinese economy is entirely dependent on the global economy and stability reflect this way of thinking. For Beijing, the United States is indeed the *indispensable nation* it claims to be, not because the values it professes are universal and represent the *end of history,* but because in a cyclical cosmic system, the interdependence of nations is essential, and a developing China cannot do without the economic hyperpower, however fragile, that is the United States of the early 21st century.
- China, unlike Western powers and the Soviet Union during the Cold War, has no intention of exporting the values it holds as universal. Marxism-Leninism and Maoism, once seen as elements of an ideology that would bring a cure to the planet's ills, have been called into question for over 20 years after their failure to usher in a more just and egalitarian society. This ideology has been broadly questioned and adapted to new challenges and new issues, resulting in a return to the old Chinese pragmatism. China is

---

[35]Anne Cheng, *Histoire de la pensée chinoise,* (Editions du Seuil), 37.

striving to invent a new economic, political, and social system by pragmatic means, and Chinese leaders are fully aware that they have no silver bullet. Moreover, messianism is not a feature of Chinese thought, and China does not seek to export the traditional Confucian values that it must now progressively rediscover for itself and adapt to contemporary realities. And so it is that China finds itself today in a process of transformation—not one of rupture—the only way, in Chinese thought, to achieve harmony. The painful experience of post-1949 China, the application to Chinese realities of the mostly imported ideology of Marxism-Leninism, and Mao Zedong's cherished permanent revolution, with which he hoped to cause a series of violent ruptures, have all left their mark on Chinese minds, encouraging a return to the Confucian philosophical tradition and a conception of Harmony (和谐; *héxié*) based on processes of economic, social, and political transformation.

• Sino-American relations are marked by profound mutual suspicion that will be difficult to overcome as long as the United States, whether the administration is Democratic or Republican, continues to pursue an imperialist foreign policy based on economic interests but dressed up in messianic garb and professing its desire to spread the gospel of *democracy and human rights* to all peoples, no matter how much they resist. Most American politicians are probably sincerely convinced of the superiority of the American economic, social, and political model, but history has shown since the Second World War that they are also able to quickly shake off the constraints that these *universal values* impose when US economic or strategic interests are at stake, as in the case of Guantanamo or Abu Ghraib, to cite only the latest tragic examples. This profoundly simplistic vision, rooted either in ignorance of world realities or in ideological blindness, as the case may be, makes the United States an oafish threat to delicate regional balances.

• The United States actually exerts a certain fascination over the Chinese elites, judging by the number of children of highly placed parents attending American institutions of secondary or higher education.[36] Notwithstanding the highly ideological analysis of some American authors,[37] a confrontation between China and the United States would not be inevitable if the latter accepted the idea that its status as sole hyperpower capable of uncontested unilateralism is temporary at best, just as in the case of a long series of empires throughout history, and that no one can halt the rise of China on the international scene, a rise that, in keeping with the country's dimensions, will have extraordinary effects. But many American politicians and

---

[36] "If China is doing so well, why do so many Chinese think of moving here?" *Washington Post*, November 17, 2012; "The China Conundrum," *New York Times*, November 3, 2011.

[37] Bill Gertz, *The China Threat, How the People's Republic Targets America* (Regnery Publishing, 2000); Richard Bernstein and Ross H. Munro, *The Coming Conflict with China* (Vintage, 1998); Ross Terrill, *The New Chinese Empire and What It Means for the United States* (Basic Books, 2003).

strategists,[38] convinced that they are the standard-bearers of *the truth* and have been charged with the historical mission of seeking "the end of tyranny in our world,"[39] cannot conceive of a multipolar world in which several powers, all concerned with development and stability, act in concert to resist destabilizing forces and do so as equals.

Aware of this American attitude, Chinese leaders show great deftness and finesse in defusing brewing crises without sacrificing their long-term national interests. On issues where it really does shoulder some responsibility (such as the textile conflict), Beijing has managed to preserve its interests while offering tokens of goodwill and negotiating a solution to the crisis. When the accusations leveled by the United States betray a hidden agenda linked to its own internal politics (such as the devaluation of the renminbi, which many American economists acknowledged would have no effect on the trade balance between the two countries), Beijing stands firm. When issues that Washington sees as particularly sensitive arise, as in the case of the attempted acquisition of the Unocal oil group by a Chinese energy concern, which the Bush administration took as a hostile strategic maneuver, Chinese leaders have known when to back off in order to ease tensions. This strategy responds to American policies that are also more cautious, even if George W. Bush did not let on about this in his very militant 1999 speech. Although the United Sates has indeed engaged in an active containment policy toward China and professed its determination to consider China a "strategic competitor," in a break with the Clinton administration's conception, it has also shown no signs of aggressiveness, clearly preferring the asymmetrical war to open confrontation.

• Sino-American relations have now entered a head-to-head phase, doubtless long-lasting, but which will not necessarily lead to open conflict, notwithstanding the inevitable long-term nature of their competition. This rivalry is not so much political as it is economic, unlike the decades-long standoff between the United States and the Soviet Union. Behind the American discourse of human rights and democratic freedom lurks a thinly disguised hegemonic power, thirsty for conquest and irritated by China's rise on several levels:

> • Since the Second World War, the United States has played a central role in Asia, opposing Soviet hegemony and supporting anticommunist regimes even when they themselves were dictatorships (in South Vietnam, Cambodia, Indonesia, etc.). China's return to Asian centrality after a century and a half of absence poses a major strategic challenge for Washington.

---

[38] "A time-honored tradition: Election year and China-bashing," *Washington Post*, October 18, 2012.
[39] George W. Bush, State of the Union Address, Washington, DC, January 31, 2006.

• The priority placed by the United States on its Eurasian strategy, so aptly described by Zbigniew Brzezinski,[40] faces patient but determined resistance from China (with collusion from Russia), in a policy that seems to be succeeding in gradually arresting American influence by a variety of means (bilateral cooperation agreements, pressure for the departure of American troops, positioning of Chinese energy concerns, etc.).

• The dramatic growth of its economy makes China a power whose natural resource needs lead it into territory traditionally reserved for the West (hydrocarbons, ores, etc.). The effectiveness of the Chinese energy strategy, which leverages Washington's weaknesses or mistakes to get its foot in the door or strengthen its presence in hydrocarbon-rich countries (Iran, Saudi Arabia after September 11, Venezuela, etc.), increasingly challenges Americans to reexamine their aggressive and unilateralist policy in light of this factor.

• The prospect of the eventual success of the Chinese development model, based on a partially liberalized economy but within an autocratic political context, would deal a blow to the theories espoused by American ideologues who claim that economic development is incompatible with political interventionism. The case of Indonesia, however, where until 1998 the United States supported a military dictatorship that was economically highly effective, illustrates the limits of these convictions. While it is certainly likely that Chinese leaders will follow the path of political openness, already underway within the party and at the grassroots and local community levels, as the reforms continue their course, the model that will emerge from this long transitional period will very likely be quite different from the Western parliamentary system held up as the only acceptable model.

For its part, China is just as irritated by American power for one major reason: the Chinese regime, run by the Communist Party, has been labeled by successive American administrations, particularly the Bush administration, as a regime doomed to disappear, as in the case of the USSR and most of the former people's republics, and the United States should encourage this inexorable process. This ideological vision shapes the asymmetrical war waged against China. But the subtlety of Chinese policy since the start of the reforms has belied this prediction and defied the Western convictions based on a sole political and economic model of parliamentary democracy and economic liberalism.

Beijing faces another major hurdle to the development of more trusting relations with Washington: the successive changes in political power in the United States, which seriously hamper any possibility of a lasting strategic rela-

---

[40] Zbigniew Brzezinski, *The Grand Chessboard: American Primacy and Its Geostrategic Imperatives* (Basic Books, 1997).

tionship between the two countries. Since the start of the reforms 30 years ago, the Chinese government has carried out a policy of emergence whose main features have not changed with the procession of party and state leaders, though there have often been adjustments to economic and strategic approaches. The perception of the nature of relations with the United States has not changed much, except when certain opportunities have arisen. In Washington, on the other hand, the succession of Democratic and Republican administrations, facing the pressures exerted on the White House and Congress by public opinion and by industrial, financial, military, religious, and other lobbies constitutes a real obstacle to the establishment of lasting cooperative relations between the two countries. In Beijing, this fuels suspicion and the certainty that each new presidential term will jeopardize previous achievements. The Clinton, Bush, and Obama administrations have only confirmed this assessment, and under these circumstances, the idea of renewing the kind of alliance China enjoyed with the United States vis-à-vis the Soviet Union in the 1960s and 1970s, a period when China was in a weaker position, is inconceivable for Chinese leaders.

Zbigniew Brzezinski, however, figures that it would have seemed natural for Beijing to opt for an alliance with the United States, a faraway power, rather than with Russia, which was too close, or with Japan, which had historically posed a threat. But this strategic choice would depend on the idea that the United States "has no designs on the Asian mainland and has historically opposed both Japanese and Russian encroachments on a weaker China."[41] Yet it is clear that while it perhaps has no such designs in the historical sense of the term, or territorial ambitions, but rather imperial ones,[42] its strategic (energy and military) interests and its democratic proselytism, which ignores local differences, in themselves constitute a threat to China and Russia. Since the 1930s, when the United States did indeed support China in the face of Japan, whose imperial aims clashed directly with American economic interests, the geopolitical landscape has undergone profound reconfigurations that invalidate Brzezinski's appeal to collective memory. In 1937, Cameron Forbes, an influential banker close to the State Department, described American economic prospects in China as "particularly bright," and noted that "China has probably never before in history offered greater promise of commerce, industry, and general economic progress than… just before the outbreak of current hostilities."[43]

In economic terms, American leaders have been convinced since the 19th century that American prosperity depends on constant expansion of the liberal model: complete opening of markets to American interests—the *Open Door Policy*—which in terms of foreign policy became what William A. Williams

[41] Brzezinski, *The Grand Chessboard*, 159.
[42] Harry Magdoff, *Imperialism Without Colonies* (MRPress, 2003); Philip S. Golub, *Power, Profit and Prestige, A History of American Imperial Expansion* (PlutoPress, 2010), 107.
[43] William Appleman Williams, *The Tragedy of American Diplomacy* (London: Norton Ed., 1984), 193.

rightly called "imperial anti-colonialism."[44] Survival of the American economy was inextricably linked to this continuous expansion. As Assistant Secretary of State Francis B. Sayre put it at the time of the New Deal, the program of expansion of commerce was "a tool to throw the full weight and influence of America against the current disastrous move toward economic nationalism."[45] For the engineers of the New Deal, the reestablishment of the economy and American prosperity depended on other nations' acceptance of American policy. Williams also points out that during the interwar period, the United States considered "any nation (or group) that defied or limited this expansion" a direct danger to its interests. The three countries in question at the time were Italy, Germany, and Japan, whose businesses had entered into fierce competition with American companies in Latin America and Asia, even before the three countries launched acts of military aggression against regions the United States could consider vital to their economic interests. America's economic structure has changed profoundly since the end of the Second World War, and agriculture has lost its importance to the US economy. The overwhelming domination of the service sector in the GDP of the United States poses a problem of trade balance to the extent that its current weak production of consumer products forces it to turn increasingly to imports, particularly from China. Chinese exports to the United States went from $69.9 billion in 2002 to $411 billion in 2012, a staggering 487 percent increase. The argument that the trade deficit is caused by Chinese dumping and the undervaluation of the renminbi attempts to conceal the structural weaknesses of the American economy and blame China for American political, economic, and social shortcomings.

If the economic and political obstacles on the road to Sino-American rapprochement are numerous, the most insurmountable ones are doubtless based on strategic issues. The slow transformation of power relationships in Asia constitutes the true long-term challenge for these relations. The United States still sees itself as the sole possible guardian of stability in Asia, but its long record of strategic errors over a decade makes it seem to Asian leaders, including its closest partners, a power whose repeated currents of radical ideology may well upset the fragile balances of a continent that Americans themselves recognize as "the seat of the world's greatest concentration of rising and recently awakened mass nationalisms."[46] Like the Americans who once supported unsustainable regimes in Asia, Africa, or Latin America in order to contain Soviet ambitions, China today forms alliances with regimes that the West finds undesirable but whose survival ensures, at least temporarily, the maintenance of these balances. The American invasion of Iraq in April 2003 clearly showed the United States' power for destabilization and capacity to plunge countries and whole regions into a chaos whose main beneficiaries are neither democracy nor the people,

---

[44] Williams, *The Tragedy*, 19.
[45] Williams, *The Tragedy*, 173.
[46] Brzezinski, *The Grand Chessboard*, 161.

notwithstanding what the unconditional partisans of American messianism, with their distant and sterilized vision of the realities of the "success of the American operation in Iraq," may have to say about it.

The risk of open conflict between the United States and China seems low, given the latter's growing economic prowess within the world economy and its deterrence capacities. Meanwhile, Beijing's determination on the Taiwan issue is doubtless strong enough to eliminate any risk of a unilateral move on the part of present or future Taiwanese leaders or American military intervention in Taiwan's defense if a crisis were to break out. However, it is difficult to rule out the possibility of a conflict set in motion by a more aggressive policy on the part of the United States if it feels that its very status as a superpower is seriously threatened by a deterioration of its domestic economic and social situation and the continuous growth of Chinese power.

# Chapter III

# *CHINESE ECONOMIC STRATEGY*

ascination, euphoria, and malaise: these three words sum up nicely the
sentiments of China's partners in the face of its extraordinary economic
rise and its as yet untapped potential. Fascination for this historically unprecedented economic development. Euphoria at the extraordinary promises
of the Chinese market for Western businesses, thanks to its demographic mass
and the nonstop economic activity of an increasingly productive population.
Malaise in the face of the social equalities generated by this economic growth,
the shakeup of the world economic order as conceived by the West, and the
*calm strength* that characterizes Chinese leaders, now freed of ideological constraints and professing their desire to participate actively in the redefinition of
this increasingly obsolete order.

China's economic emergence concerns not only public opinion and anxiety
about the effects of outsourcing in the immediate future, but also Western
leaders, who usually seem paralyzed by the phenomenon and unable to do
anything about it. These leaders use China as a scapegoat to draw attention
away from economic policies that have run out of steam or ones that are paralyzed by models that no longer work. Washington's repeated attacks against
the renminbi exchange rate and the controversies over skyrocketing Chinese
textile exports after the expiration of the Multi Fibre Arrangement cannot draw
attention away for long from a major weakness of the American economy,
its weak productivity.[1] Worker productivity in China has risen by 6 percent
annually, with 28 percent of the jobs on the planet, and by 3.5 percent in
India, with 15.5 percent of the world's jobs. The International Labor Office
set productivity growth for all of East Asia at 75 percent for the decade from
1993 to 2003, compared with a mere 14.9 percent for developed economies
for the same period. The relative consistency of this economic growth and the
demographic mass represented by China and India have led to an increasingly
hostile perception by Western public opinion and the return of the old specter
of a yellow menace. No matter how many threats are leveled at them, Chinese
leaders cannot turn back now from this economic policy to return to an approach favorable to Western interests without jeopardizing a policy of growth
that has clearly borne fruit beyond their expectations. The parties involved
must therefore keep a cool head, set aside demagogic and political tendencies,
and negotiate an adaptation of the world economy as a whole to the phenomenon, probably unique in history, of China's economic, and eventually political, emergence.

## Demographics

In the Western imagination, China is first and foremost a teeming mass of
population that threatens to spread out in all directions. Its accelerated popu-

---

[1] Albert Keidel, "China's Currency: Not the Problem," Carnegie Endowment for International Peace, June 2005.

lation growth, which started at the end of the 18th century under the Qing dynasty, was one of the factors leading to the disturbances that broke out across the country after the turn of the 19th century. From 1776 to 1850, the Chinese population suddenly jumped by 63 percent, from 268 to 437 million, a rate that had been a mere 19 percent the previous century. This unprecedented growth finds its explanation in a period of domestic peace that lasted until the eve of the great rebellions of the mid-20th century. This led to major intra-regional migrations caused by overpopulation in the urban areas and coastal regions, driving the overflow to the peripheral regions, including the hard-to-reach mountain regions. Provinces like Sichuan, Guangxi, and Hunan were completely saturated in a matter of decades. But this flow of Han population toward regions mainly inhabited by indigenous populations, mostly nonsini-cized, provoked the first major ethnic clashes. The Han and Manchu's will to progressively bring these regions under the centralized administration of the Qing also ran head on into the interests of local warlords. In the Hunan and Guizhou border region in 1795, the Miao were the first to rise up en masse against this policy, particularly the immigration of poor Han peasants in search of land. Their revolt, which lasted until 1873, symbolized the desper-ate resistance of indigenous populations against the progressive sinicization of education and religious practices imposed by the Qing. In a sign of the social ills of the period, this rebellion was shortly followed by a series of millenarian rebel movements influenced by organized crime as well as mysticism (the se-cret societies of the south, the White Lotus Revolution, the Nien and Taiping Rebellions). The violence of the domestic uprisings of the 19th century, the first wars with the colonial powers, and then the civil wars and Sino-Japanese wars of the early 20th century dramatically slowed the population growth rate, which fell to 25 percent between 1850 and 1949.

With the founding of the People's Republic of China in 1949, the Chinese population would nearly double in 30 years, from 540 million to over 800 million in 1979, whereas previously it had taken two centuries, from 1700 to 1949, to attain the same increase. But this type of growth has not always been typical of China. In the first half of the 20th century, the Chinese population

## Population growth (in millions)[2]

|               | 1700  | 1850  | 1900  | 1950  | 2000  |
|---------------|-------|-------|-------|-------|-------|
| China         | 275   | 429   | 500   | 540   | 1,265 |
| India         | 170   | 222   | 285   | 357   | 1,021 |
| United States | 3.9*  | 23.6  | 76    | 157   | 284   |
| Japan         | 26    | 33    | 43    | 83    | 127   |

*Data from 1790.

---

[2] UN, World Population Prospects 2004; Immanuel C.Y. Hsü, *The Rise of Modern China* (Oxford Univ. Press, 1995).

increased by a mere 0.8 percent, compared with 25 percent for India. Over the second half of the century, with a newly independent India and a China that had entered the socialist camp, the imbalance in population growth still favored India (186 percent for India and 134 percent for China).

Despite the tens of millions of deaths during the Great Leap Forward (1958–1961) and the Cultural Revolution (1966–1976), the accelerated population growth of the first three decades of the People's Republic placed increased pressure on natural resources, agricultural production, internal migration patterns, issues of identity, and in recent years, on the international community's perception of China. The one-child policy, put in place in 1979 within the framework of the Deng Xiaoping–era reforms, had only a modest impact on the birthrate, despite the use of coercive methods (sterilizations and forced abortions) by overzealous local government officials, a practice that seems to have dramatically decreased in recent years, probably due to greater receptivity by the Chinese toward the policy.[3] The rapid increase in quality of life in urban centers and the eastern provinces of the country doubtless encouraged couples to use contraception more consistently in order to ensure a certain quality of life, and more particularly, to cope with the widespread housing shortage. Though resistance was notably stronger in rural areas, this approach seems to have become popular in the intermediate developing regions. The drop in fertility actually started before the reforms, in 1970,[4] but it did not bring growth entirely to a halt. The current average projections of the United Nations forecast a peak in 2025 with a population of 1.44 billion people, then a period of stagnation, followed by a considerable drop to 1.36 billion in 2040.[5] India, on the other hand, is projected to see continuous population growth, reaching 1.62 billion inhabitants in 2040, up from its 2010 population of 1.22 billion. And so India's demographics will continue to resemble those of a developing country, while Chinese demographic structure will approach that of the developed countries. However, while the predicted stabilization of its population growth in the mid-21st century may ease the concerns of the international community, the internal imbalances of this same growth are of serious concern to Chinese authorities as well as all of China's partners, who see them as a grave threat to China and the international community.

## Imbalances

There are two main features to Chinese demographics: a rapidly aging population and one of the world's longest life expectancies today. The two phenomena together raise grave questions about the future of China's economic development and the social tensions that it may bring.

[3] Immigration and Refugee Board of Canada: http://www.irb-cisr.gc.ca/fr/recherche/cnd/.
[4] Wang Feng, "Can China Afford to Continue Its One-Child Policy?" *Asia Pacific Issues*, East-West Center, Honolulu, No. 77, March 2005.
[5] *World Population Prospects – The 2010 Revision*, UN Department of Economic and Social Affairs.

China has already entered a phase of demographic aging that will increase over the next 50 years. According to recent United Nations projections, 38.2 percent of China's population will be over 60 years old in 2050, compared with 12 percent in 2005. In 2050, it is estimated that 100 million Chinese will be over 80 and 218 million will be under 15. This trend became clear in the 1990s and has increased ever since. In 1990, people over 65 represented 5.57 percent of the population; this climbed to 6.96 percent in 2000, 10 years later. The average age of the Chinese, which was 34.5 in 2012, should reach 48 in 2050, overtaking Canada (45.2) and several European countries (Denmark, Finland, and France). Life expectancy, which had already reached 71.5 years in 2010, should reach 78.7 years in 2040, matching that of France today and coming in just behind the United States' projection for 2040 (82.5).

According to the same projections, the fertility rate, which was 1.56 children per woman in 2010, should increase very slowly to 1.73 children per woman in 2040, below the replacement rate, and then progressively increase to 2.01 in 2080.

Naturally, for Chinese leaders it is imperative to carry out the most precise studies possible and analyze several scenarios. This population growth influences not only their policy decisions for the development of social safety net programs and employment, but especially the energy and food consumption China must prepare for in the future.

The geographic distribution of the Chinese population is another cause for concern. The urbanization rate reached 32.1[6] percent in 2000 and 51.7% in 2011; it should perhaps reach 90 percent by the end of the century. This rapid decrease in rural population, and therefore in the rural workforce, could have major consequences on agricultural production, which Chinese authorities now prioritize.

In order to cope with its population growth between now and 2020, China must dramatically improve agricultural technologies and soil resource management. But it must also attempt to stabilize rural populations and slow the urban exodus by taking measures to improve quality of life in rural areas and putting a halt to the land speculation that is progressively reducing the cultivated land area. Still, though China is the world's largest consumer of grains, it is currently self-sufficient in this regard, and most of its current grain imports are destined for reserves in case of natural disaster or to respond to price differences between local production and international markets. If China falls behind in research and development, however, it may run the risk of having to increase markedly its imports. To place this in perspective, in 2012, world grain imports reached 296 million tons, 115 million of which went to Asia alone. The appearance of the first signs of a world food crisis in 2008 can only reinforce the fears of

[6]The state of China's cities 2012-2013, UN-HABITAT, http://www.unhabitat.org/pmss/listItemDetails.aspx?publicationID=3404.

countries like India and China. Feeding the Chinese population in the future remains up to the Chinese authorities, not the United States, as some American experts believe.[7] Even assuming that most of the country's arable lands are currently in use, technological developments in agriculture, proactive policies to recover the poorest soils (as in the case of wheat grown in the Libyan desert), and funneling capital investments back into the agricultural sector could reverse the current trend and breathe new life into Chinese agriculture. But for this to work, Beijing must create a truly comprehensive land use policy that takes into account the technological and capital needs of agriculture, the need to stanch urban migration though more rapid improvement in the quality of life in rural areas, and the need to limit the constant increase in the income gap between the city and the countryside.

The population distribution within the country has varied only very slightly since 1949. At the founding of the People's Republic, 43.47 percent of the total population of the country was distributed across 13.60 percent of the territory (the nine east coast provinces and the three municipalities of Beijing, Tianjin, and Shanghai). In 2010, the population of these provinces and cities reached 44.48 percent of the total.[8] Moreover, the five autonomous regions (Xinjiang, Tibet, Guangxi, Inner Mongolia, and Ningxia) represent 45 percent of the territory but accounted for only 6 percent of the total population in 1949 and 7.63 percent in 2010. This increase is due to the higher birthrate among ethnic minorities as well as internal migrations. The one-child policy, in fact, was not imposed on the ethnic minorities, who are allowed to have up to three children. While the Han population rose by 91.4 percent between 1949 and 1990, the Mongol population increased by 231 percent, the Hui by 144 percent, the Miao by 196 percent, and the Manchus by 310 percent. The population growth of the Uyghurs in Xinjiang was nearly identical to that of the Han (with 99.6 percent), while the rate for the Tibetans was much lower (66.8 percent) and closer to that of the Korean minority (73 percent). This proactive policy resulted in an increase in ethnic minority populations as a proportion of the total from 5.89 percent in 1949 to 8.49 percent in 2011.[9]

Several factors contribute to this persistent demographic imbalance. Historically, the Chinese population has spread along the waterways and coasts, forsaking the backcountry. The development of communications infrastructures came too late to allow for a rapid, noticeable rebalancing of this uneven population distribution. The efforts dedicated to this issue by Chinese authorities over the last decade, however, should make the inland regions more attractive in the medium term, encouraging population movement that would help

---

[7] Lester R. Brown, "Can the United States feed China?" *Washington Post*, March 11, 2011.
[8] For an accurate comparison, the populations of Taiwan, Hong Kong, and Macao are not included. Source: Sixth National Population Census of the People's Republic of China.
[9] "Communiqué of the National Bureau of Statistics of People's Republic of China on Major Figures of the 2010 Population Census[1] (No. 1)," National Bureau of Statistics of China, April 28, 2011.

reduce demographic pressure on the coastal regions. This infrastructure development, of course, is accompanied by a land use policy for energy, education, and health care that may reduce these imbalances. This policy, which has been in effect for several years, should eventually ease social tensions as well. But to the extent that the populations encouraged to migrate inland are mostly made up of Han, interethnic tensions may well arise in certain regions, as occurred in the 19th century, particularly in regions where the newcomers live alongside native Muslim populations. The Chinese government should pay particular attention to this problem in order not to displace social tensions into areas made vulnerable by the coexistence of populations of very different cultures, languages, and religions.

## Successes of the economic reforms

In 1978, the China that emerged from the Cultural Revolution was a complete economic and political train wreck. The society was traumatized, the economic structures were disorganized and unproductive, and millions of men and women, particularly intellectuals, had vanished in the turmoil. The country had taken such a severe beating that one had to wonder about its future and its ability to overcome this national catastrophe. Isolated from the international community because of Maoist excesses, and faced with a hostile environment and serious reservations on the part of Western countries, China had to confront the daunting task of economic reconstruction and the restoration of domestic and international confidence. And then China saw a man rise providentially from among the wreckage, a visionary, already 74 years old, ready to implement a strategy that would bring domestic prosperity to China and allow it to take its rightful place in the international community, never mind the naysayers.

Deng Xiaoping's launch of the concept of a *socialist market economy* (社会主义市场经济; *shèhuì zhǔyì shìchǎng jīngjì*) was meant to respond to this need. This new revolution, which resonated with a population fatigued by one political movement after another since 1949 (the Hundred Flowers, the People's Commune, the Great Leap Forward, the Cultural Revolution), aspired above all to stability and development. This was an example of China's remarkable ability to adapt to changing contexts. The *Four Modernizations* (四个现代化 sìgè xiàndàihuà), agriculture, industry, national defense, science and technology, immortalized in the Party Constitution during the Eleventh Congress in August 1977 and in the Constitution adopted in March 1978, became the new ground rules for closing the considerable gap that had grown between China and the industrialized countries over the course of the previous decades. Political reform was conspicuously absent from these basic concerns, though the straitjacket of the Cultural Revolution would gradually loosen.

The results of the first half century of economic reforms surpassed expectations. Between 1981 and 2000, annual growth in GDP reached 9.6 percent. GDP per capita went from $300 in 1981 to $5,439 in 2011, compared with $275 in India in 1981 and $1,528 in 2011.[10] Experts differ on the prospects for the Chinese economy in coming decades. Most predict, however, that it will surpass the US economy within 20 years. Others considered this prediction overly optimistic at the beginning of the 2000s, predicting instead that this would happen within 50 years,[11] barring of course a major crisis that would bring the development process to a halt. History played an ironic turn, however, when the United States plunged into a major financial and economic crisis that China weathered rather well, speeding up the closing of the gap between the two economies.

After its October 2005 meeting, the Fifth Plenum of the Central Committee of the Communist Party of China had confirmed its goal of doubling GDP by 2010, which meant an average annual growth of 7.5 percent. In 2010, it had tripled from $1.944 trillion to $5.95 trillion. The Eleventh Five-Year Plan adopted at the time had also reaffirmed the authorities' willingness to take into account the weaknesses of current development and the need to pay greater attention to the negative effects of rapid growth, particularly on social issues. This growth has profoundly and rapidly altered the structure of domestic wealth, as the proportion of the work force employed in agriculture has dropped from 71 percent in 1978 to 46.3 percent in 2000 (versus 52 percent in India). Over 90 percent of this increase is represented by the tertiary sector alone, particularly telecommunications, banking, the service sector, and commerce.

While these results are rather encouraging for Chinese economic policy, they are likely what led Party leaders to revise their plans for agriculture and take the measures necessary for the progressive recovery of internal balances. The January 1, 2006, elimination of the agricultural tax, for the first time in 2,600 years in China, aimed to jump-start the agricultural sector, and the plan worked. China produces 18 percent of the world's grains and 50 percent of its vegetables today,[12] or 20 percent of the world's food, using only 9 percent of the world's cultivated land. Taxes on agricultural products had already been lowered several times since 2004, and during the second session of the People's Conference, in March 2004, Hu Jintao had committed to eliminating these taxes for good within five years. The timetable had to be moved up to respond to the growing challenges facing Chinese rural areas and the threats that these areas' lagging development posed to the stability of the country.

Agriculture has always been the foundation of the Chinese economy. The sector required massive investment since the start of the reforms, because it had

---

[10] Figures in constant prices. Source: UNdata.

[11] Keidel, "Prospects for Continued High Economic Growth in China," Carnegie Endowment for International Peace for POSRI International Forum on China's Development, Seoul, Korea, November 10-11, 2004, 5.

[12] Colin A. Carter, "China's Agriculture: Achievements and Challenges," Giannini Foundation, 2011.

been largely neglected since 1949 in favor of industry. Its complete restructuring was essential to the success of the Four Modernizations, and this was the objective of the first phase of the reforms, until 1984. While the measures taken since 1978 to help the agricultural sector helped improve the quality of life in rural areas, the inadequacy of technological advances, the rural exodus, and the reduction of cultivated area (the area dedicated to cultivating grains went from 93.55 million hectares in 1990 to 86.57 million in 2000[13]) have had the reverse effect and reduced the positive impact of the reforms. The privatization of agricultural production, which became the rule in the countryside in the early 1980s in order to stimulate initiative and productivity, has markedly improved the situation of peasant families. However, the strong economic growth of the urban centers and eastern provinces has widened the gap between city and countryside. Generally, those who live in rural areas are the big losers of Chinese development today. But the growth differential between urban and rural China should not hide the results obtained within the framework of the reforms.

In 1978, around 260 million inhabitants of rural regions lived below the absolute poverty line, representing 33 percent of the total rural population.[14] Thanks to the reforms, by 1984 the figure had dropped to 11 percent, with a 15 percent increase in per capita income. This growth slowed after 1985, stabilizing at around 3 percent annually. These structural reforms had a rapid impact on production, particularly thanks to the nearly universal adoption in 1983 of a system of family farming and the disappearance of the people's communes in 1984, but rural areas began to lose momentum in 1985 due to the lack of resources and inadequate prices for production conditions. The central authorities struggled to win the trust of the peasants as they promised that the reforms and decollectivization were here to stay. The constant political campaigns of the previous decades had left the peasants very cautious, and they were not prepared to invest in their farms as long as fears of a return to the old system remained.[15] It took until the mid-1990s for this trust to be established and for the peasants to truly feel safe from a return to the old ideological excesses.

The effects of the reforms have been a major reduction in poverty—not only in rural areas, but nationwide. According to the World Bank, 360 million Chinese were below the poverty line in 1990; in 2011, only 170 million lived on less than $1.25 per day. Despite the growing gap between the incomes of the richest and the poorest Chinese, a syndrome that has affected the United

---

[13]FAO Country Profiles, 2005.

[14]Shengen Fan et al., *Growth, Inequality and Poverty in Rural China*, International Food Policy Research Institute, Washington, DC, 2002.

[15]Arthur Lewis Rosenbaum, ed., *State and Society in China: The Consequences of Reform* (Boulder: Westview Press, 1992), 145.

States and Europe as well over the last 20 years,[16] and the social movements that generate this phenomenon, the quality of life of the Chinese population as a whole has risen considerably over a quarter century. While the peasants have been somewhat neglected by the authorities, workers have meanwhile been privileged.

In the industrial sector, the priority was first placed on investment in large projects worth over $400 billion, so that Chinese industrial production could "approach, match, or even surpass that of most developed capitalist countries."[17] These projects were mainly centered on steel, coal, oil, and electricity production. This program, launched amid much fanfare in February 1978 on instructions from Hua Guofeng, depended on the accumulation of capital and massive importation of foreign technologies, based on the model used by Ceaușescu in Romania in the 1970s. But this policy only led to a higher budget and trade deficit and mounting inflation. In April 1979, Deng Xiaoping and his allies decided to revise this policy, whose negative effects were already being felt. They gradually tightened their grip on the reins of the Party until the official elimination of Hua Guofeng during the Eighth Plenum of the Eleventh Conference of the CPC in June 1981, when he relinquished his duties as secretary general and chairman of the Central Military Commission (he had already been relieved of his duties as prime minister in August 1980). The Plenum also adopted an act condemning Maoism as a political and economic program, stating that Mao Zedong's greatest contributions had been prior to 1957, and his greatest errors came afterward, particularly "the grave 'Left' error of the Cultural Revolution." This cleared the way for the implementation of a program oriented to the market economy, introduced by Deng Xiaoping, Hu Yaobang, and Zhao Ziyang, and inspired not only by the economic experiments of countries like Yugoslavia, but especially on those of the "little dragons" (Taiwan, South Korea, and Singapore). In 1984, public sector reforms were implemented, including partial liberalization of prices and the decentralization of decision-making authority. This policy led to the collapse of the profits of those companies, crushed under the weight of excessive consumption and investments, and a round of criticism from conservatives who interpreted this as the result of methods incompatible with socialism. The June 1989 Tiananmen Square events occurred just in time to reinforce their position and cast doubt on the whole reform program conceived by Deng Xiaoping's group. The most liberal among them, Hu Yaobang, had already been relieved of his duties as secretary general of the Party in January 1987. Zhao Ziyang took over as interim secretary general and managed to keep up the growth rate, thanks especially to a flexible credit policy, enough to keep the conservatives

---

[16] In 2010, 46.2 million Americans lived below the poverty line, 14.96 percent of the total population. Poverty affects 15.1 percent of the citizens of the European Union, a number that is constantly rising. (David Kenner, "Decline watch: How poor is America?," *Foreign Policy*, September 14, 2011.)

[17] *Quotidien du Peuple*, March 9, 1978.

at bay. His removal on June 24, 1989, after he stated his willingness to engage in dialogue with the student protesters, strengthened the conservative wing of the Party. But the conservatives were nonetheless unable to take power, and they agreed to the nomination as secretary general of Jiang Zemin, who had been against military intervention at Tiananmen Square. The reforms were too far along and too solidly rooted in public opinion to contemplate turning back, and even within the Party itself, the conservatives could not hold sway. The adoption by the Fourteenth Congress of the CPC in October 1992 of the concept of a *socialist market economy with Chinese characteristics* (中国特色的 社会主义市场经济; *zhōngguótèsè de shèhuì zhŭyì shìchăng jīngjì*) and Jiang Zemin's report on the acceleration of economic openness and modernization finished off the conservative opposition. Deng Xiaoping announced that he meant to sacrifice the small state businesses and concentrate on the large ones, privatizing those whose losses had become too great.

Thanks to this policy, the share of industrial production corresponding to state businesses dropped from 82 percent in 1978 to 36 percent in 1996. The authorities progressively focused their efforts on a short list of large businesses, with particular attention to six megacompanies that they hoped to see listed among the top 50 largest companies in the world by 2010 (in the steel, household appliances, electronics, shipbuilding, and pharmaceuticals sectors). These are the same big Chinese concerns that China's partners are worried about. In recent years, they have not only set out to conquer new markets abroad, they have also begun to take over Western companies in different sectors. Not satisfied with being the largest beneficiary of foreign direct investments among developing countries, China has actually begun to export its own capital. In 1991 Chinese investments abroad totaled only $3 billion, a figure that leapt to $424 billion in 2011.[18] These Chinese businesses have carried out a few real coups since 2004 by buying up European or American companies in trouble and saving local jobs, particularly after the crisis of 2008. Certain acquisitions that were broadly reported in the media, such as the takeover of the PC division of the American company IBM by the Chinese Lenovo group, or that of the third-largest American appliance manufacturer Maytag by the Chinese concern Haier for over a billion dollars, have raised some eyebrows in Europe and the United States, although some observers note rather condescendingly that "they still lack certain technologies, a certain know-how."[19]

The strength of the Chinese economy, which has defied predictions for two decades, is that it was able to turn to its domestic market in the late 1990s to encourage growth, something Japan had been unable to do in the 1970s. The rapid development of construction, the auto industry, and infrastructure have ensured the continuation of rapid growth, even as the world economy slows. Moreover, China has thus far been able to remain very active in industrial

---

[18] "A Closer Look at China's Overseas Investment," *World Resource Institute,* December 12, 2012.
[19] "Les entreprises chinoises passent à l'offensive," *France Matin,* August 29, 2005.

sectors requiring a large workforce at the same time that it has moved progressively toward less workforce-intensive high-tech sectors. Finally, one of the drivers of its good economic health lies in its acknowledgment of the role of competition for Chinese companies as well as foreign companies. Thus, a powerful group like Huawei, a private telecommunications giant, now competes openly in domestic and foreign markets with the largest Chinese public groups.

The health of the Chinese economy depends on several economic factors partially linked to the international economic and political situation. Its accelerated growth has a direct impact on the world economy, and the continuation of its emergence will have increasingly important consequences for the entire world economic and financial system, which will certainly have to adapt in order to prevent crises due to too many sudden changes.

## Vectors of power

### Foreign trade

The January 1, 2005, expiration of the textile quotas under the rules set by the WTO brought to the forefront the problem of trade relations between a China in a phase of rapid economic growth and other economies, those of developed and developing countries alike. These countries, with their very inconsistent performance and generally gloomy outlook, must depend on fragile balances that the emergence of China is already upsetting. In 2012, China's trade surplus had risen by 48 percent compared to 2011, reaching $231.1 billion, for a total trade volume of $3.867 trillion, up from only $289 billion in 1995.

The first victim of this trade explosion was the United States, which had a $282 billion trade deficit with China in 2011, triple what it was 10 years prior. China is now the United States' biggest supplier, but also its third-largest buyer. In 2011, China alone represented 50 percent of the American trade balance of $560 billion, down from its record level of $753 billion in 2006.

The responsibility is clearly shared. On the one hand, despite the warnings of some economists, Western policy makers have been unable to anticipate the impact of China's integration into the world economy and to look more deeply at the adaptations necessary for their economies. On the other hand, China, pressed by the demands of growth that will determine its social stability and domestic policies, refuses to apply immediately the rules others wish to impose on it in areas such as intellectual property and labor conditions, which might slow this growth. This is precisely the complaint of its partners today, whose economies are beginning to feel the effects of the Chinese economy and its rapid process of opening.

The West and Asian nations have very different perceptions of Chinese trade power. The removal of the textile quotas suddenly forced Western leaders to take a hard look at the major consequences that may come with China's integration into the world economy. This crisis has exposed the structural weaknesses of their economies, but it has also given American and European policy makers a chance to place the blame squarely on China for the gloomy outlook of their economies.

Chinese exports have grown consistently in nearly all economic sectors, making it the world's largest exporter, ahead of Germany and the United States, in 2010, well ahead of economists' predictions. The crisis led to the reversal of some trends. For instance, in 2004, China carried a trade deficit with Japan of $14 billion, which in 2012 had become a record surplus of $44 billion, partly due to tensions between the two countries that led to a considerable drop in the activities of certain large Japanese concerns, particularly in the auto industry, and the attendant drop in sales.[20] Trade with the European Union, however, has dropped by 3.7 percent, while with the United States it has risen by 8.5 percent, and by 10.2 percent with ASEAN member states. The Americans and Europeans have continuously denounced the fixed exchange rate of the renminbi, supposedly artificially maintained below market rate to unfairly favor Chinese imports. The central authorities nonetheless readjusted the fluctuation band of the renminbi to the dollar, changing it from 0.5 percent to 1 percent in April 2012. Naturally, Beijing's monetary policy is heavily influenced by interest groups in China, perhaps even by certain American industrial groups that produce for export in China and whose interests would be seriously compromised by the floating of the renminbi based on the market.[21]

The undervaluation of the Chinese currency is debatable, even in the United States, where certain economists blame its drift on shortcomings in Washington's economic policies.[22] They point to the experience of Japan, unfairly subjected to the same accusations in the 1980s. When the revaluation of the yen, under US pressure, failed to change the Japanese-American trade balance, it forced economists to look for an ad hoc explanation: "Japan does not respond to economic models."[23] This revaluation did, however, plunge Japan into an economic crisis that it was not able to extricate itself from until more than two decades later. The lesson was learned, which explains economists' caution today regarding the problem of America's trade balance. Other American voices are raised against the revaluation of the renminbi, particularly among American industrials who import components or finished products from China and are afraid that such a move would impact them directly. Even consumers in general mistrust the sort of pressure on China that may lead to a jump in prices of products made in China. These products certainly flood American and

[20]"Tensions avec la Chine: Toyota renonce à produire 10 millions de voitures," AFP, October 23, 2012; "Ordinary Chinese will also suffer from boycotting Japan," *Global Times*, September 19, 2012.

[21] "China's Export Lobbying Groups and the Politics of the Renminbi," *Freeman Briefing Report*, February, 2012.

[22]M. Baily & R. Lawrence, "Don't blame trade for US job losses," *McKinsey Quarterly*, 2005, Number 1.

[23]Oded Shenkar, *The Chinese Century* (Upper Saddle River: Pearson Education, Inc.—publishing as Wharton School Publishing, 2006), 14.

European markets, but at the same time they allow low-income families to afford products that were once out of reach. The exchange rate is just one explanation of this surplus, behind which lurks another reality: China's extraordinary domestic savings capacity.

In 2010, gross savings in China had reached the historic level of 53.9 percent of GDP, compared with a mere 9.3 percent in the United States.[24] According to the economic theory of savings, this means a very high level of investing. This domestic savings capacity places the importance of foreign direct investments to the domestic economy into perspective, as they represented only 3 percent of GDP in 2011.[25]

In this international economic context, still very favorable to China's trade balance, after a drop in exports of 11.9 percent in 2009, the year after the economic and financial crisis hit, exports have begun their rise anew. They have reached a new record of €1.34 trillion in 2011,[26] notwithstanding the central authorities' efforts to slow exports and increase imports. Imports have indeed increased significantly in recent years (up 47.5 percent from 2009 to 2010, and up 20.3 percent in 2011 from the previous year), but at too slow a rate to keep up with the growth in exports. The continuous rise of oil prices, however, could help limit the trade surplus given the considerable annual increase in hydrocarbon imports to slake China's unquenchable thirst for energy. China's growing participation in international trade is perhaps the best evidence of its integration into the world economic system. Japan and the newly industrialized countries went through a period of rapid double-digit growth for over 30 years before China ever did. And there was a time when Japan, too, was the object of the very same accusations now leveled against China by the West, but it eventually found its place in the world economy without destabilizing it. In reality, the Chinese economy poses a challenge to the world economic system not so much because of its growth rate as because of its extraordinary potential based on factors we have mentioned, particularly its demographic weight. Reactions to this Chinese economic prowess are very different in the West and in Asia, for their interests do not necessarily converge.

Asia as a whole has enjoyed major benefits from this emergence. By privileging trade with Asia, which in 2010 represented over 50 percent of its imports,[27] China is attempting to create a dynamic of détente, based on the principle of greater economic interdependence, which would allow it to work toward improvement in its political relations with its neighbors and try to overcome

---

[24] Wayne M. Morrison, "China's Economic Conditions," *Congressional Research Service*, December 4, 2012.

[25] "Foreign direct investment, net inflows (percent of GDP)," World Bank, http://data.worldbank.org/indicator/BX.KLT. DINV.WD.GD.ZS.

[26] IMF, Direction of Trade Statistics (DOTS), "http://dx.doi.org/10.5257/imf/dots/2013-05."

[27] With $514.4 billion in imports, three of China's main suppliers, all of them Asian (Japan, South Korea, and Taiwan), represent nearly a third of its total imports for 2010.

historical antagonisms. The level of economic relations among states is certainly no guarantee that conflicts will be eradicated, but it does exert a considerable influence on them. The Chinese strategy of pacifying the periphery and maintaining stability rests largely on this economic engagement, and thus far it seems to be bearing fruit. Beijing has therefore projected a phased-in expansion of this economic integration that started with Southeast Asia.[28]

Southeast Asia was indeed the first to embark on this path by accepting the principle of a free trade zone with China in 2001. With a growing trade balance in its favor, ASEAN hoped to press its advantage and continue to benefit from the Chinese dynamic. Signing in November 2001 at Bandar Seri Begawan a statement of principle announcing the creation of a free trade zone between China and ASEAN within 10 years marked the success of the strategy that Beijing had patiently followed since the early 1990s. Confirmed during the ASEAN Summit at Phnom Penh in December 2002, this free trade zone will eventually bring nearly 1.9 billion people into one market with a GDP of over a trillion dollars, or 18 percent of world GDP (20.7 percent for the United States and 21.7 percent for the European Union). With an average annual GDP growth rate of 5.5 percent for ASEAN and nearly 10 percent for China, the region remains a major hub of world economic dynamics.

Once this first stage was completed, China took advantage of the November 2002 ASEAN Summit to engage in negotiations with Japan and South Korea for the creation of another free trade zone to bring together three of the best-performing economies in Asia (the combined GDP of the three countries represented 20 percent of the world total in 2010). These negotiations were more delicate given existing tensions, but in November 2012, the three countries announced the official launch of the free trade zone project. After the 1992 diplomatic normalization between the People's Republic of China and South Korea, trade between the two developed rapidly in South Korea's favor, as the trade balance brought it a $40 billion surplus and $36 billion in Korean investments in China in 2011. Japan too has benefited from Chinese growth, but Japanese professional agricultural organizations pressure the government to slow this integration, for they fear its negative impact on Japanese agriculture. Moreover, the political crisis affecting relations between the two countries has considerably slowed the growth in their trade, causing concern among Japanese industrials. Japan and China's respective economic demands place limitations on their conflicts, which must remain within acceptable parameters in order not to jeopardize the whole partnership, as evidenced by the frequent conciliatory statements of both parties. With over 28,000 companies having invested in China, or over 6 percent of the total foreign companies

---

[28] 中国发展研究，国务院发展研究中心研究报告选 [Research on Chinese development. Extract of investigative report on the Development of China by the State Council of the People's Republic of China], *Editions du Développement Chinois*, 2004, 123.

present in the country, the Liberal Democratic Party in power must pay heed to its political supporters in the business sector, while China, for its part, cannot yet do without Japanese technological know-how. Since 2001, Korea too has sought to find its place among the economic giants by making itself the East Asian hub, thanks to its privileged geographical position. But the path to regional integration is rife with political pitfalls, so the three countries must clearly identify the complementary aspects of their economies. The creation of a free trade zone between Japan and Korea and excluding China, which has been brought up several times, would mean for China an estimated drop of 0.1 percent of its GDP and a considerable impact on its level of investments and trade balance. In the event of an "ASEAN Plus Two" free trade zone (Japan and South Korea), the drop in China's growth rate could reach 0.45 percent.[29] China's strategy of economic engagement with South Korea and Japan therefore aims to avoid letting the negotiations that have already begun end up in a free trade agreement that does not immediately include China, while reinforcing the influence of its growth on neighboring economies in order to reduce the economic impact of existing tensions, especially with Japan.

The rapid increase in trade between China and India, though the amount is still relatively low ($66 billion in 2012 compared with $1 billion in 1994, with a $29 billion trade deficit for India), reflects a trend toward improvement in relations between the Asian economic giants. The parallel economic emergence of the two most populous countries, with annual growth rates that are the stuff of Western dreams, has led Beijing and New Delhi to take a closer look at their rivalries and points in common. The agreement signed by the two countries in January 2006 on energy cooperation likewise signaled a political will to reduce sources of friction and work toward progressively harmonizing their economies. The size of the two economies makes the process rather slow and difficult, but the prospect of a common market covering a third of the world population, which Southeast Asia might eventually join as well, should finally encourage Indian and Chinese leaders to iron out their political differences. Yet India remains defensive of its position in South Asia and its economic influence, as evidenced by its reservations about China's December 2005 entry into the South Asian Association for Regional Cooperation (SAARC)[30] at Pakistan's invitation. India was the only member state to object. After the summit at Dhaka, China and Japan obtained observer status, but with only grudging agreement from India. China is now lobbying SAARC, regularly signaling its willingness to cooperate with the organization in the hopes of eventually being admitted as a full member.

Venturing further from its traditional sphere of influence, China engaged in negotiations with the Gulf Cooperation Council (GCC) in July 2004. This organization includes six Arabian Peninsula countries (Bahrain, Kuwait, Oman,

---

[29] 中国发展 … [Research on Chinese …], 125.
[30] The association includes Bangladesh, Bhutan, India, the Maldives, Nepal, Pakistan, and Sri Lanka.

Qatar, Saudi Arabia, and United Arab Emirates), which represent a market of 20 million consumers and $1.5 trillion in foreign investments. Trade between China and these countries has grown considerably, with China representing 10 percent of GCC member states' trade in 2011, up from 2 percent in 1992.[31]

But negotiations have stagnated since 2006, due to the expectations of both sides. For China, this agreement should throw open the doors of trade with the Gulf monarchies, which represent only a small total number of consumers (31.8 million inhabitants in 2009) but a strong potential for consumption, with a GDP per capita of $17,700. It should therefore allow China to reduce somewhat its trade deficit with the GCC, which reached $20 billion in 2011. But for GCC member states, the imbalance is skewed by China's energy dependence, which represents 60 percent of their total exports. China has thus far refused its partners' demands to integrate the service sector into this agreement. The GCC member states' concern is that the agreement should not benefit only China by facilitating the exportation of goods to the GCC, while GCC states can export only services. This free trade agreement, which has not yet been signed despite several announcements to that effect, is of particular importance to China because of its interest in the Gulf monarchies' energy reserves during this current phase of economic development, with its constantly growing level of consumption. Moreover, this agreement could be a first step toward similar arrangements with other Arab states.

China's numerous projects for bilateral agreements, in Africa, Latin America (it has signed agreements with Chile, Peru, and Costa Rica to date), and Central Asia, underline the economic strategy adopted by Beijing with an eye not only to opening new markets, but also to strengthening its political relations on the different continents in order to build its economic emergence on the foundations of growing relations of interdependence, in order to get its foot in the door of globalization.

## Financial reserves

China's economic emergence over the last quarter century has generated extraordinary growth in its cash reserves. Its public finances are considered healthy, with a budget deficit for 2011 of 1.64 percent of GDP, and public debt at 25.8 percent[32] (in India, by contrast, the figures are 5.3 percent and 68.5 percent of GDP, respectively). The public finance reform launched in 1994 has allowed for more transparent management and the growth of state revenues though indirect taxation. Despite some increase, public expenditures remain inadequate, particularly in the areas of social services and debt service.

---

[31]"The GCC turns East," *Arab News*, December 16, 2012.
[32]IMF, http://www.imf.org/external/data.htm#data.

But this good financial health has allowed China to accumulate cash reserves at an impressive rate: from $403.3 billion in 2003, they rose to over $3.3 trillion by the end of 2012, having surpassed Japan long ago ($1.268 trillion). The People's Bank of China has invested nearly three–quarters of its reserves in US Treasury bonds and other assets held in dollars.

In December 2012, with $1.2 trillion (21.6 percent) of Treasury securities held by foreigners (7.2 percent of the total American public debt of $16.68 trillion), the People's Republic of China had become the United States' largest foreign creditor. China has also become the main financier of the American budget deficit alongside Japan ($1.12 trillion) and the Gulf oil monarchies. This hold over American public finances is worrisome for certain powerful circles in the United States, particularly the neoconservatives who see China as the incarnation of evil. In an article published in 2005, *New York Times* editorial writer Nicholas D. Kristof claimed that China's holding of a major proportion of American public debt (through its purchase of Treasury bonds) gives it "leverage over us" and "undermines our national security."[33]

But using that leverage would require great skill on the part of Chinese leaders, due to the great interdependence of these economies. A slowdown in Chinese purchase of assets could result in a serious destabilization of the American economy. Naturally, a long-term slowdown in American economic growth would have a considerable impact on the Chinese economy and trade balance as well, so Beijing must manage these financial balances very carefully. American economists have long warned policy makers of the risk that foreign investors will lose interest in American currency due to the exploding American debt.[34] Even former Secretary of the Treasury John Snow insisted repeatedly that the budget deficit must be reduced in order to avoid "paying a huge price on the financial markets."[35] While China is really not interested in making hostile moves against the American currency, it could begin a gradual shift to other currencies, which would be a serious challenge for the American administration. And in the event of a major crisis with Washington, it does have at its disposal a means of applying considerable pressure.

## Foreign direct investments

Since it opened to foreign investors in 1979 and reformed its exchange rate, China has attracted considerable capital, becoming in 2012 the greatest beneficiary of foreign direct investments (FDI), ahead of the United States. In 2011, Asia provided 87 percent of the FDI going to China. An Asian hub, Hong Kong was naturally the main source. In 1980, China's share of FDI going to

---

[33] "A Glide Path to Ruin," *Washington Post*, June 26, 2005.
[34] "The true national debt," *Washington Post*, February 25, 2013.
[35] AFP, January 5, 2006.

the Asia-Pacific region was equivalent to that of Singapore or Malaysia. After Deng Xiaoping's decision to launch reforms in early 1992 in order to restart economic development in the wake of events in 1989 and 1990, this share reached 50 percent in the early 1990s, rising from $4 billion in 1991 to $41 billion in 2000, before falling back to 25 percent in 2011 (India represents 6 percent of the total).[36] This relative drop is due to the overall increase in FDI in the Asia-Pacific region. Asian states have become concerned about the attraction China could eventually exert on the flow of FDI, given its accelerated development. However, it appears that these fears are unfounded thus far, for several reasons:

• A major share of these FDI come from the Chinese diaspora, which would not necessarily have invested its capital in non-Chinese economies in any case.
• China's economic development has doubtless contributed to the increase in foreign investments in other Asian economies that supply it with the inputs necessary for its growth (particularly raw materials and components to be assembled in China).
• Educational level and scientific development exert a considerable influence on FDI, which tend not to be drawn to lower-performing economies.
• The increase in FDI in China appears, however, to have had an impact on Singapore, where the bulk of investments that came from the Chinese diaspora have been funneled toward continental China, to the detriment of the city-state.

According to the World Bank,[37] the Chinese diaspora originally provided around 70 percent of FDI in China in the 1980s and 1990s, mostly coming from Greater China (Taiwan, Hong Kong, Singapore, and Macao) and Southeast Asia. This capital is naturally funneled first and foremost to the regions from which this diaspora comes, that is, the provinces of the east coast. The economic and political opening of China, along with reforms, has allowed Chinese abroad to rekindle their relations with the homeland and with tradition, honoring their ancestors through investment in the villages and cities their families come from, where they have usually maintained solid ties of solidarity, including with local authorities. From 1980 to 1991, the provinces of Guangdong and Fujian saw FDI growth rates of 13 percent and 11 percent, respectively. Between 1986 and 1992, monies coming from Chinese individuals and companies abroad represented 90.8 percent of Guangdong's

[36] "FDI flows crucial to Asia's development – UNESCAP," *The Manila Times*, January 5, 2013; Chengang Wang, Yingqi Wei, and Xiaming Liu, "Does China rival its neighbouring economies for inward FDI?," *Transnational Corporations Journal*, University of York, March 2007.
[37] "Are Foreign Investors Attracted to Weak Environmental Regulations? Evaluating the Evidence from China," World Bank Policy Research Working Paper 305, February 205.

total FDI.[38] By the end of the 1980s, Chinese from Fujian alone represented around 35 percent of the diaspora (nearly 9 million people, or 30 percent of the total population of the province). The attraction that the eastern provinces exerted over investors lay not only in family ties, but also in their geographical position, easy access to ports for imports and exports, and the greater density of communications infrastructure. While the proportion of FDI corresponding to the diaspora has diminished since 1994 due to measures taken by the Chinese authorities to encourage foreign investment in general, it still represents a major share.

### FDI in China in 2012

| Origin | Total (billions USD) |
|--------|------|
| Hong Kong | 71.28 |
| Japan | 7.38 |
| Singapore | 6.53 |
| Taiwan | 6.18 |
| United States | 3.13 |
| South Korea | 3.06 |
| Germany | 1.47 |
| Netherlands | 1.14 |
| United Kingdom | 1.03 |
| Switzerland | 0.80 |

*Source:* Ministry of Commerce of the PRC, January 2013.

On the other hand, the landlocked provinces and those populated by ethnic minorities, which have historically maintained only very little contact with the diaspora, have been the most neglected by investors. Moreover, the native populations tend to maintain family- or clan-based relations along cultural or religious lines with Central Asian states little affected by the economic development, unlike Southeast Asia, which hosts a major Chinese community. This is why the Chinese authorities, encouraged by Prime Minister Zhu Rongji, launched the China Western Development program (西部大开发), meant to mitigate the growing gaps in development between the east and the west of the country. The target area includes 11 provinces, autonomous regions, and municipalities with a population of nearly 370 million, but a per capita income of only 40 percent that of the eastern provinces. Despite the development disparities, the situation of the western provinces has improved somewhat since the start of the reforms. Per capita GDP for the province of Qinghai rose from 428 renminbi in 1978 to 990 in 1999, and then to 6,426 in 2002. In Tibet, it rose from 375 renminbi in 1978 to a high of 29,522 renminbi in 2011.[39] These few results show a growth trend even in the isolated provinces, though this progress is still inadequate in light of the formidable growth of the coastal provinces.

---

[38] *Statistical Yearbook of Guangdong,* 1993.
[39] *China National Bureau of Statistics Database,* accessed March 2013, http://219.235.129.58/welcome.do.

A visit to the western provinces reveals an obvious improvement in infrastructure, thanks to a major investment program, and in living conditions as well, despite the persistence of pockets of severe poverty. Investors in Greater China have also begun to reach the interior of the country, including remote areas in the far reaches of Chinese territory, as evidenced by the food processing plants recently seen in Shihezi (located a few hundred miles from Kazakhstan)—the fruit of Taiwanese investments. A growing number of Chinese and foreign investors should be drawn by the increasing openness to Central Asia and the creation of free trade zones such as the one that was established in a two hundred-hectare section straddling the prefectures of Ili Kazakh, in Xinjiang, and Almaty, in Kazakhstan. The link that could eventually develop between the great urban centers of the east coast and Central Asia is promising, for energy as well as movement of goods, but this will require lasting stability and a real effort toward development on the part of the former Soviet republics, rich in natural resources but run by autocratic regimes that neglect national development in favor of clan interests.

## Distribution of FDI in China 2006–2008 (percentage of total)
### Top 5 and bottom 5

| | |
|---|---|
| Jiangsu | 17.1 |
| Guangdong | 13.5 |
| Shandong | 7.8 |
| Zhejiang | 7.8 |
| Liaoning | 7.1 |
| | |
| Ningxia | 0.0 |
| Gansu | 0.1 |
| Guizhou | 0.1 |
| Xinjiang | 0.1 |
| Qinghai | 0.2 |

Source: "Three Essays on FDI in China," University of Nebraska, January 21, 2011.

The relatively minor degree to which Chinese growth depends on FDI and the massive volume of investments from the Chinese diaspora ensures China some stability in this regard. The United States does not have the critical mass necessary to wield the weapon of FDI against China in the event of serious tensions. Further, the profits earned by American companies in China make the American economy just as dependent on Beijing's goodwill, if not more so. The powerful American industrial lobby is equipped to pressure politicians, particularly in Congress, in order to chill the administration's occasional hostile tendencies on economic issues. In their book *The Coming Conflict with China*, which was widely commented on and highly controversial at the time, Bernstein and Munro insisted that this very industrial lobby was largely responsible for the weaknesses they attributed to the Clinton administration vis-à-vis Beijing on human rights issues.

## Development assistance

From its founding until the late 1970s, China pursued a development assistance policy loaded down with ideological baggage. After the Bandung Conference in 1956, this policy was driven by a desire for solidarity with *third world countries,* as Mao Zedong saw it. Then, after 1960, its driving force was China's rivalry with the Soviet Union for the leadership of the socialist world. For two decades, aid was granted according to the political regimes in power and their relations with the West and Moscow. And so aid to Ghana was suspended until the fall of Nkrumah in 1966, and aid to Indonesia was suspended in 1965 after the military coup.

The Cultural Revolution led to a break with several African countries concerned about its possible influence on African youth and African students in China. Indeed, between 1956 and 1976,[40] Africa received over half of Chinese development assistance. In 1978, Beijing reoriented its development assistance policy in a more pragmatic direction, while still keeping up all of its assistance to its traditional partners. However, a very clear shift took place in the late 1990s, with a greater focus on development assistance driven by China's growing energy concerns. While Africa is still generally a high priority, greater attention is paid to those countries possessing considerable hydrocarbon resources, such as Sudan, Angola, or Nigeria. In recent years, China has dedicated major assistance efforts to certain countries whose strategic importance is no mystery. This Chinese aid is gladly welcomed by developing countries, for several reasons:

- Unlike the growing trend in Europe and the United States,[41] China places no political conditions on its aid, in keeping with its historical position since the Bandung Conference of noninterference in the internal affairs of other countries.
- Infrastructures built by China are considered by international experts to be inexpensive, high-quality, and quick to build.[42] This contrasts with those built with Western aid, which are costly, often inadequate, and usually very slow to build. In 2008, tied aid (where projects must be built by companies from the donor country) from OECD member states had dropped to 18 percent from its 1999 level of 46 percent. This practice, which used to be the norm, usually raises the price of products and services charged to recipient countries by over 20 percent. The lower cost of infrastructure built with Chinese aid than that built with the assistance of Western companies reduces the financial burden on the recipient country.

---

[40]François Joyaux, *La tentation impériale* (Paris: Imprimerie Nationale, 1994), 323.
[41] The conditions supposedly placed on Western development assistance to certain countries are apparently only cosmetic, as shown by the cooperation of certain European countries with states such as Gabon or the Central African Republic.
[42]Esther Pan, "China, Africa, and Oil," Council on Foreign Relations, Washington, DC, January 18, 2006.

- After a peak in 2010, development assistance from the developed countries as a proportion of their GNP has seen a notable decline, largely due to the world financial crisis. Despite appeals from Jacques Chirac during his presidency and from the secretary general of the United Nations, addressed particularly to American leaders, only 0.2 percent of the GNP of the United States went to development assistance in 2011 ($30.7 billion), equivalent to 3.6 percent of their military expenditures (around $838 billion in 2011).[43] Under these circumstances, China's marked interest in developing countries is appreciated by most of these countries' governments, even if it is partially motivated by strategic interests, as Western aid has always been.

In Asia, Chinese aid has been funneled to countries with which Beijing has traditionally enjoyed good relations, such as Myanmar, Pakistan, and Cambodia. In 2009, a third of Chinese development aid went to Asia. In December 2001, several cooperation agreements were signed with Myanmar during Hu Jintao's official visit to Rangoon. This country was strategically very important to China because of the planned construction of a gas and oil pipeline linking Ruili, in the province of Yunnan, to the port of Kyaukpyu, which would allow China direct access to the Indian Ocean for its supply of oil and gas from the Persian Gulf, bypassing the Strait of Malacca, which the Chinese like to call the "Malacca Barrier." In May 2011, during new Burmese President Thein Sein's visit to China, the two countries announced the decision to establish a *comprehensive strategic partnership*.[44] Construction work on the 750-mile oil pipeline began in May 2012. Pakistan, for its part, received $150 million in aid in 2004 for the construction of the second phase of its nuclear facility at Chashma, in Punjab. But the construction of the Gwadar deep-water port became the particular focus of Chinese aid, given its strategic importance.

In Africa, every official visit by a Chinese leader usually leads to the signing of economic and technical aid agreements with China, whether in the form of grants, loans at concessional rates for infrastructure projects, or loans at commercial rates. The Chinese development assistance strategy does not focus only on energy projects, however, as evidenced by the aid regularly received by countries such as the Central African Republic and Eritrea. The clearest example of this is the construction of the new African Union headquarters at Addis Ababa with Chinese cooperation to the tune of $200 million,[45] inaugurated in January 2012 for the 18th African Union Summit. This gesture by Beijing was particularly well received in Africa. Ethiopian Prime Minister Meles Zenawi described the building as the symbol of "the rebirth of Africa."

---

[43] "FY 2011 U.S. Federal Budget." The site http://www.usgovernmentspending.com sets US defense spending at $964.8 billion for 2011.

[44] "中缅宣布建立全面战略合作伙伴关系" ["China and Myanmar announce the beginning of comprehensive strategic cooperation"], *Huanqiu shibao*, May 27, 2011.

[45] "The Chinese-African Union, Why is China spending $200 million for this new over-the-top headquarters for the African Union?" *Foreign Policy*, March 19, 2012.

And yet it is in Latin America, which still represents only 13 percent of Chinese development assistance, that China's entry has been most spectacular, particularly in light of its disinterest in the continent during the 1950s, when it was considered the exclusive domain of the United States and the Soviet Union. China has committed to major development assistance projects in the region. In November 2004, Hu Jintao visited Argentina, Brazil, Chile, and Cuba, signing 39 agreements along the way, and the Chinese president announced investments worth $100 billion over the next 10 years, particularly in social projects. This strategy rivals the Monroe Doctrine and is raising eyebrows in the United States, but between the rise to power of socialist or anti-American parties in Latin America and the policies of Venezuelan President Hugo Chavez, who sought to build an anti-American bloc in the continent, Washington finds itself in less of a position to object. The energy and mining resources of Latin American countries are a powerful incentive for Beijing to pursue this policy based particularly on development assistance.

Overall, China's strategy has met with undeniable success, and as its economic growth continues, its interest in the developing countries grows stronger, and those countries may expect to see greater aid from Beijing than from Western countries in the medium and long term. Moreover, Beijing still has room to use this leverage thanks to its cash reserves, which allow it to adjust the level of aid to diplomatic priorities without overburdening its own financial balance. However, it must now reconcile this new plan, with its emphasis on the social sector, with its own domestic social issues, for the sake of its stability and its diplomatic goals, which are closely linked to its growing energy needs. Chinese public opinion, which increasingly finds its voice via Internet, regularly expresses opposition to development assistance given the economic and social problems that exist within China,[46] which is still a developing country, as its leadership frequently reminds its partners.

---

[46] "Providing foreign aid a way to survive," *Global Times*, July 21, 2012.

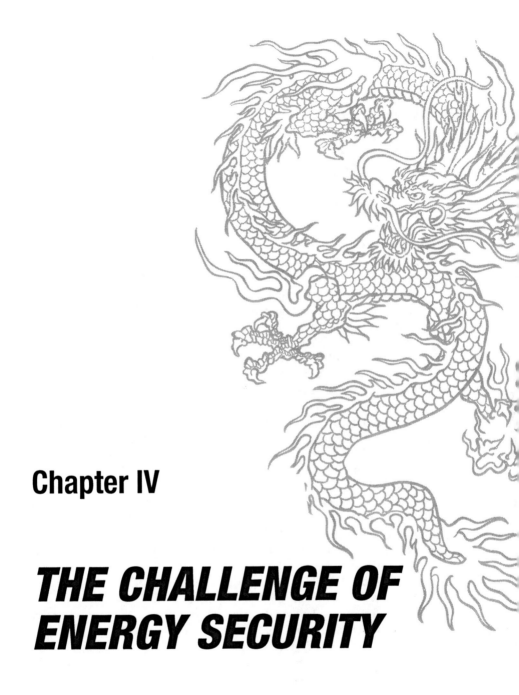

# Chapter IV

# *THE CHALLENGE OF ENERGY SECURITY*

T he hydrocarbon market is now a leading factor in the strategic choices of the international community's principal actors. The most powerful among them seek to secure their long-term futures, and the fortunate proprietors of existing reserves compete against one another for optimal profits. After jumping up sharply between 2005 and 2008, oil prices have remained high, which experts have attributed to various factors (the decrease in the dollar, the announced decline of oil reserves, speculation), including increased consumption by emerging countries. The price per barrel reached a peak of $147 in July 2008, versus $38 in 2004. This jump in prices allowed oil-producing countries to make significant profits, and increased the costs to the main oil-importing countries. Western experts agree that the rapid economic growth of China and India poses a serious threat in the medium term to the distribution of worldwide oil reserves. In 2011, oil consumption declined within the OECD(–1.2 percent), but it continued to rise in countries outside the OECD (+2.8 percent), with China remaining the motor driving this rise (+5.5 percent, or 505,000 barrels per day), although the increase in its consumption was weaker than during the previous decade. Tensions in the Middle East, in particular surrounding the issue of Iran, helped keep prices elevated during 2011–2012, and experts agreed that prices would remain steady, between $100 and $110, in the following year.

China is one of the main victims of this situation, due to an explosion in its energy consumption over the past few years. In the middle of the first decade of this century, China experienced an upsurge in oil consumption (in 2004, it imported twice as much as in 2003). Unable to meet the needs of its industrial and agricultural sectors, China saw its dependence on imports rise continuously, from 29.3 percent in 2000 to 52.8 percent in 2009, and to over 60 percent in 2012 (US dependence on imported oil in 2012 was 40 percent).[1] In fact, between 2000 and 2010, oil consumption doubled, after already having exploded by 97 percent between 1995 and 2004 (versus 62 percent in India), while in Japan and Europe, a movement toward reducing consumption was beginning to take shape thanks to proactive energy-saving policies. According to some projections, in 2030 China will have to import 88 percent of its oil requirements,[2] which will naturally have a significant impact on its foreign policy and strategic choices. Between now and 2030, worldwide oil demand should reach 116 million barrels per day, versus 32 million in 2005, with 42 percent of this increase coming from Chinese and Indian consumption.

In addition to economic development—particularly in industry—the rapid rise in living standards for a significant portion of the population and the gradual formation of a true middle class in urban areas also contribute significantly

---

[1] "Chinese Crude Imports Rise 6.8 Percent in 2012," Xinhua, January 13, 2013; "Where the U.S. Imports Its Oil from, in One Map," *Washington Post*, January 19, 2013.
[2] Ryoichi Komiyama, "Asia Energy Outlook to 2030: Impacts of Energy Outlook in China and India on the World," The Institute of Energy Economics, Japan (IEEJ). World Energy Council, http://www.worldenergy.org/documents/p001038.doc.

to increases in consumption. In 2012, the Chinese authorities declared that there were 114 million automobiles on Chinese roads[3]—an increase of 7.66 percent over the year before—versus 5.54 million in 1990. In 2030, this figure should reach 200 million. In 2009, China overtook the United States to become the largest market for new automobile sales.

It was in 1993 that everything changed for China and it became a net importer of oil. The rate at which its energy consumption grew exceeded all predictions by the experts. They had thought that China would become second worldwide in terms of oil consumption in 2020, but by 2003 it had already arrived at that position, moving ahead of Japan and coming in behind the United States—though still very far behind the United States, since China's consumption represents only 50 percent of that in the US (9.66 million barrels per day versus 18.56 million in 2012). But the rate of Chinese economic growth regularly defies all analyses. While the US Department of Energy announced in 2004 that Chinese oil consumption would reach 10.6 percent of worldwide consumption by 2025,[4] but that figure has already been reached and surpassed in [sic] 2011 (at 10.97 percent). With over 23 million barrels per day, in 20 years China and India alone will represent over 20 percent of worldwide energy demand.[5]

Faced with this extraordinary growth in its consumption, China cannot, however, count on its own resources. In 2011, its production of crude oil represented only 4.9 percent of the worldwide total, and does not seem likely to increase significantly in the two decades to come, despite undeniable efforts to develop the exploration and exploitation of its reserves. China's pursuit of economic development at the same rate as during the last three decades is now more than ever conditioned by the stability of its energy supplies. Given these circumstances, Beijing has been forced since the end of the 1990s to take into account certain parameters, both internal and external, in order to redefine its energy policy and re-situate it within the larger context of the strategic movements of other major consumers, in particular, the United States, Japan, and India. This policy is now based on two axes: first, an emphatic effort to develop its own resources and create strategic reserves and, second, to secure and diversify its supplies in the wake of the invasion of Afghanistan and then Iraq by American forces. Whereas relations between China and India in the energy domain today seem to be following a path of cooperation, one that will likely avoid the tensions associated with growing rivalries, China's relations with Japan and the United States are tending toward increasingly strong disagreements that could occasionally lead to veritable political crises.

The Unocal affair, which was the talk of the energy world throughout the first half of 2005, revealed the depth of the antagonisms that increasingly

[3]"China's Motor Vehicles Top 233 Million," Xinhua, July 17, 2012.
[4]United States Department of Energy, *Annual Energy Outlook, USA,* (Washington, DC, 2012).
[5]IEA, "World Energy Outlook: Fact Sheet Oil," 2007.

characterize China's relations with the rest of the international community, and with the United States in particular. By using political pressure to force the Chinese oil company CNOOC to withdraw its offer to buy Unocal, the 9th largest American energy group—though its offer was clearly superior to that of its competitor, ChevronTexaco—American authorities chose to drive a stake into the heart of liberal doctrine. By opposing this acquisition, the Bush administration recognized that the opening up of markets in all sectors to American capital, something constantly demanded of America's partners, would not be reciprocated. For the rest of the international community, this dramatic admission of hypocrisy by the champions of economic liberalism highlighted the economic threat that Washington's unilateralist policy represents. Moreover, this American muscle-flexing to protect a company depicted as strategic reinforced the Chinese leaders' conviction that the long-term struggle for energy survival among the major consumer countries had begun, and that it would be merciless.

## *China's own resources*

China has vast energy potential, but achieving it will require huge investments, primarily to access these resources, which are often located in regions far from the main centers of consumption, but also to modernize their exploitation. China has recently emphasized the development of nuclear and renewable energies in an effort to overcome its energy weaknesses and reduce its dependence on oil imports in the long term. Chinese citizens have also been asked to make an effort to save energy, especially to curb electricity consumption, in order to respond to the significant shortages in major urban centers, notably Beijing.

- Coal: With 3.52 billion tons, China was in 2011 the world's largest producer of coal, accounting for 49.5 percent of global production. It is also the world's largest consumer of coal (47 percent of the total), but the extent of its production allows it to rank among the principal global exporters of coal (9.28 million tons in 2012) and at the same time guarantee 95 percent of its own consumption. The majority of coal mines—there are a total of 12,000, 80 percent of them "small"—that supplies 70 percent of total energy consumption and 80 percent of national electricity production,[6] lie in regions far from the major urban areas and are for the most part situated in the northeastern provinces. Exploiting them requires considerable investments to mechanize and modernize extraction and transportation. Today, the recourse to coal as the principal source of energy poses serious safety and environmental problems for China. In 2011, mine accidents resulting from dilapidated facilities and insufficient regard for safety rules killed 1,973

---

[6] In 2011, China became first worldwide in electricity production, ahead of the United States.

miners, a slight improvement over previous years. In spite of the central government's efforts to make those in charge sensitive to these issues,[7] the management of mines by local public or private actors remains rudimentary and inadequately controlled. In recent years, within the framework of sector reform, the central government has closed dozens of mines considered insufficiently profitable or too dangerous, and has striven to improve the management of the most important ones so as to make their exploitation profitable and render the sector more attractive to foreign investors. In 2012, the authorities declared the temporary closing of thousands of small mines in order organize an inspection of safety conditions, and proclaimed its desire to definitively close 625 that year. But the success of this policy will require a sustained effort to enable China to attain a number of accidents equivalent to those of countries like Australia or the United States.

China's proven coal reserves amount to approximately 125 billion tons, or 12.6 percent of global reserves, and its potential reserves are estimated at 4 trillion tons, placing China third globally (at 13 percent), behind the United States (22.6 percent) and Russia (14.4 percent), allowing it to contemplate the future of this domain with serenity. But the negative impact that the mass utilization of coal has on the environment and on human health requires the Chinese government to take more determined action to eventually guarantee greater diversity in energy production.

• Oil: The situation is far more worrisome in the case of oil, which China depends on for 38.5 percent of its energy consumption. With nearly 2 billion tons at the end of 2011, or 0.9 percent of global reserves, China's proven reserves fall below those of the United States (3.7 billion) and Russia (12.1 billion).[8] China, which since 2003 has been second globally, after the United States, in terms of oil consumption, with 9,758,000 barrels per day consumed in 2011, is today only fifth worldwide in terms of oil production (4,090,000 barrels per day in 2011, or 5.1 percent of global production). Its consumption continues to rise, and could reach a total of 12 million barrels per day by 2020, whereas production might go up to only 4 million barrels. This extraordinary growth in demand led the Chinese authorities to reorganize the hydrocarbon sector, beginning in 1998, giving high priority to energy research and to the implementation of an active policy of supply-source diversification.

China's oil resources are distributed very unequally across its territory. The bulk of its reserves lie in the west, in the Xinjiang Uyghur Autonomous Region; in the northeast, historically an oil-producing region; and in the China Seas. However, for now the onshore fields represent 90 percent of

[7] In 2004, authorities published 11 texts dealing with safety problems in coal mines.
[8] The figures given here are from BP, *Statistical Review of World Energy*, June 2012.

China's proven reserves, and the Daqing field, in Heilongjiang Province, in the northeast, alone accounted for one-fifth of national production, or 40 million tons, in 2012. This oilfield, which has been exploited since 1955, is young, and its production should continue to increase in the years to come thanks to some recently discovered small fields and to improvements in mining technologies.

The Xinjiang region, situated at the border with Central Asia, is poised to become the second national center of oil production in the coming years. Its reserves, which are concentrated in the Tarim Basin, have been estimated at 34 percent of China's total reserves. Today, there is no concrete proof to support this estimate, and the data have been revised downwards, though without certainty. But even if the Tarim Basin isn't the El Dorado China has dreamed of, the region remains its principal hope for noticeably reducing its dependence on hydrocarbon imports.

The Chinese government places great hope in offshore mining, and this sector has been opened wide to foreign investments. The two main zones of exploration and production are the Bo Hai Gulf, east of Tianjin, and the estuary of the Pearl River on the South China Sea, whose reserves could amount to 2 billion barrels. Most major Western oil companies have participated in this offshore exploration, and are already contributing to production, some of them for over a decade now. Beijing would like to expand its explorative operations even further, but these ambitions run up against those of its neighbors in maritime zones where territorial disputes still exist. This is particularly the case in the South China Sea, in the Xisha Archipelago (Paracel Islands), the Nansha Archipelago (Spratly Islands), and in certain islands in the Sea of Japan. The improvement in relations between China and Vietnam until recently made it possible for the two countries to sign a demarcation agreement on December 25, 2000, regarding the territorial waters of the Gulf of Tonkin, thus bringing an end to decades of conflict and armed incidents. The agreement opened the way for China to explore this zone, and allowed it to solicit bids on 10 blocks in 2004. However, the rise in incidents between Vietnamese and Chinese ships in the region has led to heightened tensions over oil and gas exploration, and risks considerably hindering efforts to develop and exploit energy resources.[9]

Important efforts are currently underway to explore the most promising regions. In 2004, significant discoveries were made in the East China Sea (280 million tons around the Shengli field). Chinese oil groups are pursuing an active exploration policy in partnership with the major Western companies, but today it remains unlikely that China will be able to significantly reduce its energy dependence in the years to come by exploiting its own resources in this sector.

---

[9] "Dispute Flares Over Energy in South China Sea," *New York Times*, December 4, 2012.

- Gas: At the end of 2011, China's proven gas reserves amounted to 187 trillion cubic feet (5.3 trillion cubic meters), or 1.5 percent of global reserves, with most of these reserves lying in the west, north, and center of the country. The Tarim Basin, in Xinjiang Province, alone accounts for approximately 25 percent of onshore reserves, over an area of 204,634 square miles. The Chinese authorities intend to make this region the country's primary center of gas production, and they give it high priority when making investments to develop production. The two other major production centers are situated in Sichuan (20 percent of the country's proven reserves) and in Inner Mongolia, in the Ordos Basin. The offshore reserves represent about 20 percent of total proven reserves, and are mostly located in the Bo Hai Gulf, East China Sea, and in the north of the South China Sea.

Despite these relatively abundant resources, gas represents only a negligible part of national energy production, and about 4 percent of energy consumption. It is generally consumed in the producing regions themselves. Gas production has expanded considerably in the past 10 years, going from 953.5 billion cubic feet (27 billion cubic meters) in 2000 to 3,418.5 billion cubic feet (96.8 billion cubic meters) in 2010.

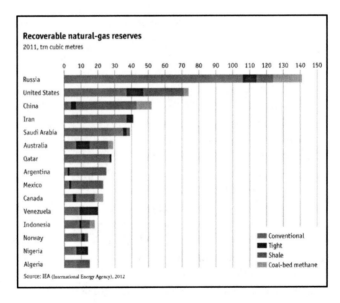

**Recoverable natural-gas reserves**
2011, trn cubic metres

Source: IEA (International Energy Agency), 2012

- The Chinese authorities nevertheless wish to pursue an increase in production and to accelerate the development of infrastructure to transport the gas toward the main centers of consumption in the east of the country. At the end of 2010, there were 24,855 miles of gas pipelines for internal transport, and others are under construction—in particular, one that will reach the Indian Ocean by way of Myanmar. In 2012 China imported 29 percent of its natural gas, 1.5 trillion cubic feet (0.04 trillion cubic meters), which suggests that the country will have an ever stronger presence in international markets, and encourages Beijing to augment its cooperation with bordering countries possessing significant reserves (Russia has the largest reserves worldwide, and Iran is second).

• Nuclear power: With 1.1 percent of total production, the nuclear sector currently represents only a very nominal portion of Chinese energy production, but the government has decided to implement a policy to rapidly develop nuclear energy production by calling for massive foreign investments. China already possesses 16 functional nuclear reactors, all of which are located in the coastal provinces of Zhejiang, Shandong, and Guangdong, and 40 percent of the world's nuclear reactor construction projects are in China. The first reactor, whose construction was decided on in 1974, was not put into use until 1991. China's installed production capacity is 6,296 megawatts electric (MWe), and Beijing intends to quadruple production between now and 2020, bringing it to 36,000 MWe with 32 new reactors, thus guaranteeing the nuclear sector a 4 percent share of national energy production. The implementation of this high-priority program, which benefits from $48 billion in investments, has sparked strong competition among the main exporters of civil nuclear technology, particularly the United States and France. In July 2004, the government approved construction of two new reactors at the Ling Ao site, in Guangdong, the first two sections of which had been built with the participation of French companies. In September, it approved the construction of six new reactors at Yangjiang, in Guangdong, with a total investment of $8 billion; Yangjiang will eventually become the largest Chinese nuclear site. The importance of these contracts for Western companies has led the United States to authorize American companies to bid on them, even though Washington had outlawed the sale of nuclear equipment to China after the events of Tiananmen Square in 1989. The United States has given strong priority to these contracts, and the American Export-Import Bank, a public credit organization, took on a $5 billion credit commitment, the highest amount ever by this organization. In order to tip the scales in favor of the AP-1000 reactor proposed by Westinghouse and its partner, Bechtel Nuclear, the Bush administration did not hesitate to engage in some intense lobbying. During his 2004 visits to China, Vice President Dick Cheney supported the proposal—Bechtel having been one of the main financiers of George W. Bush's electoral campaigns. The prospect of seeing American companies excluded from these promising calls for bids led Washington to adopt a pragmatic attitude and to mute its usual calls for the respect of human rights.

- Hydroelectric Energy: China's hydroelectric resources are the largest in the world, but today they produce only 15 percent of the country's electricity—694 billion kilowatt hours (kwh) in 2011. According to some sources, hydroelectric potential could rise to 300,000 MWe, thanks to China's important network of approximately 1,500 rivers, which are nonetheless very concentrated in the southeast and east of the country. By 2020, total installed production capacity could reach 420 gigawatts (GW). Beijing has decided to increase hydroelectric production very significantly in the years to come, and its Eleventh Five-Year Plan provides for a 160 GW increase in installed production capacity. It also gives priority to energy savings and to the rationalization of electricity use, particularly in businesses. Over the last few years, several regions in China have in fact experienced electricity shortages, in spite of the national resources. In 2004, 24 of the country's 31 provinces were affected by disruptions in electricity supplies. This shortage is explained in part by the development of sectors such as steel and automobiles, which are particularly heavy consumers of electricity, but also, for example, by an increase in coal prices and a drop in hydroelectric production in 2011.

A number of large-scale projects have been completed or are being planned, but most of them pose serious environmental problems, and over a dozen were suspended in January 2005. Local authorities had put these projects into operation before their environmental impact was assessed, as required by a law enacted in 2003.

- Renewable Energy: Under pressure from a rise in domestic demand and increasingly strong calls for environmental protection, the Chinese authorities have implemented a program to develop renewable energies, notably solar energy, wind electricity, and geothermal power. In 2011, Chinese authorities dedicated $51 billion to renewable energy—one-fifth of total global investments in this domain. The Twelfth Five-Year Plan (2011–2015) envisions a $473.1 billion investment in clean energy, with the objective of reaching 20 percent of total energy consumption in 2020. However, the massive losses recorded by companies in the solar energy sector in 2011 as a result of fierce price competition among manufacturers endanger this strategy. The four largest Chinese solar companies (Suntech, Trina, Yingli Green Energy Holding Co. Ltd., and Canadian Solar Inc.) lost a total of $1.7 billion in 2011. This situation explains the trade war between the United States and China over the manufacture of solar panels, which has led Washington to impose high taxes on the products of many Chinese companies accused of dumping.[10]

---

[10] "Trade Panel Approves Duties on China Solar Products," Reuters, November 8, 2012.

Within the framework of the "Development Plan for New Energy Sectors in China," the Chinese authorities are planning for the production of nonfossil energies to reach 15 percent of domestic consumption in 2020, versus 9 percent in 2009. However, this sector requires significant foreign investments, and several international financing organizations—including the World Bank, the Global Environment Facility, and the Asian Development Bank—have initiated projects in this domain. Nevertheless, this component of Chinese energy production will remain very marginal in comparison with hydrocarbon consumption.

## The reorganization of the hydrocarbon sector

Over the last decade, a fundamental reorganization of this sector has been undertaken in order to make it more efficient at the national level and more competitive internationally. In 1998, the Chinese government organized the entirety of the hydrocarbon sector around two vertically integrated strands, China Petrochemical Corporation (Sinopec) and China National Petroleum Corporation (CNPC). CNPC is focused more on crude oil production and Sinopec more on refining. Two other companies complete this system, China National Offshore Oil Corporation (CNOOC) and China National Star Petroleum, created in 1997. The entire sector is under the supervision of the State Energy Administration, created in 2003.

In order to make these state-run companies more competitive, the government decided to free them from certain activities that they had traditionally carried out in nonproductive areas not directly linked to their principal goal, such as managing hospitals or lodgings for personnel. Furthermore, very significant staff reductions were carried out, leading to thousands of employees being laid off. Then, in order to strengthen the financial capacities of these companies, from 2002 their capital was opened to foreign investments, to allow an injection of billions of dollars. However, the Chinese government kept a majority stake in each of the three major companies: Sinopec, CNPC, and CNOOC. These foreign investments have undoubtedly permitted the development of these companies' operations, but without being enough to contribute real solutions to Chinese energy problems.

China's refining capacity constitutes a key element of its economic development and of its energy independence policy. Until now it has been insufficient, but it is expected to reach 15 million barrels per day in 2015, versus 11.6 million barrels per day in 2012. Several refinery construction projects have thus been undertaken in the past few years, particularly in cooperation with Saudi Arabia. China's capacity to refine low-quality oil imported from the Middle East (Iraq, Iran, Saudi Arabia, or Kuwait) is quite insufficient, and considerable investments are required to create such capacity or to upgrade existing refineries. With the rapid exhaustion of low-sulfur oil reserves in Oman and

Yemen, two of China's important suppliers, it is imperative that China augment its capacity to refine Saudi Arabian crude; and Saudi leaders, who are eager to occupy a greater, and eventually dominant, place in the Chinese market have responded favorably to Chinese expectations in this domain. After several years of negotiations and feasibility studies, a three-way partnership including Saudi Aramco (Saudi Arabian Oil Company), Fujian Petrochemical Company Limited (FPCL) and ExxonMobil was finally signed on March 30, 2007, creating two joint enterprises in China, based in the province of Fujian, as well as a refinery and a chain of gas stations—the total cost of all these projects amounting to $5 billion. The first of these joint enterprises, the Fujian Refining & Petrochemical Company Limited (FREP), is responsible for treating mainly Saudi Arabian crude oil, and began operations in August 2009 at 240,000 barrels per day. The project also included the expansion of an existing refinery in Quanzhou whose capacity was 80,000 barrels per day.

This operation is especially important because it is the first project integrating refining, petrochemicals, and oil marketing that has been implemented in China with foreign participation. It falls within the framework of the commitment Saudi Arabia made in 2006 to supply the Chinese strategic reserve with 100 million barrels—10 days of the kingdom's oil production. This Saudi supply represents over a third of the strategic reserve that China finished putting into place in 2012, the rest of the supply coming probably from Kazakhstan and Russia.

Thus, in order to strengthen its energy security within a global context of saturated refining capacity, China must master its needs as best as possible, both at home and abroad.

## A planetary strategy

In 1957, China imported 60 percent of its oil consumption, before becoming itself an oil exporter thanks to its policy of energy resource development during the 1960s and 1970s. In 1985, its exports reached a peak of 6.21 million tons annually. But increased consumption due to the first effects of China's economic reforms and stagnation in production brought an end to this energy independence, and in 1993 China once again became a net importer of oil. Indeed, between 1993 and 2003, Chinese oil production increased at an annual rate of just 1.6 percent. Taking into account the foreseeable weak growth in Chinese national production between now and 2020, this dependence, which has not stopped growing, could reach between 3,215,000 and 4,620,000 barrels per day in 2020—more than Venezuela's current production. According to official sources, in 2012 China imported 271 million tons of crude oil, an increase of 6.8 percent over the previous year.[11]

---

[11]"China Crude Oil Imports Rose 6.8% in 2012," *Wall Street Journal*, January 13, 2013.

Determined to guarantee its energy security, China decided in 2001, within the framework of the Tenth Five-Year Plan, to create strategic oil reserves that would allow it to overcome potential difficulties with its oil supplies, including interruptions in the case of conflict. Beijing's initial objective was to bring these reserves up to 30 days of consumption and then, by 2020, to 90 days, about 630 million barrels. Thanks to its foreign exchange reserves (over $3.31 trillion), China could, without too much effort, withdraw the $20 billion needed (at February 2013 prices per barrel) to constitute a stock of 210 million barrels, equivalent to 30 days of imports. Chinese oil companies maintain stocks covering between 10 and 30 days, but on a fluctuating basis, so the government decided to quickly develop permanent reserves, like those in the United States and Japan. The volatility of the situation in the Middle East, on which China still depends for over 50 percent of its supplies, has prompted Chinese leaders to henceforth pay particular attention to energy security. In the first phase (2004–2008), the construction of four reservoirs intended to stock reserves of 100 million barrels was completed. The second phase, which aims for a capacity of over 200 million barrels, is underway and should be completed in 2013. In order to create these reserves, Beijing had to increase its imports by approximately 650,000 barrels per day, at a time when the OPEC countries seemed to be at their maximum production capacity, faced with a growing demand from

## Principal Suppliers
## of Oil to China and the United States
## (in barrels/day)

| China | | United States | |
|---|---|---|---|
| | **2011** | | **2011** |
| Saudi Arabia | 1,005,000 | Canada | 2,200,000 |
| Angola | 623,000 | Mexico | 1,216,000 |
| Iran | 555,000 | Saudi Arabia | 1,099,000 |
| Russia | 395,000 | Nigeria | 968,000 |
| Oman | 363,000 | Venezuela | 951,000 |
| Iraq | 276,000 | Iraq | 470,000 |

*Source*: United States Energy Information Administration Web site (Washington, DC, 2013).

China and from emerging countries. Confronted with market realities, China's needs have justified its attempts to seduce certain partners, such as Venezuela, into diverting exports toward China and away from other clients—in particular, from the United States, which generally absorbs 40 percent of Venezuelan exports[12] (this represents only 8 percent of total American crude oil imports).

---

[12] "Venezuela Oil Exports to United States Fall to Record Low," *Herald Tribune*, March 4, 2013.

Since the beginning of the 1990s, China has also undertaken a policy to expand its companies abroad by accelerating partnership contracts with foreign states and companies, and by pursuing acquisitions of foreign companies. The most important of these operations was CNOOC's attempt, in 2005, to acquire the American energy giant UNOCAL for an estimated $13 billion, but the Chinese company permanently withdrew its offer under political pressure from the US government.

In order to reduce its dependence on hydrocarbons from the Middle East, which in 2012 represented 51 percent of its imports and could go up to 70 percent in 2015, China is working to diversify its supply sources, first by trying to access resources located in its immediate proximity (Central Asia and Russia, in particular), which would be easier to transport and less subject to the vagaries of international politics, and second by seeking out for the first time new suppliers in regions that China has neglected until now (Africa and South America, in particular).

In its immediate vicinity, China has bet on the region's two main holders of hydrocarbon reserves, Kazakhstan (1.8 percent of global oil reserves and 0.9 percent of natural gas reserves) and Russia (5.3 percent and 21.4 percent, respectively). Chinese companies have thus taken a position in the Kazakh market, and have signed a number of contracts for exploration and participation in production. Until now, imports of liquefied natural gas from Kazakhstan have remained relatively low compared to China's needs, but once the infrastructure is built and put into operation, the country should, by 2030, rank among China's top suppliers.

In 1997, CNPC signed a contract with Kazakhstan for the three-phase construction of a 1,739-mile oil pipeline from Atyrau, near the Caspian Sea, to Xinjiang, and for a project to develop reserves with a Chinese investment of $6 billion. At the same time, CNPC took control of Aktobemunaigaz, outbidding the American companies Texaco and Amoco and the Russian company Yujnimost. Also in Kazakhstan, Sinopec paid $615 million to British Gas (BG Group) to be able to participate in a gas and oil field. A 621-mile oil pipeline inaugurated in December 2005 will transport 10 million tons of oil to China per year (200,000 barrels per day) from the Kumkol field, in the center of Kazakhstan, and then, in a second phase, from the Caspian Sea. This oil pipeline was financed equally by Kazakhstan and China. The Kumkol field is operated by the company PetroKazakhstan, which was purchased in 2005 by the Chinese group CNPC.

The situation with Russia is more complicated for a number of reasons, but especially because of the American and Japanese desire for Russian oil. For China, Russia is now a strategic partner of the utmost importance, whose oil and gas resources could contribute to considerably reducing the energy constraints that hinder China's economic development. Nevertheless, this partnership requires constant effort to establish an atmosphere of trust after decades of conflict and suspicion, which only began to abate with the dissolution of the Soviet Union. Russia, for its part, is managing its long-term interests and developing its oil and gas infrastructure so as to respond to the needs of American, Japanese, and Chinese markets without privileging one over the others. This delicate balancing act became particularly clear in 2004, with Russia's decision to retain the Japanese project for an oil pipeline connecting Angarsk to the Pacific Ocean, the construction of which began in 2006. For two years, China and Japan had been in a fierce competition over this project, with Beijing hoping for the construction of a 1,491-mile-long Taishet–Daqing pipeline and Tokyo supporting a 2,566-mile-long Taishet–Nakhodka pipeline. The latter would in fact make it possible to ship Russian oil to the shores of the Pacific without passing through Chinese territory, and to serve the Japanese, Korean, American, and even Southeast Asian markets, but also to supply the regions of Russia's interior along the way. Both China and Japan proposed financing the construction of the Russian part of this oil pipeline; then Tokyo also proposed investing in exploration in eastern Siberia and putting $8 billion into the gas and oil projects Sakhalin I and II. Russia ultimately decided in favor of Japan, and on December 31, 2004, made public its decision to build the pipeline connecting Taishet, near Krasnoyarsk, to Nakhodka via Skovorodino along the Amur River. It will transport up to 80,000 tons per year, whereas the Chinese project would have transported 20,000 tons to Daqing in an initial phase, and then 30,000 tons by 2010; the Chinese were so disappointed that Moscow judged it necessary to offer Beijing compensation. The Yukos affair offered the opportunity.[13] By injecting $6 billion of the $9.35 billion total cost of acquisition, Chinese banks surreptitiously financed the oft-criticized purchase of a 76.79 percent share in the crude oil subsidiary Yuganskneftegaz at a December 19, 2004, auction, through a shell company, Baïkalfinansgroup, which was itself bought on December 23, 2004, by the last major Russian oil company, Rosneft. In return, Rosneft committed to delivering 48.2 million tons of oil to China by 2010. In addition, on October 14, 2004, Presidents Putin and Hu Jintao had signed an agreement to the effect that Russia would deliver a minimum of 10 million tons of crude in 2005 and 15 million in 2010 via the Russian rail transportation company RZD. However, these commitments, which to this day have not been carried out, could never compensate for the oil pipeline project and the hopes for supplies from Russia, even though Moscow did in the end decide to build a section of the Taishet–Nakhodka line through China. This section was completed in September 2010, and connects Skovorodino, in Siberia, to the Chinese oil field in Daqing over a distance of 656 miles. It has been in operation since January 1, 2011.

[13] The Russian oil group Yukos, led by Mikhail Khodorkovsky, an industry baron close to the United States, was put into liquidation by the courts in 2004 due to its debts, which were more than $27 billion, over the protests of shareholders, who saw this as a veritable expropriation. With this operation, which undoubtedly benefited the national group Rosneft, the Russian state regained control over most of the Russian oil and gas sector.

The issue of this oil pipeline has confirmed the complexity of the geopolitics of oil. By retaining the Japanese project, Moscow gave priority to developing its gas and oil infrastructure, the most important precondition for economic recovery in the 10 years to come, and it accepted the better offer. This decision will undoubtedly have consequences for Beijing's attitude toward Russia in the coming years, and Moscow has in all likelihood lost a few points with the Chinese in terms of trust. The convergence of China and Russia's strategic interests should have led the latter to favor China's offer. But in spite of the very rapid political rapprochement that has taken place between the two capitals in the past few years, Moscow has remained very cautious and, despite the obvious importance of the Chinese market over the long term, did not want to risk depending entirely on China for such a large part of its exports. The American market is very attractive to Russia, as the construction of a new oil pipeline from western Siberia to the port of Murmansk testifies. This pipeline will allow Russia to increase its exports to the United States by 80,000 tons per year, although only one port is now available for transporting Russian crude to the United States, Vysotsk, which has a capacity of 12,000 tons per year. By choosing Nakhodka as the terminus of the pipeline, Russia was able to diversify its export markets, and this consideration took precedence over political considerations. The decision, however, most certainly strengthened the Chinese leaders' perception of their country's energy fragility, and of the absolute necessity of diversifying its energy sources as much as possible. This sentiment had already convinced Chinese leadership to pay more attention to other oil-producing regions, in particular those that had always been neglected.

Beijing's leaders have also been particularly active in Africa since 2003, increasing official visits and signing more contracts both in the energy and raw materials sectors, as well as in the domain of development aid. In December 2004 and April 2005, agreements were signed with Nigeria,[14] the world's sixth largest exporter of oil; and in March 2005 with Angola, 30 percent of whose oil production is purchased by China, just behind the United States. Since the fall of Colonel Gadhafi's regime in 2011, relations with Libya, where CNPC had already been present for several years, have become tense, but under the pressure of market realities, exports to China have quickly started up again, and China plans to import about 1 million tons per year beginning in 2013.[15]

Finally, China's policy in Latin America is exactly the same, and China is using the gradual worsening of relations between certain South American governments and Washington to make inroads into a territory considered to be the private turf of the United States. The first target of this plan was naturally Venezuela, whose President Hugo Chavez had terrible relations with the US government, which holds the world's sixth largest oil reserves, and which is

---

[14]In 2004, Chinese businesses invested $1 billion in the Nigerian economy.
[15]"土新年外交谋求能源进口多元化" ["Turkish Diplomacy Will Turn Toward Diversifying Energy Imports for the Year to Come"], 人民网 [People's Net], January 14, 2013.

eighth in terms of production and fifth in terms of exports. Caracas is thus an ideal partner within the framework of China's source-diversification policy, and important advances have been made in Beijing's favor. During a particularly noted visit by Hugo Chavez to China in December 2004, the two countries signed 27 cooperation agreements regarding gas and oil, opening wide the prospecting and refining sectors to China; and the Venezuelan president even announced the development of an oil pipeline across the Panama Canal, which would allow Caracas to deliver more oil to China and to reduce its exports to the United States. At the time, Venezuela even planned to bring its production up from 2.9 million barrels per day to 5 million barrels in order to meet the needs of the Chinese market. This goal was not realized because in 2012 Venezuelan crude production stagnated at 3 million barrels per day. President Chavez implemented an accelerated rapprochement with Iran, as Venezuela was already Iran's closest ally within OPEC, and the two countries had chosen to prioritize the development of closer ties with China in the energy domain, in reaction to Washington's repeated attacks on the regimes of Tehran and Caracas. Hugo Chavez's threats and the rapid degradation of relations between Washington and Caracas were taken seriously, and in November 2004 Richard G. Lugar, a Republican Senator from Indiana and the chairman of the Senate Committee on Foreign Relations, requested a study of the consequences of a hypothetical interruption in oil supplies from Venezuela and of the alternative solutions for the United States in such an event.

Along with its actions toward Venezuela, China has extended its ambitions to Peru (signing a cooperation agreement on the prospecting and mining of oil and gas, and on the development of the refining and petrochemical industries, during Vice President Zeng Qinghong's January 2005 visit to Lima), Argentina (signing an agreement during Hu Jintao's official visit to Buenos Aires in November 2004), Brazil (with Sinopec signing a $1 billion agreement for the construction of a 856-mile gas pipeline across the country, completed in January 2012), Ecuador (with China having purchased over half of Ecuador's production in 2011, and Quito committed to exporting 130 million barrels annually to China for the next six years), and to Bolivia (with Shengli International Petroleum Development announcing its intention to invest $1.5 billion in the gas sector). In 2012, the Sinochem Group bought the oil assets of the French group Total in Colombia for approximately $1 billion. Continuing this operation, China also acquired shares in the Cusiana field and oil pipelines. However, security conditions in Colombia, where three Chinese workers and their interpreter were kidnapped by FARC (Revolutionary Armed Forces of Colombia) following the refusal of the British subsidiary of Sinochem to pay the guerrillas a tithe of $10 per barrel, remain a disincentive for Chinese companies.[16] The hostages were not freed until November 2012.

---

[16]"FARC Kidnap Chinese Oil Workers," *Colombia Reports*, June 9, 2011.

Chinese ambitions now extend throughout South America, and have so far been well received because they are not accompanied by any political conditions: Beijing maintains a line of noninterference in the internal affairs of other states.

Finally, in the Middle East, which supplies about 60 percent of its imports, China has seized the opportunity arising from the uneasy relations between Washington and several Arabic capitals since the Iraq War to strengthen its own presence there. Saudi Arabia in particular has received special attention, given its reserves (16.1 percent of global oil reserves and 3.9 percent of natural gas reserves) and the dramatic chill in American-Saudi relations since September 11, 2001. In 2002, Saudi oil exports to the United States dropped by 6.7 percent and the kingdom became China's leading supplier, going from 49,000 barrels per day in 1999 to 1.05 million barrels in 2011. In 2012, it accounted for 20 percent of Chinese oil imports.

China was late in grasping the consequences its extraordinary growth in energy consumption would have for its security, as well as the threat to its economic and military development represented by its increasing dependence on hydrocarbon imports. Beijing had for several years been engaging in a strategic review of its energy sources, but it was quite clearly the military intervention in Iraq that drastically accelerated this realization.

In its policy to diversify supply sources, China clashes head-on with Washington, which is also trying to reduce its own dependence—which is not as great as China's—on the Middle East. For example, the United States considers that it has "vital—in fact, rising—national interests in West and Central Africa, concentrated in, but not restricted to, Nigeria and Angola."[17] Indeed, the region's proven reserves have doubled over the last 10 years, and are now at over 60 billion barrels. Consequently, Washington has boosted its diplomatic activities and security commitments in these two regions of Africa. As for Chinese diplomacy, it has become more and more active on issues that directly affect its energy interests and has, for the first time since its entry into the Security Council, opposed its partners—without, however, taking the step of blocking a Council resolution with a negative vote. The case of Darfur is particularly illuminating. China has invested $3 billion in Sudan, the largest investment it has ever made outside its borders, and undoubtedly the most promising. In fact, according to experts, Sudan's oil production, which was 453,000 barrels per day in 2011, only represents 6.7 percent of the country's reserves (6.7 trillion barrels). Sudan is thus a very important asset to Beijing's long-term diversification policy, which justifies Chinese political commitment to the Khartoum regime.

For this dynamic strategy to secure its energy supplies, China is subject to harsh criticism from its main adversaries, in particular the United States, which condemns China's relations with countries classified as "rogue states," such as Iran, and its refusal to formally integrate into its foreign policy subjects such

---

[17] J. Stephen Morrison and David L. Goldwyn, *Promoting Transparency in the African Oil Sector* (Washington, DC, Center for Strategic & International Studies, 2004).

as good governance or human rights. The United States sees this attitude as hindering the efforts of international organizations to promote greater transparency within these regimes, as well as improvements in their political and economic systems. Among these countries, Iran and Sudan are particularly singled out. However, the international community's "normalization" of relations with the Libyan regime of Colonel Gadhafi, which led to the arrival en masse of Western companies in Tripoli (122 companies submitted requests for approval to participate in the Libyan regime's calls for bids, including BP, Royal Dutch Shell, Chevron, ConocoPhillips, and ExxonMobil) dramatically underscored the pragmatism of major hydrocarbon consumers such as the United States and the European Union. Until his fall, the Libyan leader did no more than renounce—at least temporarily—his plan to manufacture weapons of mass destruction, while the autocratic political regime in place in Libya since 1969 did not soften one bit. As the Libyan case and others demonstrate, this mind-set of Western governments toward the nature of political regimes only applies to countries where these governments are confronted with difficulties other than the simple question of human rights. Neither the Europeans nor the Americans have ever displayed a critical attitude toward political regimes like Gabon's, where the president has remained in power in a nondemocratic context for 41 years, or Angola's, where oil profits are confiscated by a political elite that represents only an infinitesimal part of the population. This practice of doublespeak and double standards is constant when it comes to human rights and good governance, and denunciations of certain regimes only mask other strategic considerations that are connected to American or European national interests, but completely disconnected from the real problems of the countries in question.

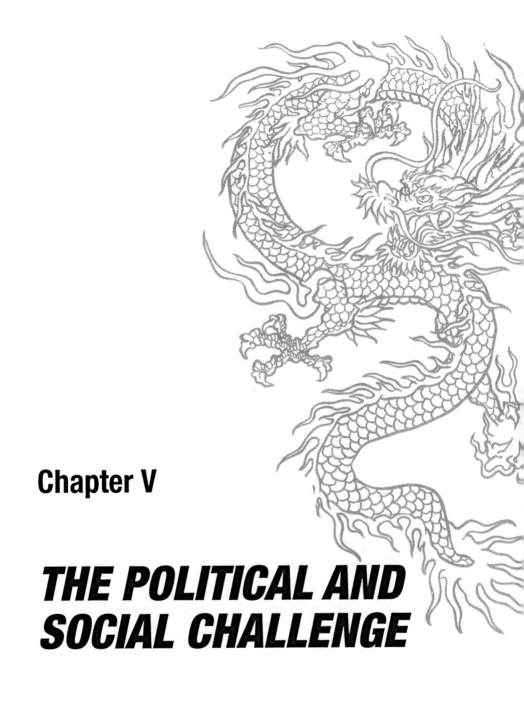

# Chapter V

# *THE POLITICAL AND SOCIAL CHALLENGE*

In December 1978, the Third Plenum of the Eleventh Congress of the Chinese Communist Party decided, at the instigation of Deng Xiaoping, who had been reinstated in July 1977, to set China on a new path of economic reforms, thus initiating a major change from the old order, that of the Maoist years and of the absolute primacy of politics. Since the middle of the 1950s, Chinese life had been shaped by slogans, political campaigns, purges, and conspiracies within the Party, and by a permanent uncertainty in a society where no one could feel safe from sudden changes of direction. The Cultural Revolution was the culminating point of these torments, and had profoundly destabilized and weakened China, calling into question the very foundations of the revolution. In the fall of 1976, when the Gang of Four was arrested after the death of Mao Zedong (in September), China was in shambles. In 1978, its GDP was $147 billion and it was 34th worldwide in terms of exports. At the time, agriculture employed 70 percent of the labor force and industry nearly 20 percent.

When the Party announced its reform program and its "Four Modernizations" in 1978, the reception was simultaneously enthusiastic and cautious. This new policy presupposed the participation of the entire Chinese population, including those the system had crushed: intellectuals and researchers, Party members who had opposed the Gang of Four's leftward drift, and students who had been sent en masse to the countryside years before. All had to draw a line under the past and take part in the rebirth of the Chinese nation by putting their skills to the service of the fatherland. This was what Deng Xiaoping and those close to him had in mind when they initiated a veritable new revolution that was intended to transform China so as to enable it make up for lost time and to defend the accomplishments of the revolution and of the first years of the People's Republic. But this policy also silently included another, fifth, modernization: the modernization of the political system. Deng Xiaoping, a revolutionary from the very beginning, did not intend to attack the dogma of the one-party state. On the contrary, he wanted to restore the legitimacy that the party had begun to lose through the excesses of the Cultural Revolution and to act pragmatically to accomplish the Party's goals. For him, the most important goal was to rebuild an economy worthy of the name by confining ideology to sectors where its task was to consolidate national unity, and where it could not interfere with economic development. To do this, it was necessary to distance the Party from the economic domain and to allow realism to take precedence over ideological dogmatism. His ally Hu Yaobang, director of the Party's school for cadres, was entrusted with this delicate mission of reforming ideology to suit it to the country's new requirements.

However, this ideological transition required officially calling into question the Cultural Revolution's past errors in order to isolate conservatives within the Party who would resist such changes. Attacks against the ultraleftist ideology of the supporters of the Cultural Revolution, and against the new "feudalism," multiplied in 1979 and in the early 1980s, but they remained under the control of Deng Xiaoping and his allies. It would have been impossible to combine a program of economic reforms, which would profoundly upset the old structures, with a program of immediate political reform, which would have endangered the stability of the country, and thus the progress of the reforms. But by deeply altering the existing system (dismantling collectives, decollectivizing land, opening special economic zones to attract foreign investments, etc.), these reforms called into question ever more profoundly the orthodox Marxist principles that had guided the Party's decisions in all areas since 1949. The Chinese leaders connected to Deng Xiaoping were, however, very aware of the economic failure of Marxist orthodoxy in the USSR and in other socialist countries—a failure that was soon to be confirmed by the political turnaround in the Soviet Union after Mikhail Gorbachev's arrival to power in 1985, and by the dissolution of the USSR in 1991. The challenge faced by Chinese leaders was considerable: to give the Chinese economic system the means to meet the needs of the population and to gradually bring China into the international economic order; to maintain the country's stability at all costs in order to guarantee domestic security and development; and to allow those regions considered to be the natural motors of the Chinese economic rise (i.e., the eastern coastal regions) to boost reforms and to create wealth, while maintaining national unity and domestic solidarity. In fact, the system of social protection was gradually dismantled, and larger and larger parts of the population found themselves marginalized in an increasingly liberal system. The concept of "Chinese-style socialism" promoted by Deng Xiaoping was certainly attractive to the Chinese, but its consequences weighed more and more heavily on the most disadvantaged segments of society.

At the end of the 1980s, it seemed obvious that Marxist-Leninist ideology had been profoundly adapted to the conditions specific to China, and that the economic-social system still remained to be invented in a country stricken with corruption, in which the peasantry was beginning to test the limits of reforms, and in which some intellectuals were demanding more political participation. In reality, the reforms had either gone too far or not far enough. In 1989, the model was paralyzed and pressure was mounting. With the events of June 1989 and the reestablishment of order that followed, China experienced a new rupture.

## *Tiananmen and the process of reforms*

During the first decade of reforms, two groups benefited from the new policies: peasants, thanks to the decollectivization of agriculture, and intellectuals, thanks to Hu Yaobang's rehabilitation of thousands of those who had been imprisoned or exiled during the Cultural Revolution and to the new freedom of expression authorized by the Party.

Peasants saw their standard of living rise significantly through the end of the 1980s, but especially between 1980 and 1985. As the darlings of the regime, they benefited from the full attention of the Party, which was determined to win back the trust of those who had previously been the very basis of the revolutionary movement's triumph. But at the end of this decade, peasants still had to deliver their harvests to the state at low prices, and the state, in return, was unable to supply them with basic commodities at reasonable prices.

Intellectuals had overall enthusiastically supported the reforms, having obtained growing freedom over the years despite very strict supervision. During this acquisition of greater freedom of expression, they tried to rely on the differences among the various clans that coexisted within the Party, to obtain the support of those leaders most open to political reform. As for the conservatives, they opposed any fundamental change in the system because they feared the impact on the Party's authority and a return to the chaos of the Cultural Revolution. Though they encouraged the importation of Western science and technology, they categorically refused to accept the West's political and cultural values. Deng Xiaoping himself prioritized administrative reform. His openness to the concerns of intellectuals was limited to whatever direct contributions they could make to his program of economic reforms, and nothing more. Moreover, in March 1979 he had set the limits to be imposed on this exercise: all debates had to respect four principles—support for socialism, for the principles of the democratic dictatorship of the people, for the Party and Marxism-Leninism, and for the thought of Mao Zedong. The leadership of the Party, a fundamental condition of stability during the phase of reforms, could not be called into question.

Deng Xiaoping was first and foremost concerned with avoiding disorder and protests against the Party's role, and thus against the political system that was born in 1949 with the founding of the People's Republic. Indeed, a mass movement could have weakened the political leadership and profoundly destabilized China at a crucial moment in its rise. There is no doubt that the hesitation and procrastination of intellectuals and students during the spring of 1989, as the conflict with the authorities was taking shape, largely caused the movement's ultimate failure. Another element that perhaps predetermined this failure was the very Confucian attitude of these intellectuals and students, who refused any alliance with peasants or workers—social categories they treated with scorn.[1] They even refused to allow anyone who did not belong to their movement and their class to enter Tiananmen Square. In spite of the Party's great vigilance precisely to prevent an alliance of intellectuals with peasants and workers, if the students had accepted this strategy it might have profoundly altered the response by the authorities, since the army would undoubtedly have

---

[1] Jean-Philippe Béja, *A la recherche d'une ombre chinoise* (Paris: Editions du Seuil, 2004), 152.

been even more reluctant to use violence against these different categories of the population. The historical mission of the army was, after all, to be an *army of the people.*

The repression of the student movement beginning on June 4, 1989, temporarily marked the victory of the conservative clan, and weakened both Deng Xiaoping and his political vision: yes to economic reforms, no to challenging the authority of the Party. Conservatives sought to prove that the political chaos and the risks the Party had just incurred were the direct consequence of liberal-leaning economic reforms. During the months following the events of Tiananmen Square, there was a certain wavering in public opinion regarding the Party. For the first time since the end of the Cultural Revolution, the legitimacy of the Chinese Communist Party had been compromised in the eyes of a significant portion of the population. The stability of the country had truly been in danger, but the People's Liberation Army had saved it, without enthusiasm, and saw its own reputation tarnished in return.

In the end, a campaign undertaken to convince the Chinese that the troublemakers had been manipulated from abroad, and that they represented a movement intent on harming China's interests at precisely the moment when it was emerging from its past difficulties, hit the bull's eye. The collapse of the European socialist bloc between October 1989 and December 1991 also strengthened the conservatives' convictions that their reactions in June 1989 had been justified: they had quite simply saved the Party. In January 1992, Deng Xiaoping went back on the offensive with a series of political speeches, known as the "Talks of Deng Xiaoping" (南方谈话; *nánfēng tánhuà*), made during a trip to the south of the country, in which he settled the question of special economic zones and their capitalist or socialist nature by forcefully insisting on the priority given to economic development and the pragmatism necessary to bring China out of its underdevelopment. In this way, Deng Xiaoping gave a new, clear signal of his commitment to a market- and production-oriented economy. From then on, those who had revolted in 1989 chose once again to stand with the Party in order to support the continuation of economic reforms and national development. Others, for the most part refugees living abroad, continued their efforts to mobilize against the Chinese regime, with mixed success.

The events of Tiananmen Square nevertheless provoked a strong reaction from the international community and led to the imposition of commercial sanctions, particularly in the military domain, by the United States and the European Union. In spite of French and German efforts since 2004 to lift these sanctions, the opposition of Great Britain in 2005—although the Blair government had declared itself in favor the year before—caused these attempts to fail, to the great satisfaction of the US government. These sanctions have become a relatively limited means of exerting pressure on China due to the attitude of Russia, which seized this opportunity to become, during the two decades following 1989, the largest supplier of military equipment to China, with exports to Beijing representing between a quarter and half of its total arms exports, depending on the year.[2] American leaders continue to demand apologies from the Chinese Communist Party for the 1989 repression, a requirement that Chinese leaders have until now treated with contempt, inviting the US government to renounce all interference in their domestic affairs. Indeed, such demands demonstrate the haughtiness with which some within the US government, as well as in certain European countries, pursue their unilateralist and colonialist approach to relations with China, as Henry Kissinger emphasized in May 2008 in an interview with the *Financial Times,* saying: "It is imperative to realize that we cannot do in China in the 21st century what others thought to do in the 19th, prescribe their institutions for them and seek to organize Asia."[3]

The idea that China should fit into a political and economic mold imagined by Westerners, who possess the "democratic truth," indeed remains very present in the minds of Western leaders and largely dominates their strategies toward China.

## *The Chinese Communist Party faced with demands for reforms*

The deep transformations effected in the economic domain since the beginning of the reforms, as well as their social impact, have gradually brought China closer to a more liberal economic model, which Deng Xiaoping theorized under the name "socialism with Chinese characteristics" (中国特色社会主义; *Zhōngguó tèsè shèhuì zhǔyì*) or "market economy with Chinese characteristics" (中国特色的市场经济; *Zhōngguó tèsè shìchǎng jīngjì*). This very pragmatic adaptation to economic realities, and the renunciation of the part of the Marxist vulgate in the economic domain that had shown its limits in terms of efficacy, extricated China from underdevelopment and allowed it to achieve the extraordinary economic takeoff that we have seen in the last 30 years. Economic growth thus became the first priority of the Chinese authorities because it guarantees social and political stability. The authority and legitimacy of the Party's power have been strengthened as a result, all the more so because it has very clearly chosen as its central objective the reduction of poverty—the main challenge facing all political regimes in developing countries, whether they are liberal or socialist. The objectives of improving the living conditions of the population on the one hand, and returning China to the international scene as a great power on the other, have allowed the Party to justify authoritarian

---

[2]"Russian Arms Exports in 2011 Total $13.2 Billion," RIA-Novosti, February 15, 2012. China is not Russia's biggest client in this domain. In 2011, Russia's biggest clients were: India (25 percent of Russian exports), Algeria (15 percent), and Venezuela (10 percent).
[3]"Lunch with the FT: Henry Kissinger," *Financial Times,* May 24, 2008.

government measures, which have so far proven their worth. Indeed, in liberal democracies, the democratic system itself—parliamentary consultation and the power of public opinion—has shown its limitations when it comes to reforms. It is very difficult to carry out fundamental reforms in Europe today because of the citizens' exercise of their right of expression (in particular, through public demonstrations), which often leads politicians, who are essentially concerned with getting reelected, to give in to public pressure and renounce reforms that are nevertheless indispensable. At the risk of outraging militant democrats, we must recognize that citizens are not always qualified to judge the merits of reforms they do not always really understand. The extreme complexity of economic and social issues, in particular, makes ordinary citizens in liberal democracies entirely dependent on the analyses offered by politicians or the media for their opinions about the proposals made by a given political party. The democratic game is consequently perverted by this situation, which causes public opinion to adopt sudden positions and then make equally spectacular reversals. Public opinion in parliamentary democracies is thus subject to the influence of an active minority, as Bryan Caplan brilliantly demonstrates in his work *The Myth of the Rational Voter: Why Democracies Choose Bad Policies*.[4]

In China, the Party's guidance has made it possible to carry out major reforms within very short time frames, which explains the changes we have seen in the last 30 years, the likes of which, even Western economists admit, no country has ever experienced in the past. Naturally, the political regime is not exempt from criticism, particularly concerning human rights, but the choice that was made—which of course was also made to preserve the Party's authority—was for the well-being of the majority, in exchange for restrictions on the freedom of a minority. This choice can be criticized, but to this day it has proven its worth with regard to economic development and the improvement of the daily lives of the Chinese people. After three decades of economic and social reforms, the need for true political reform is now being felt and expressed by a growing number of Chinese actors, including within the Party itself.

Nevertheless, to "give back to Caesar what is his," it is necessary to emphasize that the implemented reforms have also had an impact on the Chinese political system and on public freedoms. Economic changes have brought about parallel changes in the political system, which Westerners do not perceive because they are obsessed with the formal terminology and the word "Communist," which is attached to the party in power in China today. The principal of "stability above all else" (稳定压倒一切; *wěndìng yādǎo yíqiè*), dear to Chinese leaders since its formulation by Deng Xiaoping in March 1987,[5] has until now guided the decisions and strategy of the Party. It has, in particular, made it possible to close ranks within the Party and to convince Party leaders not

---

[4] Bryan Caplan, *The Myth of the Rational Voter: Why Democracies Choose Bad Policies* (Princeton University Press, 2007).
[5] Deng Xiaoping's return to this slogan on February 26, 1989, rang out as a warning to the student movement.

to air their disagreements in public, as was the case until June 1989, so as to preserve unity and thus stability. The techniques of manipulation for personal ends that culminated with the Cultural Revolution were certainly put to an end. The recourse to mass movements in order to strengthen or take power within the Party, following the model of the political campaigns of yesteryear, was abandoned in favor of politics that are more technocratic, more rational, and entirely dedicated to economic development and social questions. There was a gradual return to traditional Chinese values, particularly to the Confucian tradition, which was called to the rescue in order to strengthen the nation's social unity.

Today, it is legitimate to question the limits of economic reforms and development processes that are generating a noticeable improvement in the living standards of the population, including in the rural areas, but which is also sparking calls for greater transparency of political—and especially legal—institutions. Over the last quarter-century, the Chinese population has dedicated its energies to seizing the opportunities offered by economic reforms and to responding to Deng Xiaoping's call to enrich itself—or at least to live in better conditions—while at the same time refraining from making any claims that would be too overtly political. The numerous social movements today are generally directed against the heads of public or private enterprises or against local authorities accused of corruption. The ever easier access to means of communication (cell phones, Internet, trips from one province to another) allows for the wide and rapid communication of information about these movements. The foreign press is quick to jump on the slightest demonstration of discontentment that degenerates into a violent confrontation, and the American and European media are quick to relay this type of information. Contrary to a belief widely held in Western public opinion, it is now impossible for local or central authorities to conceal for very long any discontentment expressed by certain categories of the population; and the communications strategy of those in power has very noticeably evolved toward greater transparency. These days, the authorities regularly announce that investigations have been initiated to find those responsible for police violence or for the despoliation of peasants by local authorities—thereby demonstrating an increasing sensitivity to the need to answer to public opinion for their actions in areas involving public freedoms. The events of 2011–2012 in the village of Wukan, in the province of Guangdong, shed new light on the political evolution underway. After having demonstrated against local Party heads, confining them, and then turning Wukan into a fortress against police forces from outside, the villagers obtained the right to organize an election of their village committee, with the support of Prime Minister Wen Jiabao, who declared his desire to thus "better respond to the guarantees demanded by rural populations against the illegal confiscation of their land." He also maintained that "if the people can run a village well, they can run a township; if they can run a township, they can manage a country."[6] This election has become emblematic not of political demands—as one leader of the village revolt, Zhuang Liehong, declared ("our action was not a revolt, just an attempt to defend our rights")[7]—but of the common people's growing resistance to the plundering they have suffered for too many years at the hands of corrupt local authorities.

For the Party, the question of political reform appears to be a real concern now, but the fear of a loss of control that could provoke turmoil and instability, and thereby endanger all the successes achieved over the last three decades, has persuaded the Chinese leaders to advance haltingly, adopting a rhythm considered suitable for China and justifiably refusing to give in to the Western demands that are mostly based on an exogenous and reductive view of Chinese problems. As Kissinger said in the interview cited above, China has had 4,000 years of continuous government, and the political establishment, in whatever form, has developed specifically Chinese administrative capacities that cannot be contested today, and which it would be wise to recognize in order to develop a balanced dialogue with China.

The concept of democratic centralism, for example, which may today seem somewhat outmoded, remains an important subject of debate within the Party.[8] This principle is based on absolute obedience, and its application is thus profoundly incompatible with a process of democratization. However, the Party has so far refused to renounce it, as it has renounced other principles previously deemed untouchable—such as the collectivization of agriculture or a planned economy—during the reform process. This is primarily out of the Party's concern to eliminate centrifugal tendencies, which have been manifest several times in the past, during the Cultural Revolution and during the first decade of reforms, and which could threaten China's very existence as a unitary nation. Hu Jintao's visible desire after his accession to all the posts of power (General Secretary of the Party, President of the Republic, Chairman of the Central Military Commission of the Party and of the National Assembly) to surround himself with experts in such fields as law, the political history of Europe or the United States, and science and technology[9] was already a sign of the true concerns of the Chinese leaders and their increasing attention to political reform, which is considered inevitable in the long term but difficult to put into practice. Hu Jintao's incontestable popularity, due to his charisma and his style of government based on transparency and social justice, was an important asset in this project of reform. A Party technocrat who spent many years in the

[6] "Wen Hints at Greater People Power in China," AFP, March 14, 2012.

[7] "Chine: la grande désillusion des révoltés de Wukan," *Le Figaro*, December 15, 2012.

[8] 郑挺秀 [Guo Tingxiu], "坚持和健全民主集中制是增强领导班子活力的不竭动力" ["To Preserve and Strengthen Democratic Centralism Is to Strengthen the Inexhaustible Strength of the Dynamic of the Leading Group"], *理论前沿* [*Theory Front Review*], November 14, 2004.

[9] Ji Wei, *The Politburo's Group Study Sessions* (Center for Strategic and International Studies, Washington, DC, April 30, 2004).

country's most deprived provinces, Hu Jintao was a young leader who was able to promote a young generation of local and central managers who had come out of the Communist Youth League and were charged with the difficult task of henceforth giving priority to social justice over GDP growth. Thus, Hu Jintao called for the founding of a "harmonious society" (和谐社会; *Héxié shèhuì*), which naturally sounds familiar to the Chinese and reminds them of the Confucian concepts of Supreme Harmony (太和; *Tài hé* ) or Great Harmony (大同; *Dà tóng*). The Confucian concept of a "society of great harmony" represents the ideal of a perfect society in which the people enjoy social well-being within a framework of state ownership. Society at large takes care of the weak and destitute, and everyone tries to serve it as much as possible. This aspect of the Confucian social program quite clearly aligns with the precepts of socialism as it was developed by 19th-century thinkers, but there is a stumbling block: the idea that in such a society the people elect the most capable and most virtuous individuals to positions of leadership. In China's current situation, given the challenges to be met, it is the Party—an emanation of the People—that is in charge of identifying the leaders most capable of leading the country on the path to development. Already during the Fourth Plenum of the Sixteenth Congress of the Party, Hu Jintao insisted on the need to strengthen the Party's "governing capabilities" in order to confront the many problems it faces (rampant corruption, economic disparities, bureaucratic inertia, and ideological inconsistencies) and to give priority to social justice—themes that the new General Secretary of the Party, Xi Jinping, took up as soon as he acceded to power.

Thus, reform of the political system has been very gradually undertaken by the Party in order to encourage a greater participation by citizens in local life, under the Party's control, and in order to fight against the problems currently plaguing certain categories of the population. This process is certainly very slow, but it constitutes an embryo of participatory democracy intended to render local life more transparent while limiting the risks of destabilization. Naturally, it is not at all a matter of calling into question the role of the Party, but rather of responding to the aspirations of a population that increasingly rejects the political nominations of local leaders and demands to choose the leaders themselves from among their peers. In rural areas, this reform has become indispensable in the attempt to calm the anger over the social consequences of economic reforms. General Secretary Xi Jinping's insistence on the fight against corruption, which threatens the very existence of the Party,[10] confirms the line taken by Hu Jintao, but it is now obvious to the new leaders that this fight must be fought on all fronts and mercilessly.

---

[10]"习近平：腐败问题越演越烈 最终必然会亡党亡国" ["Xi Jinping: Corruption is developing, it is stronger and stronger, and it will not fail to eventually cause the death of the Party and the country"], Xinhuanet, November 19, 2012.

## *Society confronted with reforms*

At the social level, the reforms put into place in 1978 destabilized a social-ist system that had many weaknesses but that had made it possible to meet the basic needs of over 90 percent of the population in terms of health and education. After 25 years of reforms, the gap between rich and poor, as in the liberal economies of Europe and America, has not stopped growing, and pro-test is brewing. According to the National Bureau of Statistics, 45 percent of the country's wealth is in the hands of the richest 10 percent, and the poorest 10 percent have only 1.4 percent of the national wealth. This ratio testifies to China's entrance into the global liberal economic system,[11] and it is causing Chinese leaders to pay more attention to the serious social imbalances that have appeared during the era of reforms, in order to slow down a trend that could, in the medium term, constitute a threat to the stability of the country. However, China has made considerable progress over the past few years in the struggle against poverty, which has declined at an annual rate of 2.6 per-cent.[12] The Asian Development Bank (ADB) announced in December 2012 that between 1990 and 2008 China experienced the greatest rate of reduction of extreme poverty in Asia—from 84.6 percent to 29.8 percent. According to ADB, 700 million Asians still live on less than $1 a day, and its report specified that "the bulk of the success achieved throughout the region in the past years is the result of a strong reduction of poverty in China."[13]

The situation is most worrisome in the countryside. According to official data, in 2012 incomes in rural areas were still over four times less than in urban areas.[14] With 656 million people, or 51 percent of the total population, living in rural areas, the increasingly frequent incidents often involve tens of thou-sands of demonstrators. Local authorities in all the provinces have often taken advantage of the deregulation of the economy to make lucrative private deals for themselves, scorning the law and their constituents. Although the statistics on such problems would have previously been classified, they are now made public, and are referred to by the Chinese president and members of govern-ment in order to reinforce the struggle against corruption and abuse. Thus, in 2010 there were 180,000 "mass incidents." Thousands of bureaucrats at the central and local levels have been punished, sometimes by the death penalty for major corruption scandals, but the task is daunting. China's geographic and demographic size invites local law-breaking that is sometimes difficult to identify with precision, particularly when there is complicity among the local

---

[11]In the United States in 2012, the richest 10 percent of Americans held 80 percent of financial assets and 1 percent of them held 34.6 percent of the national wealth. Between 1979 and 2007, the highest 1 percent of the population saw its pretax income double, while the lowest 80 percent saw their income drop by about 20 percent.

[12]Asian Development Bank, *Key Indicators for Asia and the Pacific 2012* (Manila, August 2012).

[13]Asian Development Bank, *Asian Development Outlook 2012: Confronting Rising Inequality in Asia* (Manila, 2012).

[14]"2012年基尼系数为0.474 城镇居民收入差距超4倍" ["The Gini coefficient was 0.474 in 2012, and the income gap between cities and the countryside was over 4"], 北京晚报 [*Beijing Wanbao*], January 19, 2013.

Party representatives, the police, and the legal system, with all of them usually finding ways to profit financially from the abuses. But the increasing violence of popular demonstrations and the threat they pose to regional political stability are encouraging the central authorities to demonstrate more firmness regarding corruption, so as to provide justice to ordinary citizens harmed by an all-powerful political-legal apparatus. In January 2006, the Party secretary of the province of Guangdong, Zhang Dejiang, announced that local authorities had provoked social unrest through their actions, and had not respected "the three red lines" of expropriation (obtain the necessary administrative authorizations, make sure the peasants occupying the land are in agreement, and guarantee appropriate compensation), and that they would be dismissed.[15] At the end of 2005, Prime Minister Wen Jiabao himself declared that "expropriation by local authorities is the greatest threat to the stability of rural areas," and added that "we must absolutely not commit a historic error on the question of land."[16] He thus recognized not only the reality of these illegal practices, but also the ideological problem they pose for the Communist Party, which owed its victory over the Nationalists in 1949 specifically to its fight against social injustices toward the Chinese peasantry, and which had made this fight the very basis of its legitimacy.

It was on the strength of these considerations and concerns that the Party decided to revise its approach to the economic program launched by Deng Xiaoping—the call to individual enrichment—by insisting on the need to guarantee a better distribution of the wealth being produced, and to pay more attention to the rural areas and their problems, principles that had already figured prominently in the 11th Five-Year Plan, created in 2006. Although the goal of doubling the GDP between 2006 and 2010, which the Chinese leaders had set for themselves, had been achieved (it went from $2.7 trillion to $5.87 trillion), social conflicts have never stopped spreading and today are the principal threat to the stability of the country. Concrete measures have been taken to reduce the gaps in development between the cities and countryside and to accelerate improvements in the living conditions of the rural population.

The historic abolition,[17] on January 1, 2006, of the 5 percent tax on agricultural production and of other taxes so as to revitalize the rural economy and try to stabilize the population there—in the hopes of slowing down the rural exodus that over the next 20 years could involve nearly 300 million peasants—was a gesture intended to reduce tensions and satisfy the demands of the peasants. The idea expounded by economic policy makers was to allow the industrial sector, which was undergoing a new stage in its growth, to support the

---

[15] 张德江硬话背后的硬道理, 中国青年报电子版 [*The hard reasons behind Zhang Dejiang hard talk*], January 26, 2006.

[16] 温家宝严斥地方可能犯下历史错误 [*Wēn Jiābǎo blame is maybe a historical mistake*], January 20, 2006.

[17] The very official publication the *People's Daily* did not hesitate to state in its October 8, 2005, edition that this measure brought an end to "2,000 years of an intolerable situation," a rather uncharitable view of the first five decades of the People's Republic.

development of agriculture. Over the last few years, the area of land being farmed has not stopped shrinking, leading to a stagnation in agricultural production. The insufficient profitability of agriculture due to the high cost of seeds and other production inputs, the temptations of the city, and the expropriations (most often for real estate speculation) have all motivated peasants, especially the young, to leave rural areas and join the massive floating populations in the urban agglomerations. In 2010, the authorities counted 242,230,000 migrants (农民工; *nóngmíngōng*), amounting to 17 percent of the labor force, a very large increase over previous years. The authorities see the low incomes of these migrants as a cause for concern, given the potential force such a population could muster. According to a study done by the National Population and Family Planning Commission, the average monthly salary of migrants less than 35 years old was only 2,513 yuan in 2011, or $397.[18] This salary represented a 29.4% increase over 2009, but still does not allow a worker to cover all housing and health costs, which have gone up significantly in recent years. In February 2012 a long-awaited memorandum granted migrants from the countryside the right to obtain residence permits in small and medium-sized cities, thus finally allowing them access to public services—in particular, health services and education for their children. Public opinion exerted strong pressure on the authorities in the past few years to reform the system of the family record booklet (户口; *hùkǒu*), a permanent residence permit issued during the Maoist era and now obsolete in the face of the demographic and sociological changes of the last 30 years.

The example of the province of Heilongjiang, in the northeast of the country, is significant in this respect. Out of a workforce of 9,430,000 in 2004, 4,700,000—50 percent of them—were in "excess" for the province. Every year, Heilongjiang, which has now reached 38 million inhabitants, sees its workforce increase by between 70,000 and 90,000 individuals. In 2004, 3,570,000 people left the province, either for other regions or to go abroad; 110,000 did the latter, though one may assume that many of them crossed the border to move into the far-eastern provinces of Russia, which are currently being depopulated.[19] The salary differential between rural and urban residents reached a factor of four in 2012, and it has not stopped growing because recent measures by the central government have not yet gone into full effect. In 2011, the size of the urban population officially surpassed that of the rural population for the first time, testifying to the rural exodus underway.

The situation of the workers in the cities is clearly better than that in the countryside, even if it is still precarious for several million of them. Economic reforms have translated into the closing of a number of state businesses that had become unproductive, leading to the layoffs of millions of workers (known as

---

[18]"Report Reveals Measly Pay for China's Migrants," Xinhua, August 7, 2012.
[19]"加快农村剩余劳动力转移需要制度作保障" ["To accelerate the transfer of surplus labor from the countryside, the system must provide protection"], 中国信息 [*China News Journal*], December 16, 2005.

*xiagang*, 下岗), who are now considered long-term unemployed and have joined the ranks of occasional workers. For the year 2010, official Chinese sources counted 5,470,000 xiagang and 9,200,000 unemployed in the urban areas, equivalent to an unemployment rate of 4.2 percent nationwide—a rate that has remained stable since 2000.[20] Some American authors question these figures.[21]

Official statistics for rural areas are scarce and seem unreliable. Certain critical sources put the number of unemployed in the countryside at 150 million in 2005, the number of xiagang in urban areas at 20 million, and the new entrants into the labor market at 14 million each year.[22] Today, several million former employees of state businesses live in very precarious conditions, often working as day laborers in the major metropolitan areas. This situation is presented as temporary and as the result of the indispensable conversion of the Chinese economy from a planned economy indifferent to criteria of profitability to a rationalized economy, dynamic and competitive internationally.[23] Certainly, the criticisms regularly expressed in the Western media of the Chinese authorities for the layoffs they carried out in order to stabilize public corporations testify to the rather shockingly bad faith in light of the state of European economies. Moreover, it was precisely to avoid the mass layoffs that were not absolutely inevitable that the state banks were encouraged to approve loans to state businesses in dubious financial condition. This policy made it possible to limit the impact of the reforms on the competiveness of state enterprises by shifting the financial problems to the banks. The latter, which in 2011 thus held 492.9 billion yuan in nonperforming loans,[24] or 40 percent of the total loans granted by Chinese banks, have entered into a process of semi-privatization thanks to their very gradual opening to foreign capital, within the framework of WTO regulations, which should eventually save most of those threatened with bankruptcy. The government's policy for dealing with the unemployment problem has clearly made it possible to attenuate the effects on the population of the shift to an economy that is more and more liberal, even if several million workers have not been able to avoid these effects entirely. Those who do have jobs, however, still work all too often in precarious conditions in spite of the new labor code adopted in 1995. The situation of miners is often on the front page due to the terrible working conditions in private mines, which are regularly highlighted in the Chinese press.

In spite of these difficulties and the current weaknesses in Chinese development, the population's living standards have incontestably risen over the last

---

[20]*2010 年度人力资源和社会保障事业发展统计公报* [*2010 Statistical Report on the Development of Social Protection and Human Resources*] (Beijing: Ministry of Labor and Social Security, People's Republic of China).

[21]Derek Scissors, "Chinese Growth, GDP, and Other Things the U.S. Should Doubt," Heritage Foundation Brief, January 18, 2013. According to the author, the unemployment figure may be five times greater.

[22]"处在生死边缘的中国下岗工人" ["The Chinese Xiagang at the edge of life and death"], January 29, 2006, http://www.dajiyuan.com.

[23]"下岗与失业有什么不同" ["What is the difference between the Xiagang and the unemployed?"], October 30, 2003, http://www.china.com.cn.

[24]"More Bad Loans in China," *Forbes*, February 3, 2013.

three decades, and the trend continues, thanks to a strong rate of growth and to investments made by the authorities in the interior provinces, which are disadvantaged because of the heavy concentration of economic development in the eastern provinces. Consumption in urban centers continues to grow, and is encompassing increasingly sophisticated products. In the real estate sector, for example, home ownership has doubled over the last five years and is now at 80 percent (versus 67 percent in the United States and 61 percent in Japan).[25] Household consumption, on the other hand, is still relatively weak compared to the GDP due to the deep-rooted tradition of saving, which has made China first globally in terms of savings (with a gross savings rate of 53.9 percent of GDP in 2010, versus 9.3 percent in the United States), while private consumption has fallen to 35 percent of GDP. This tradition has also been reinforced by the insecurity felt by the Chinese in the face of increased health and education costs and the uncertainties regarding the pension system. In 2012, however, the middle class[26] included approximately 300 million people, or 25 percent of the population,[27] and could reach 600 million in 2020 given the high rate of urbanization (51.3 percent in 2011), which makes it possible to hope for an increasingly significant ripple effect on the Chinese economy. The Chinese countryside is also beginning to see an emergence of more wealthy households, even if city dwellers absorb the lion's share of disposable income while making up only 50 percent of the population. Certain products are the objects of veritable consumption frenzies identical to what has been observed in Europe, as in the case of cell phones (with 1.06 billion cell phone accounts in August 2012[28]), purchases of which have gone up by over 70 percent annually over the past few years. Another sector undergoing strong growth and representative of a new China is domestic Chinese tourism, which counted 3 billion travelers in 2012 (generating $407.94 billion), surpassing the more than 80 million Chinese who traveled outside of Chinese territory the same year (this figure, however, includes trips to Hong Kong and Macao, which make up about 70 percent of the total), which is expected to drop to 200 million by 2020. After the opening of direct contacts between the two sides of the strait, continental tourism to Taiwan underwent a massive increase in 2012: up 45 percent from the year before, with 2.6 million citizens of the People's Republic traveling to the island. The Chinese can now travel as tourists to 90 countries, including those of the European Union, which has opened its doors to them since September 2004. In addition, the recent introduction of consumer credit has given an impetus to the acquisition of many household products and automobiles.

---

[25]James R. Barth, Tong Li, and Michael Lea, *China's Housing Market: Is a Bubble About to Burst?* (Santa Monica: Milken Institute, 2012).
[26]Those whose annual income is between 60,000 RMB and 500,000 RMB.
[27]Helen H. Wang, "The Chinese Middle Class View of the Leadership Transition," *Forbes*, September 11, 2012. Some authors give the higher figure of 474 million in 2012, without, however, specifying their salary criteria.
[28]"China Has 1.06 Billion Mobile Phone Accounts," *China Daily*, August 28, 2012.

It is the size of this potential Chinese market that is especially attractive to foreign companies that dream of selling a toothbrush to every Chinese, or of selling the 2,000 airliners that China will need in the next 20 years. In spite of the warnings of Western Cassandras who have enumerated China's major weaknesses, the Chinese have continued their economic development over the years by striving to fix social problems on the basis of the priorities of the moment, and in such a way as to never endanger the overall edifice itself. After having successfully made the transition from a planned economy to a market economy while limiting the social consequences as much as possible, the authorities are now striving to reduce the inequalities that have appeared in this transition process, a considerable task whose success depends, now as ever, on the maintenance of overall stability. Agricultural production must be stimulated; the rural exodus must be slowed down; social protection must be quickly extended to rural areas; the trend of school dropouts in the countryside, due to the high cost of previously free education, must be rectified; claims made against abuses by authorities must be handled more transparently; and the field of democratic expression must be enlarged, while its effects on social and political stability remain under control. The response to all these challenges will shape both the pursuit of general development and the emergence of an undoubtedly innovative Chinese model, a form of "Confucian socialism" (儒家社会主义; *rújiā shèhuì zhǔyì*), whose specificities would correspond to the characteristics of the most populous state on the planet, and whose economic development during the last quarter-century has taken place at a speed without precedent in history.

## *The problem of the rule of law*

The question of human rights is the subject of intense debate between China and its detractors, between those who support the total and immediate application of the rules decreed by international organizations and those who favor a more gradual approach that takes into account China's fragilities, and between those who defend a universalist conception of human rights and those with a more pragmatic view. In order to approach this issue calmly, it is necessary to first distance oneself from the moral concerns that seem to govern the criticisms expressed by Westerners. This is necessary not because these concerns are irrelevant or unjustified, but because, rather than signs of good intentions, they are signs of a general political strategy to destabilize China during its gradual integration into the international community, and to maintain political leverage over it, as the arms embargo proves. Torture is no more intolerable when it is used extensively in Chinese police stations to force suspects to confess than when it is used in Iraqi prisons to distract American soldiers, who take out their anxiety and boredom on random prisoners. In the latter case, however, the tor-turers were obeying the orders of a government that had reduced a nation, Iraq, to ashes in the name of democracy and human rights. The Pentagon's subcon-tracting of prisoner torture to third-party states, a phenomenon that is today acknowledged, is only the most recent proof of American cynicism regarding human rights. In December 1997, the international community gathered in Rome to ban antipersonnel mines, millions of which had been deployed in 60 countries and had been responsible for the deaths of 26,000 people each year, the overwhelming majority of them civilians. The United States refused to sign this agreement, alongside Afghanistan, Russia, China, and Vietnam.[29] We could add to this sad list its support for criminal regimes in Asia, Africa, and Latin America out of pure strategic interest, or its refusal to accept the juris-diction of the International Criminal Court, whose usefulness has been made clear by the matter of Iraqi and Afghan prisons.

Once these so-called moral motivations have been eliminated, it is pos-sible to examine the situation of human rights in China, which requires an indisputable effort on the part of the authorities, as they themselves recognize. The June 1989 events of Tiananmen Square have taken on a symbolic aspect in this domain. They have caused China to be penalized with sanctions and a period of isolation, whereas the massacre of some 5,000 Kurds at Halabja by Iraqi forces in March 1988, one year earlier, had not resulted in such measures against Saddam Hussein's Iraq, which was at the time a Western ally in resisting the revolutionary Iranian Shiite wave.

The death penalty, which is widely used in China and which, let us remem-ber, is supported by a large majority of the Chinese population, figures among the primary concerns expressed by human rights organizations. Indeed, China does hold the world record, with several thousand executions each year. As one French China expert, Jean-Luc Domenach, rightly emphasized in 2004, the death penalty is not the subject of much debate within Chinese public opin-ion, which considers it a "fair" punishment. The debate is beginning to arise among wealthy urbanites and democrats, as well as among businesspeople, as the practice is bad for international business.[30] It is true that the stories that haunt the Western media about the conditions in which executions are carried out feed these criticisms. In 2011, pursuing a very gradual reform in this do-main, China eliminated the death penalty for 13 types of crime.

Judges and lawyers in China seem to be increasingly sensitive to this issue, and demand more independence in making their rulings, based on the central government's own renewed calls for a greater respect for the rule of law. The Chinese government has implemented a reform that aims to reduce the abuses observed for years in the local courts, whose sentences could not be appealed

---

[29] Chalmers Johnson, *Blowback: The Costs and Consequences of American Empire* (New York: Owl Books, 2001), 68–69.
[30] Jean-Luc Domenach, "Peine de mort: la Chine évolue lentement," *Alternatives Internationales*, no. 17, October 2004.

and which too often practiced summary justice. The Supreme Court has thus set itself the goals of reducing the number of death sentences, reducing the number of them carried out, and eventually abolishing the death penalty.[31] But there is still a long way to go, especially in rural areas. The law enacted on January 1, 2007, which requires that all capital punishment sentences handed out by ordinary Chinese courts be submitted to the Supreme Court, has allowed an important step to be taken toward improving the objectivity of judgments; and, according to the Chinese authorities, it should reduce the number of executions by at least 20 percent.[32]

Another important matter is torture, which is widespread in China. The director of the National People's Congress Committee on Internal and Legal Affairs put out a report in 2005 based on a study of the application of criminal procedure law in six provinces; it emphasized that the most serious problem was the continued use of torture to extort confessions.[33] Following this report, the National People's Congress made revising the law one of the top priorities of its mandate; this was finally done in 2006 and enacted in 2007. At the same time, the public prosecutor established a pilot program that requires video recordings to be made of the entirety of interrogation procedures, and that a lawyer be present. This decision, initiated by the public security forces of three regions and by Beijing University of Political Science and Law, underscores the will of the central authorities to strengthen the protection of the rights of the accused and suspects, in a country where torture has always been used and where the very principle of the right of defense is not really perceived as a supreme value. Of course, the objection can be made that this right of defense, and the respect for citizens, is violated every day in China; but one cannot deny that considerable progress in this domain has been made over the last 25 years. As we have seen from the American troops' violent acts against prisoners in Iraq and Afghanistan, the respect for prisoners' rights is first and foremost a matter of law and of supervision, not of a tradition of "democracy" or civilization. The Chinese central authorities are on a long and difficult path toward improving the respect for human rights in the legal domain, and the progress made in this direction is cause for optimism. Economic development and the continuing advances in the standard of living and quality of education for the Chinese population promotes the deepening of the legal reforms underway.

Another topic under consideration in China today is the existence of reeducation-through-labor camps. The system of *laogai,* established in the 1950s in order to isolate criminals and political prisoners assigned to construction or manufacturing activities, and which makes possible the detention of

---

[31] 对中国死刑制度的思考 [*Reflection on the Death Penalty in China*], 中国法院网 [Network of Chinese Courts], October 2005.
[32] 新华社 [Xinhuashe], October 31, 2006.
[33] "Law Revised to Ban Confessions by Torture," *Judicial News* (The Supreme People's Court of the People's Republic of China), July 19, 2005.

prisoners for over four years without trial, remains one of the most disturbing aspects of the Chinese legal system. But the secrecy that surrounds this issue does a disservice to China, because it is impossible to seriously evaluate the scope of the phenomenon and the real conditions of detention, leaving some to imagine practices worthy of American prisons in Iraq. However, China's detractors are hardly convincing on this matter. In an interview given in October 2005, the famous Chinese dissident Harry Wu, for example, limited himself to general remarks and acknowledged that he could not give precise details:

> *It is difficult to know the exact number, but they are everywhere. Every totalitarian regime needs to keep control over the population. It is a mechanism necessary for keeping people terrified and passive. The USSR had its gulags, Nazi Germany had its concentration camps, China has the "laogai." The system has lasted since 1949 and almost no one outside China's borders is aware of it.*[34]

Comparing the current Chinese regime to Soviet and Nazi dictatorships remains one of the favorite themes of Chinese dissidents living in the United States, but this approach is both absurd and scandalous. It is amusing and very telling about the strategies of these enemies of China to note that, in order to illustrate the content of this interview, the site published some supposedly current photos of executions and, as if the images weren't strong enough, photos of executions preceded by torture that dated from 1905! No outside source can determine precisely the number of detention sites or the number of prisoners concerned, and the Chinese authorities classify this matter under the category of "state secrets." However, in 2008, in a rare mention of this penitentiary system, the authorities declared the existence of 350 reeducation centers holding 160,000 prisoners. The new leaders of the Chinese Communist Party, who came out of the Eighteenth Congress, in November 2012, nevertheless announced that reform of the reeducation-through-labor system was underway,[35] but that a complete and immediate abandonment of this system inherited from the previous era of reforms is still not certain. The international community is showing itself to be more and more sensitive to this question, especially Western public opinion, which activist organizations are trying to sensitize to this issue because of the strong suspicion that these prisoners participate in the manufacture of certain exported products. It seems reasonable to think that this aspect of the Chinese legal and political system is largely obsolete today, and that its reform is urgent for China's image and for the respect of its citizens' fundamental rights.

---

[34]Caroline Stevan, "Harry Wu s'exprime à propos du laogai chinois, de la peine de mort et des prélèvements d'organes sur les prisonniers, exécutés," October 19, 2005, http://www.interet-general.info/spip.php?article5564.
[35]"China to Reform Reeducation through Labor System," Xinhuanet, January 7, 2013.

The debate over human rights in China is a dialogue of the deaf because its protagonists have very different objectives and all of them stand their ground. The Chinese authorities underline the economic results obtained after thirty years of reforms and the real improvement in the standard of living of the population as a whole in order to justify their concern about stability and their lack of leniency toward anyone—individuals or organizations—that, through their opposition, could endanger the country's development. The *White Paper on Human Rights in China*, published by Beijing in October 2005, emphasizes the social gains and the abundance of media in the country (over 50 billion national and regional newspapers sold in 2012; over 6 billion books published in the last few years; over 560 million Internet users at the end of 2012), which contradicts China's image abroad as a police state characterized by great intellectual poverty. This abundance of publications can be observed in Chinese bookstores in every city in the country; and the systematic translation of foreign books, from philosophy to management, is amazing. Management and economy, as well as foreign literature, dominate the bookshelves. It is nevertheless true that all these publications are carefully censored in order to expunge anything that could contradict official discourse concerning China itself. In this area, as in Internet usage, the Chinese authorities remain cautious. China's increasing openness to the world should rapidly convince Party leaders of the futility of total control over the media, now that the Chinese can travel, meet foreigners, and have access to foreign publications. Intellectuals and cadres already escape this censorship thanks to their growing globalization. In reality, it is the workers and peasants who are most subject to this censorship, as they cannot communicate in a foreign language, even if some of them (still very few) have begun to travel abroad as tourists. Though it is not good for overall stability to contemplate a drastic opening, particularly considering the anti-Chinese campaign brewing abroad, the strategy of gradual liberalization, controlled but perceptible, is a courageous and responsible choice by the Party. Moreover, the very strong attachment that the vast majority of Chinese feel toward their country, both in China and in the diaspora—as we saw once again during the recent events in Tibet—represents a real guarantee for the Chinese leadership that the Western media and anti-China organizations can have only a weak influence over them. The trust between the Chinese people and today's Party leaders will only be strengthened by the current pursuit of political openness, which is appropriate for a new stage in the history of Chinese socialism.

Among the criticisms of the Chinese regime, the Western discourse on human rights is also political cant. Incapable of reasoning over the long term, Western human rights organizations and their allies daily denounce human rights violations and, most often prisoners of a completely ideological approach to the Chinese political system, they refuse to recognize the progress made in this domain, as in that of the economy. As we have seen, official Chinese sources themselves admit these violations and maintain that they are trying to address them by taking adequate measures to punish abuses. In the last few years, religious freedom in particular has been the subject of systematic denunciations by American organizations and leaders, regarding both the Muslims in the west of China and Christians, especially evangelical Christians.

## Religion in China

During the Cultural Revolution, religious freedoms were suppressed and all believers, regardless of their religion, suffered systematic persecution. Deng Xiaoping's accession to power was a veritable liberation for them, and religious freedom was rapidly reestablished. The places of worship reopened their doors, and religious leaders resumed their activities within the political framework established by the Party. The training of priests and imams is in fact supervised by the Party, which does not tolerate any foreign interference, either by the Holy See or by Islamic authorities.

Over the course of the past decade, the religious phenomenon has spread like wildfire throughout the country. The reforms, the gradual effacement of the orthodox socialist model, and the appearance of social problems connected with the impact of reforms, led to a veritable crisis of faith. The Chinese found themselves suffering from a lack of spirituality, and embarked on a search for values. In spite of the vigorous return of classical Chinese culture and philosophies to satisfy this quest for meaning, the competition from imported religions is very strong. The authorities have opened the door especially to evangelical proselytism, mainly of American origin, which is based on solid organizational structures and benefits from very significant financial support. The presence in the White House for eight years of a president with close ties to evangelical sects naturally favored their expansion, and they used this religious freedom to cover Chinese territory with houses of worship and to send numerous missionaries to China.

During his official visit to China in November 2005, George W. Bush attended a religious service in Beijing organized by a Protestant association. One of the American evangelists present, Luis Palau, declared to the press that "Chinese people enjoy more religious freedom than people overseas imagine." He specified that he had "total freedom to speak at every church and every (religious) gathering in China. Nobody told me what to say and what not to say." These statements, which go against the image that Washington wants to present of the situation of religion in China, were condemned in the United States, and Palau was obliged to issue a correction on his return.[36] Although religious freedom is effectively recognized in China today, the sermons of many evangelists inciting contestation of the Chinese regime pose a real problem. For the authorities, the openly anti-Communist activism of these evangelical

---

[36]"U.S. Evangelist Regrets Remarks on Religious Freedom in China," CNSNews.com, November 30, 2005.

movements, which receive substantial subsidies from abroad, justifies the regular arrests of preachers accused of subversion. In the provinces, the thirst for faith has favored the emergence of numerous false prophets who take advantage of the credulity of some residents in order to extort funds and organize veritable cults that are sometimes powerful enough to represent a real threat to local authorities.

The situation with regard to the Catholic Church is at once more complicated and simpler. It is more complicated because of the coexistence of two churches, one official and the other underground, which have opposed one another for decades on the matter of relations with the Vatican. The Chinese Patriotic Church has, since its creation in 1957, rejected the authority of the Pope, and it refuses the instructions and teachings of the Vatican. Indeed, the Party does not want to accept what it considers to be foreign interference in domestic religious affairs. In 2005, Beijing and the Vatican resumed negotiations in order to try to overcome their enmity and establish diplomatic relations after 60 years of ignoring one another. But the process always stalls over the question of the Holy See's power to ordain priests, which Beijing continues to oppose. Also at stake for Beijing in these negotiations is the Vatican's breaking of relations with Taiwan, which would represent a major defeat for the Taiwanese leaders. The Chinese authorities have thus set two conditions for dialogue with the Holy See, in the words of the spokesman for the Chinese Ministry of Foreign Affairs:

1. There is only one China in the world, Taiwan is part of China, and the Vatican must end its relations with Taiwan.
2. The Vatican must not interfere in domestic Chinese affairs, even under the pretext of religion.

Under these conditions, negotiations quickly became bogged down, in spite of the gestures each side made from time to time. It is, however, in the interest of the Chinese leaders to normalize relations with the Vatican and to give greater religious freedom to Catholics, whose activities are less politicized than those of evangelicals and stem from a central authority, the Holy See, with whom it is possible to negotiate. Chinese bishops' inability to attend synods in Rome, even if their requests for travel authorization are not usually officially rejected, demonstrates the limits of these relations and Beijing's determination to get the Catholic hierarchy to relent on the nomination of bishops and the recognition of Taiwan.

As for Protestants, the great variety of their churches, their murky relations with political powers in the United States, their militant anti-communism, and the memory of the Taiping Rebellion in the 19th century make them more suspect. In other times, as Voltaire noted, Chinese Emperor Yongheng had adopted defensive measures when faced with subversive preachers:

*As soon as he was on the throne, he received requests from all the cities of the empire against the Jesuits. He was warned that, under the pretext of religion, these monks were conducting a great deal of business, that they preached a doctrine of intolerance ... that they had been the soldiers and spies of a Western priest reputed to be sovereign over all the kingdoms of the Earth; that this priest had divided the kingdom of China into bishoprics; that he had made pronouncements in Rome against the ancient rites of the nation, and that, finally, if these unprecedented enterprises were not repressed as soon as possible, a revolution was to be feared.*[37]

Strangely, even though American foundations regularly announce the arrests of preachers and followers, which generally occur during underground meetings, Beijing seems to show great tolerance toward them. Protestant missionaries have multiplied these past few years in China, financed by American evangelical organizations, and there have been hundreds of thousands of conversions. In 1949, there were only 700,000 Protestants in China. Today, some Western sources estimate that there are 500,000 conversions annually.[38] Most sources agree that the number of Protestants is somewhere around 30 to 40 million today. Evangelicals represent a true challenge for Chinese authorities because their motivations are not only religious, but also largely political. Their preaching is often directed against the Chinese regime and calls for contesting its legitimacy. Beyond the freedom of religion, it is fundamentally a crusade led by groups financed by activist organizations in the United States, some of them closely tied to the Bush administration,[39] under the mandate of that American president. So, it seems logical that the response to them would be political in nature—that is, law enforcement measures intended to repress what Beijing considers attacks on the stability of the country. Although this attitude, could, of course be criticized on a religious level, it is also easy to understand that this political aspect of evangelism helps generate suspicion and repression.

In addition to the problem of Islam, which I will address in another chapter, there is the matter of the Falun Gong (法轮功) sect, which has become so famous. The founder of this sect, Li Hongzhi, appeared suddenly in 1992 in the city of Changchun, proclaiming his "discovery": the possibility of ascending, under his leadership, to the "paradise of Falun." China has seen dozens of millenarian sects, and this one could have disappeared as quickly as it had appeared. But it undoubtedly found fertile ground in the crisis of faith that had affected the Chinese since the reforms of the 1980s, especially given that Changchun is located in one of the industrial regions most affected by the

[37] Voltaire, "L'empereur de la Chine et le frère Rigolet ou relation du bannissement des jésuites de la Chine, par l'auteur du Compère Matthieu," in *Œuvres choisies*, Edition du Centenaire (Paris: Mai, 1878), 825–826.
[38] "God's Grace in China," *Grace Magazine* (London, June 2005).
[39] In 2004, the Web site of the American ambassador to China presented a 27-page interview with David Aikman, author of *A Man of Faith: The Spiritual Journey of George W. Bush*, which dealt extensively with the American president's "rebirth" thanks to the Evangelical Church.

economic reforms and restructuring of state-run businesses, which had thrown millions of employees onto the labor market. In four years, the sect won over about a million followers throughout the country.

In Europe, a simple reading of Li Hongzhi's statements would have sufficed to classify his movement as a cult, just like Rev. Sun Myung Moon's Unification Church or the Church of Scientology. In 1999, the Chinese authorities, frightened by Falun Gong's rapid development among a population destabilized by the social impact of the reforms, and by the sit-in organized by thousands of followers in front of the Party headquarters in Beijing, decided to outlaw the sect and to repress those disciples who continued to pursue their practices. "Li Hongzhi's project is built on virtue and grand promises. The goal of the National Union of Associations for the Defense of the Family and of Individual Cult Victims (UNADFI) is to determine whether this movement could pose a danger to some of its followers. To this end, we point out five key features of the doctrine" (as quoted from the Web site):

1. The movement's mission, its nature, its goals, its organizational structure, and its lack of transparency.
   The spiritual project is hidden under a cloak of qigong.
   The Master claims to be Buddhist but holds that people today can no longer cultivate themselves and practice [Falun Gong] using Buddhist law.
   The movement claims to have no hierarchy, but it has a very efficient organization led by many volunteers devoted to the Master. Before the repression in China, there were 1,900 practice stations; in the United States, Falun Gong infrastructure can be found in almost every state; in Paris and its suburbs, there are 13 practice stations.
2. The Master is an exceptional Being.
   From the age of four, he received the wisdom of masters from other universes!
   Today, it is he alone who publicly transmits the righteous law!
   He is the one who allows virtuous believers to transform the cells of their bodies into energy.
3. The Master keeps virtuous believers in good health in order to allow them to deepen their spirituality.
4. Even if virtuous believers cannot use their supernatural powers, the notion remains a temptation, and some are persuaded that their health has improved and that the effects of aging on their bodies have been lessened (white hair, age spots, menopause).
5. The Master suggests that followers gradually master their conjugal and parental feelings (these are attachments!), and replace them with compassion, the sort of compassion we have for our neighbors!

We are therefore led to conclude that adherence to Falun Gong may pose certain dangers to the equilibrium of its followers and to their effective integration into society.[40]

[40] Chine: Falungong, http://www.prevensectes.com/falun.htm.; "Que sait-on de? Falun Gong," Bulles N°72, January 2002, http://www.unadfi.org/que-sait-on-de-falun-gong.

Raphaël Liogier, director of the World Religion Watch in France (*l'Observatoire du religieux en France*) deems that Li Hongzhi's "teaching is closer to a spiritual totalitarianism that cultivates a cult of personality in the name of qigong."[41] In 1999, the guru claimed that his movement was not an organization and did not have any specific structures. Today, the sect has become a veritable multinational, benefitting from funds from its followers and from other associations, such as American evangelical organizations. In the West, Falun Gong has followers among those disillusioned by the model of development and by the social crisis, and it benefits from its hint of exoticism. The fight to defend the sect is carried out in the name of religious tolerance and defense of human rights in China, but it is clearly used abroad to increase pressure on China (naturally, Li Hongzhi lives in the United States). Indeed, the Chinese government uses violence against followers of the sect in China, which feeds the criticisms by human rights organizations, themselves insensitive to the accusations of manipulation made against the sect and to the danger it represents, according to some observers, to its own members.[42] But, once again, the debate over Falun Gong is not situated at the level of morality, but is rather part of a strategy of destabilization.

In general, the problem of political reform has for many years remained one of the major points of opposition between China and its Western partners. It will be quite difficult for China to bring these points of view closer together as long as economic growth remains an absolute priority, as it does for economic reasons—it is necessary to profit from the next 20 years to pull China out of underdevelopment before problems related to its demographic transition begin to kick in—and for domestic political reasons. Greater priority is therefore given to social rights, to the fight against unemployment and insecurity, than to political freedoms. It must also be emphasized that, in trying to impose their vision of democracy on China, Westerners usually ignore the fact that none of the East Asian regimes they supported in the past that emerged with strong economies—from Singapore to South Korea—were liberal democracies or open economies at the time. The changes these countries made at the political level came in the wake of economic development, never before.

It is likely that we will see occasional social crises in the 20 years to come, in connection with the different phases of economic growth that China will go through, but nothing suggests an economic crisis of sufficient scale to have major negative consequences on the political system. Western countries have also experienced major crises (the great crash of 1929, for example, or the oil crisis of 1973) and near-insurrections (May 1968 in France, for example), but if these crises temporarily weakened their economies and sometimes caused deep social transformations, they never sent these countries back into underdevelopment. China's great strength, inherited from the Confucian tradition,

---

[41] *L'actualité des religions*, September 1, 1999.
[42] "Sous la gymnastique douce de Falun Gong, une doctrine dure," ["Under the gentle gymnastics of Falun Gong, a hard doctrine"], *Le Courrier* (Geneva), August 25, 2001; "Le Falun Gong, arme de la CIA contre le 'Grand dragon rouge,'" ["Falun Gong, CIA weapon against the 'great red dragon'"], *Réseau Voltaire*, August 22, 2008, http://www.alterinfo.net.

is to be able to learn from its failures. It has proven this with the reforms begun in 1978, and then with the regular adjustments made in these reforms since then in order to correct errors and take into account the real situation of the country. We can bet that this will also be the case in the event of more serious social crises.

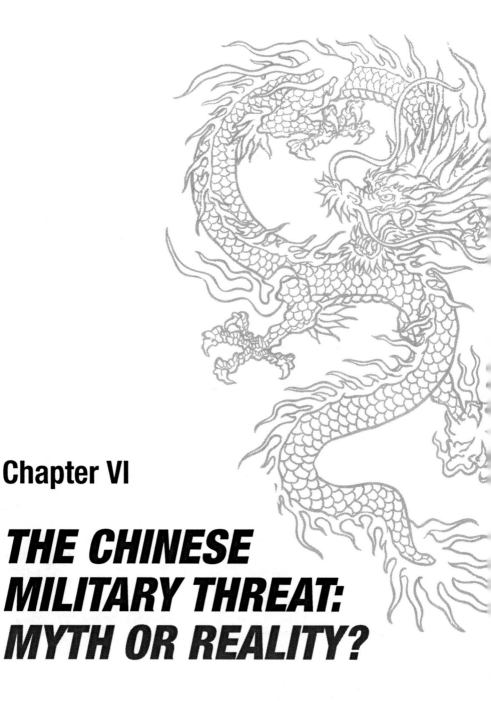

# Chapter VI

# *THE CHINESE MILITARY THREAT: MYTH OR REALITY?*

At the beginning of March 2013, the report presented to the National People's Congress by the outgoing prime minister, Wen Jiabao, which gave an assessment of the prior fiscal year and outlined future directions, announced a double-digit spike in spending on one area: a 10.7% increase for defense, amounting to an annual budget of $115.7 billion. The report mentioned the need for China to ensure the defense of its territory.[1] The new general secretary of the Communist Party of China (CPC), Xi Jinping, who is close to military circles, needs more than ever the support of the most prominent figures in the People's Liberation Army (PLA) to fortify his power in the decade to come. Overseas, the reactions to this Chinese military effort have naturally been critical, and China's neighbors are particularly worried, even though China never ceases to affirm its desire to resolve regional conflicts—especially conflicts over territory—in a peaceful manner. Recent tensions in the South China Sea and Beijing's increasingly muscular approach to these disputes—notably by sending warships into the area and making declarations intended to dissuade coastal states from opposing Chinese claims—have justifiably strengthened suspicions and have helped increase Washington's options for intervention in the region. However, the Chinese military budget must be compared with that of the United States ($656.2 billion in 2012) or with Japan's ($53.3 billion, half of China's, for a country with 3.89 percent of China's territory and 9.38 percent of China's population, and with a history of conquest in the Asia-Pacific region that is still a source of cruel memories).

China's program of military modernization, begun in 1978, has given rise to many questions in the United States and in Europe. Western experts compare approaches to the question, in conference after conference, without being able to agree on a consensual response. The debate is dominated by ideological considerations and a desire to dramatize that obscure the arguments and limit any understanding of the developments underway. Every year since 2000, the US Department of Defense has published a report for Congress entitled "Report on the Military Power of the People's Republic of China" (and since 2010, "Military and Security Developments Involving the People's Republic of China"), which takes stock of Chinese military power and sustains the belief that China is a threat to US security. Jean-Loup Samaan, a researcher at the NATO Defense College and formerly of the RAND Corporation, has meticulously detailed the Pentagon's fabrication of the theme of the "Chinese threat" and the motives behind it.[2]

In Washington, Eurasia has been clearly identified for over a decade as the main target of American hegemony. In his first foreign policy speech, candidate George W. Bush declared on November 19, 1999: "Today I want to

---

[1] "China Makes Increased Spending a Top Priority as People's Congress Meets," *Washington Post*, March 5, 2013; "中国安全需要10.7%的军费增长" ["China's Security Requires 10.7% Growth in Military Spending"], 环球时报 [*Global Times*], March 6, 2013.

[2] Jean-Loup Samaan, ed., *La menace chinoise: une invention du Pentagone?* (Paris: Editions Vendemiaire, 2012).

talk about Europe and Asia ... the world's strategic heartland ... our greatest priority." A bit further on, he added: "Beijing has been investing its growing wealth in strategic nuclear weapons ... new ballistic missiles ... a blue-water navy and a long-range air force. It is an espionage threat to our country."[3] The US government starts off from a purely ideological postulate: China is an officially Communist state, one of the last survivors of the Cold War. Communist regimes are driven by an aggressive proselytism and seek to overturn democratic regimes through political subversion or force in order to extend their own model of society throughout the world. China, led by a Communist party, is thus today the principal menace to the international community, and its military modernization is aimed solely at ensuring its definitive hegemony in Asia, which would replace the hegemony held by the United States before spreading to the rest of the world. On the Eurasian continent, the postulate goes, China is all the more threatening because it has allied itself with the other great regional power, Russia, which very actively contributes to its military modernization.

The attitude of Europeans in this domain is more ambiguous. Most of the continent's leaders are not convinced that China will eventually represent a military threat. They are on the whole persuaded that a strict application and strengthening of international rules on arms sales, as well as international agreements on regional security and on limiting the arms race, could gradually establish a framework restrictive enough to halt or eradicate hegemonic designs by any power. The ongoing polemic between the Americans and some Europeans over lifting the arms embargo that was imposed after the events of Tiananmen Square in May–June 1989 has its source in precisely this difference of opinion. For the United States, which has made itself the champion of long-term predictive strategic analysis, it is necessary to halt China in its military modernization in order to prevent the rise of a great power capable of truly opposing the directions currently imposed by Washington in many domains. For Europe, it is enough to ensure the respect of the code of conduct on arms sales adopted in 1998 in order to reintegrate China into the international community, while at the same time limiting technology transfers in sensitive sectors. The European approach is indeed political, and not commercial. The lifting of the embargo would in fact be of only limited economic interest, given how few states' arms industries would be likely to benefit, as they would have to share a market that is after all rather narrow. The main effect of the embargo, besides sustaining China's sentiment of being excluded from international debates on collective security, has been to encourage Beijing to accelerate and strengthen its own scientific and technological research, even recruiting foreign experts—particularly Russian experts, who are numerous in the market—and

[3] Governor George W. Bush, "A Distinctly American Internationalism," Ronald Reagan Presidential Library, Simi Valley, California, November 19, 1999.

to accelerate the development of its own defense industry. Moreover, since the Europeans, France and Germany in particular, do not have a military presence in the Far East, as the United States does, their approach to Chinese military power is more nuanced and less focused on the question of Taiwan than is Washington's. The effect of the pressure exerted by the Americans during the first half of 2005—when France was beginning to build a European consensus for lifting the embargo—was to cause Great Britain to reverse its initially favorable position on this issue and to force a postponement of the decision. The simultaneous rise of strongly Atlanticist European leaders—in Germany, France, and Italy—finally put an end to the possibility of the embargo being lifted.

Russia, China's obliging and yet cautious neighbor, has for its part seized the opportunity offered by the Western embargo to position itself as a weapons supplier to Beijing. This market represents a significant commercial interest for Moscow, and also makes it possible, at least for the moment, to create a strategic Chinese-Russian axis that will limit American military expansion in Central Asia. However, this strategic complicity may have it limits: the Russian leaders might start to reconsider their supplying of military technology once Chinese modernization reaches a critical level, when China would be capable of representing a possible threat to Russia's own military capacities. As was shown by the June 2012 conviction by a St. Petersburg court of two Russian scientists accused of having communicated secret information about the intercontinental Bulava missiles to the Chinese,[4] relations between the two countries are still marked by the mutual suspicion inherited from age-old imperial rivalries and from the Sino-Soviet rivalry.

In the end, China contents itself with emphasizing the inoffensive and responsible nature of its military modernization, which, for the Chinese leaders, simply amounts to making up for the considerable time lost during the "revolutionary" years. In fact, "China's peaceful rise" (中国和平崛起; *Zhōngguó hépíng juéqǐ*) would be the culmination of a natural historical process after China's subjection to more than a century of Western and Japanese imperialism that lowered it to the rank of a semicolonial country. Today's development will simply allow China to take its place in the international community, at a level reflecting the height of its human and economic potential, without this rise threatening the security of its partners. Instead, China is reviving the traditional imperial policy of ensuring the pacification of its borderlands, which in the past was done through the payment of a tribute, and today is being done through strong economic interdependence without coveting any direct influence on regions outside this periphery. But the accumulated time lost over decades in the military domain is motivating China to build a credible military power that could, on the one hand, face the regional conflicts that are likely to occur (Islamist terrorism, Taiwan, latent conflict with Japan) and, on the

---

[4] "Two Russian Professors Convicted of Divulging Missile Secrets to China," *Washington Post*, June 20, 2012; "Secrets of Russia's Bulava delivered to China?," *Pravda*, June 25, 2012.

other hand, dissuade the United States, which periodically declares its hostility to the Chinese regime openly, from any direct or indirect intervention in Chinese affairs.

Confronted with these different viewpoints, it is interesting to quickly review the decades that followed the founding of the People's Republic of China, in October 1949, and the vicissitudes of the development of the People's Liberation Army (PLA) until 1978.

Traditionally, the soldier's profession was viewed with contempt in China. A proverb expressed this sentiment perfectly: "Good iron is not used to make nails, honest men do not become soldiers" [好铁不打钉, 好人不当兵; *Hǎo tiě bù dǎ dīng, hǎorén bù dāngbīng*]. In fact, the imperial army was generally in the hands of local lords, and was composed of good-for-nothings who lived off the population and were notorious for abuses of all kinds. Rich or noble families refused to let their children choose the army as a profession, naturally preferring that they enter the Mandarin civil service. When the Republic succeeded the Qing dynasty in 1912, the warlords' troops and the troops of the Kuomintang, the Nationalist Party, perpetuated the tradition of plundering and terror.

Mao Zedong was aware from very early on of the decisive importance of the army for his conquest of power, and devoted special attention to the formation of a "red army" that would be called the "Revolutionary Army of Workers and Peasants" (中国工农革命军; *Zhōngguó gōngnóng gémìng jūn*) beginning in 1928, several months after the Nanchang uprising of August 1, 1927. This army played an essential role not only on the military level, of course, in the war against Japan and the fight against the Kuomintang, but above all in the political conquest of hearts. As a result, for the first time in China's history, the army adopted an exemplary attitude vis-à-vis the population and constituted a veritable "People's army." In December 1929, in his speech entitled "On Correcting Mistaken Ideas in the Party," Mao declared:

> They [who hold the purely military viewpoint] think that the task of the Red Army, like that of the White army, is merely to fight. They do not understand that the Chinese Red Army is an armed body for carrying out the political tasks of the revolution. Especially at present, the Red Army should certainly not confine itself to fighting; besides fighting to destroy the enemy's military strength, it should shoulder such important tasks as doing propaganda among the masses, organizing the masses, arming them, helping them to establish revolutionary political power and setting up Party organizations. The Red Army fights not merely for the sake of fighting but in order to conduct propaganda among the masses, organize them, arm them, and help them to establish revolutionary political power. Without these objectives, fighting loses its meaning and the Red Army loses the reason for its existence.[5]

---

[5] *Selected Works of Mao Tse-Tung*, Volume 1 (Beijing: Foreign Language Press), http://www.marxists.org/reference/archive/mao/selected-works/volume-1/mswv1_5.htm.

But even if the army did play a decisive role, under no circumstances was it to get the upper hand over the Party. In all circumstances, the Party remained the governing political body giving impetus to the army: "Our principle is that the Party commands the gun, and the gun must never be allowed to command the Party."[6]

It was only beginning with the 1955 reorganization, in the aftermath of the 1954 Constitution, that the Chinese armed forces took on a more professional appearance, adopting the Soviet model. The introduction of conscription, replacing simple revolutionary voluntarism, made it possible to select candidates and maintain criteria of quality. A hierarchy was established within the army, and professionalism began to win out over politics. With almost 3 million men under its flag in the middle of the 1950s, the Chinese army was now a force to be reckoned with in the region, as it proved in 1962 during the war with India. However, the Party maintained true authority over the army in order to preserve political orthodoxy. A large proportion of officers were also Party members (90 percent of the oldest officers and 30 percent of the youngest in the 1950s).[7] But this situation, which had been encouraged by Marshall Peng Dehuai—the Defense Minister removed from office in 1959 at the Lushan Conference for having openly challenged the line taken by Mao Zedong—did not survive the Sino-Soviet split and the onset of the Cultural Revolution. Lin Biao, who succeeded Peng Dehuai in 1959 as defense minister, defended the Maoist vision of an army entirely devoted to ideological work, even at the expense of military training. He reinvigorated ideological work within the armed forces both to ensure their loyalty to Mao Zedong and to be himself in Mao's good graces. The success of the military campaign against India in 1962, and then the detonation of the first Chinese atomic bomb in 1964, seemed to prove that the process of repoliticizing the PLA was not detrimental to military expertise. The army even became an example for the Party itself, which took inspiration from its organization to improve its own functioning. Thus, in February 1964, the campaign "Learn from the People's Liberation Army" (学习解放军; *Xuéxí jiěfàng jūn*) was launched. The army's prestige was at its height.

Despite the attempts of some military leaders (Zhu De, Chen Yi, Ye Jianying, Xu Xiangqian) to distance the PLA from the major political movements that periodically swept through China from 1957, the army was crushed under the weight of ideology and the infallibility attributed to Mao Zedong when it came to strategy. The army's loyalty to the founder of modern China never wavered, in spite of sporadic protests that were quickly stifled. In February 1966, just before the official launching of the Cultural Revolution, the sudden intrusion into military affairs by Mao's wife, Jiang Qing, one of the heads

---

[6] "Problems of War and Strategy," November 6, 1938, in *Selected Works of Mao Tse-Tung*, Volume 2 (Beijing: Foreign Language Press), http://www.marxists.org/reference/archive/mao/selected-works/volume-2/mswv2_12.htm.

[7] Jacques Guillermaz, *Le Parti Communiste chinois au pouvoir*, Volume 1 (Paris: Editions Payot, 1979), 208.

of this new radical political movement,[8] reinforced the PLA's politicization in the service of Mao Zedong and the supporters of the Cultural Revolution. Lin Biao's potential rivals within the PLA were pushed aside thanks to various controversies over policy toward the Vietnam War[9] or over what position to take on literary questions. Beginning in 1966, the Cultural Revolution group took control of the military structure and of the cultural sector. Mao Zedong himself threw the PLA into turmoil by calling on it to "support the large masses of the Left," and to stop serving as a refuge for "a handful of Party members who hold power and are taking the path of capitalism," and to give "active support to the large revolutionary masses of the Left in their struggle to take power."[10] The Army could no longer avoid the destructive spiral surrounding it without being crushed. At the Ninth Party Congress, in April 1969, 12 of the 20 members of the Politburo belonged to the army.

After the disappearance of Lin Biao in September 1971,[11] and then that of the chiefs of the General Staff, the PLA gradually weakened and its political role diminished. The post of Defense Minister remained vacant until 1975, when it was filled by the old Marshall Ye Jianying, Vice Chairman of the Party's Central Military Commission (CMC). The PLA then regained its role of defending the stability of the country, under the Party's direction, especially when it came to eliminating the "Gang of Four" in 1976. Until then, the Defense Minister had been the most powerful figure in the PLA, not because of his ministerial position but because of his parallel function as Vice Chairman of the CMC. It was thus natural that the army would claim its part in the reforms beginning in 1978, and military modernization was one of the "Four Modernizations" (四个现代化; Sìgè xiàndài huà), but military authority remained entirely in the hands of the CMC, the Party body responsible for military affairs.

With the implementation of reforms beginning in 1978, the PLA entered into a transitional phase, and its role and influence were called into question. At the moment of Hua Guofeng's replacement in August 1980—he was forced to resign by Deng Xiaoping's clan—the question of the balance of power between the Party and the army arose in a dramatic way. The Party had come out of the Cultural Revolution considerably weakened vis-à-vis the Chinese population. As for the army, in spite of its relative weakness, it continued to matter. Those who wanted to rule the country needed the support of the generals. Hua Guofeng's failure had been in part caused by his inability to assert his

---

[8] During a forum on literature and the arts in February 1966, Jiang Qing took charge of cultural activities within the PLA although until then she had only had sporadic and distant relations with military circles.

[9] The army chief of general staff, Luo Ruiqing, who was close to Lin Biao and was a veteran of the war against Japan, was eliminated for having recommended that the PLA actively prepare a defense of Chinese territory against an eventual American attack from Vietnam. This proposal contradicted the Maoist theory that the enemy should penetrate deep into Chinese territory and then be destroyed by popular war, cutting off its supply lines and gradually defeating it.

[10] Simon Leys, "Les habits neufs du Président Mao," in Essais sur la Chine, rev. ed., Robert Laffont, ed., (Paris: 1989), pp. 54–55.

[11] Lin Biao is said to have been killed on September 13, 1971, when the plane in which he was escaping along with his wife after a coup attempt crashed in Öndörkhaan, in Mongolia.

authority over the military leaders, in spite of Marshall Ye Jianying's declared support for him. When Deng Xiaoping returned in mid-1977 to his positions as Vice Chairman of the CMC and Chief of the Army General Staff, the generals turned away from Hua even more. When Deng became Chairman of the CMC, in December 1980, order was reestablished and the high officers of the PLA swore allegiance to him. Deng's objective was to reestablish unfailing discipline within the Army and to restore the Party's complete control over it.

High-ranking officers had always obeyed Mao Zedong and, when faced with the choice between Mao and the Party, they refused to choose the Party over him. The rehabilitation of Liu Shaoqi, which fundamentally called into question the choices made by Mao during the Cultural Revolution, provoked strong discontent among the generals of the old guard, those who valued above all the reputation of the "Father of the Revolution." The first reductions of the PLA's budget, in 1980 and again in 1981, accentuated the military's dissatisfaction. When the *Liberation Army Daily* published an article in September 1982, just prior to the Twelfth Party Congress, denouncing "certain comrades responsible for the cultural sector" who were accused of supporting liberal bourgeois points of view,[12] Deng Xiaoping considered the army to have crossed a line. Several days after the Congress, Wei Guoqing, Director of the PLA's General Political Department, as well as the Chief of General Staff of the Marines, were dismissed. Deng became aware of the failure of his strategy to regain control of the army. Profound structural changes were necessary.

During the Cultural Revolution, the most prominent army officers had played a defining political role thanks to their revolutionary past, which guaranteed them strong legitimacy. Historically, it was the PLA that allowed the Chinese Communist Party to gain legitimacy with the population and to come to power with popular support. For the first time, the Chinese had found a disciplined army respectful of persons and property, and led by mostly exemplary officers. For the first time, soldiers constituted a veritable army of the people. This defining role played by the army in the conquest of power translated into the massive presence of high-ranking officers in the Party structure after liberation. The PLA's association with the excesses of the Cultural Revolution had greatly damaged its image. During the first years of the People's Republic, the PLA had, willingly or not, supported the political movements that had, over the years and through various reversals of situations, touched every level of the Chinese population. Its reputation was seriously tarnished, and only a return to a policy of professionalization could help improve its reputation and restore its legitimacy. From then on, instead of being called upon to actively participate in the class struggle within China and to support the worldwide revolution abroad, the army was asked to retreat from the political activities in which the Cultural Revolution had involved it, and to fully dedicate

---

[12] *Liberation Army Daily,* September 1st, 1982.

itself to its reorganization and to national defense within the framework of the "Four Modernizations" program. The 1982 Constitution created the CMC, which was placed under the direct authority of the Standing Committee of the People's National Congress (Article 94), and in his speech to the new Congress, Peng Zhen, who was reinstated in 1979, specified that "the Party's leading role in the life of the state, which is explicitly affirmed in the Preamble, naturally includes its direction of the armed forces." This decision was key for the PLA because it broke the link that had until then placed it under the exclusive control of the CMC, and transferred control to the state, making the army simply a part of the state, as in most other countries. By taking the helm of this new structure while remaining chairman of the CMC, Deng Xiaoping ensured a harmony between Party and state decisions. As a consequence, the CMC gradually came to be made up of career soldiers rather than civilians—and thus, politicians—reducing the heterogeneity within it and encouraging a consensus among career soldiers who shared a common experience and tended to develop military policy in a more institutional manner.

## *The popular liberation army in transition*

The political transition that had been prepared throughout the 1990s, and which sanctioned the arrival of a new, "fourth generation" of leaders, took place in several stages between November 2002 and March 2005, when Jiang Zemin officially retired from his final post, as head of the State Central Military Commission, and was replaced by Hu Jintao. The latter, at the age of 61, thus completed the process of harmonizing the entire Party structure (he became General Secretary of the Communist Party of China at the Sixteenth Congress in November 2002 and Chairman of the Party Central Military Commission in September 2004) with the State structure (he became President of the Republic in March 2003). Jiang Zemin, on the other hand, was 67 in 1993, when he became President of the Republic. Despite not having a military or revolutionary past (Jiang Zemin had joined the Party prior to liberation, in 1946, as a student), Hu Jintao succeeded in establishing himself as the leader without provoking any political turmoil, and in winning great popularity for his competence and for his positions, particularly on social issues. This fourth generation of Chinese leaders is now dominated by technocrats with little or no military experience. They joined the Party after the 1949 liberation, and thus have no revolutionary legitimacy. Their collective priority is to enable China to become a great power and, so that this could happen, to maintain the Party's authority in a pragmatic way. They are deeply convinced that only a single strong Party is capable of providing the momentum necessary for economic development and of maintaining this objective in the long term. For these relatively young and pragmatic leaders, the army is only one aspect of Chinese power enabling them to ensure China's territorial integrity against possible outside threats; to affirm China on the regional scene as a power whose concerns must be taken into account; and to contribute to the technological and scientific development of the country, particularly in space technology. In this context, the army must be controlled by high-ranking officers who are themselves technocrats; and for this to happen, it was necessary to facilitate the gradual departure of those who were repositories of revolutionary legitimacy so as to guarantee that there would be a profound change in the relations between the Party and the army. This operation of rejuvenation and professionalization began in early 2002, even before the Sixteenth National Party Congress. A vast shift in personnel directly affected the highest ranks of PLA leaders. The change in directors of four of the PLA's general departments, in the heads of the Academy of Military Sciences and of the National Defense University, and of many officers at the level of the eight military regions was completed during the Congress by the departure of six members of the Party Central Military Commission (CMC) and the arrival of three new members.[13]

As in the Party, the governing bodies of the military sector have become younger overall (average age of 60 instead of 70), which has had indisputable consequences for the approach to modernization and to relations with other countries, particularly with the United States. All the generals who were members of the CMC in 2002 had in common the fact that they had conscientiously climbed the ranks of the PLA without political parachuting. Thus, these were officers who were entirely dedicated to their mission, who were devoted to military modernization, and who had experience managing sensitive issues (the 1989 Lhasa rebellion for Liao Xilong, the antiseparatist operations in Xinjiang in 1990 and 1992 for Guo Boxiong, and the 1989 Beijing uprising for Liang Guanglie; also, all three had conducted military exercises against Taiwan).

With this new team under the leadership of Hu Jintao, a civilian, the Party clearly confirmed its maintenance of the historical line: the Party always commands the gun. But the arrival of this new generation of officers had, of course, an important impact on the policies, doctrines, and strategies that were adopted. Just before the Eighteenth Congress in November 2012, a shifting around of staff at the top of the army solidified a new direction in military affairs. The promotions of certain generals, such as Ma Xiaotian, generally considered to be outspoken—he had, notably, declared in a televised interview in Hong Kong in May 2012 that the United States had no business in the South China Sea—or Zhang Youxia, who drew attention to himself for having criticized the PLA's lack of combat experience in the the the *People's Daily*, seem to indicate a tendency toward greater firmness in the area of defense, especially with regard to the United States.

---

[13] Stephen J. Flanagan and Michael E. Marti, eds., *The People's Liberation Army and China in Transition* (Washington, DC: National Defense University Press, 2003), 43.

# *The evolution of the doctrine*

Chinese thinking on military doctrine and strategy is today largely determined by its confrontation with the United States, which is unfolding in an atmosphere of mutual suspicion and latent hostility. Beijing has integrated several parameters that condition China's strategic vision at the beginning of the 21st century:

- China is more secure today than it has been since the beginning of the 19th century.
- The economic development begun in 1978 is indispensable to its sustained emergence on the international scene, and is heavily dependent on the stability of the country.
- Contrary to the predictions of Chinese analysts, the end of the Cold War did not result in the formation of a multipolar world, but in the increasing power of a single actor, the United States, which opposes Communist China on principle. It will be many years before China can catch up with American military power; thus, China must still build its power.
- For several years, the strategic balance of power in Asia has favored China, which increasingly dominates the Asian continent, whereas the United States dominates maritime Asia.
- Taiwan is a major crisis factor: Beijing can still be content with the current status quo and must absolutely prevent a war, which would be inevitable if Taiwanese authorities were to unilaterally proclaim their independence. To avoid this crisis, it is necessary to keep the pressure on Taiwan to discourage its leaders from taking such an initiative and to develop relations with them based on a convergence of interests, particularly economic interests.

These considerations largely guide the strategic approach of the Chinese leaders and the shaping of military doctrine. The Maoist theory of "active defense" (积极防御; *jī jí fáng yù*) has always dominated Chinese military thinking, from the founding of the People's Republic to the present day.[14] Elaborated in March 1953 by Mao Zedong before the Congress of the Party Commission on Military Affairs (党军事委员会; *dǎng jūnshì wěiyuánhuì*), this concept took into account China's relative military weakness and the need for the PLA to be capable of striking first in order to destabilize the enemy and limit the damage to national territory, preferably by attacking the enemy on its own soil, from the rear. Moreover, this surprise offensive should make it possible

---

[14] An article published in October 2002 on the Chinese Web site www.qianlong.com, with an extract from the book 当代实际军事与中国国防 (*Real Military Affairs and Chinese National Defense*) affirmed by way of introduction that "中国的军事战略是积极防御的军事战略" ("Chinese military strategy is a strategy of active defense").

to shock the enemy, disorganize its defense, and then quickly withdraw into Chinese territory without making any territorial gains. This strategy was used successfully twice: during the Sino-Indian War of 1962 and against Vietnam in February 1979. The basic idea of this strategy is to take the initiative on the battlefield and to keep it. Aware of its military inferiority vis-à-vis the United States, China remains attached to this concept, even if it would be more difficult to apply in the event of a conflict with the United States given the geographic distance and Chinese technological inferiority in terms of intercontinental missiles. However, this strategy could foreseeably be used against American military bases and logistical-support facilities located on China's periphery (in Central Asia, Southeast Asia, and Japan), or against the American naval presence off the eastern coasts of China.

From the end of the 1970s, changes in the nature of the threat led the Chinese leadership to significantly modify the doctrine and strategy of the PLA, while maintaining the concept of active defense as its main course of action. Rapprochement with the United States made the USSR the principal external threat, and the concept of "popular war in modern conditions" (现代条件下的人民战争; *Xiàndài tiáojiàn xià de rénmín zhànzhēng*) was adopted. This was a suite of active defense concepts concerning the risk of conventional land war, supported by nuclear weapons.

But developments in the USSR led to a new direction in strategy. In 1985, during an expanded meeting held between May 23 and June 6, the CMC decided to renounce the preparation of a nuclear war with the USSR after Mikhail Gorbachev's election as the head of the Soviet Communist Party in March and his announcement, barely one month after his election, of a unilateral moratorium on the deployment of intermediate range nuclear missiles in Europe. In addition, an agreement signed on July 23 of that same year between China and the United States outlining peaceful nuclear cooperation between the two countries perceptibly reduced tensions in this area. After this accord, Deng Xiaoping announced the reduction of the PLA by 1 million men, a strategic decision that gave a strong signal to Moscow and Washington of a willingness to deeply reform the Chinese military apparatus.

The demonstration of American technological prowess during the 1991 Gulf War struck the Chinese generals and led to a new change in doctrine. The overwhelming technological superiority of the United States encouraged the emergence of a new concept: "local war under conditions of high technology" (现代高技术局部战争; *xiàndài gāojìshù júbù zhànzhēng*). This meant giving priority to the mobility of forces and to rapid strikes, developing naval and air power, and possibly expanding the use of nuclear weapons. The airstrikes against Yugoslavia in 1999 reinforced this Chinese analysis and accentuated the PLA's feeling of fragility in the face of the American technological giant. From then on, military modernization was accelerated and the acquisition of modern technology became a priority.

Military modernization

For the Beijing authorities, the aim of the PLA modernization process begun in the early 1980s has been to renovate an obsolete military apparatus that had been politicized to the extreme by the Cultural Revolution. The objectives are thus to acquire or manufacture modern weaponry worthy of a great power and to professionalize the military staff.

The Chinese military budget is regularly the object of joint American-Japanese offensives, which were particularly vigorous under the Bush administration, although the subject had already been brought up by China observers under previous administrations. Washington systematically denounces the opacity of the real Chinese military budget for two fundamental reasons: the absence of nongovernmental sources and the fact that defense spending is spread out across several ministries and departments. Some major expenses do not, in fact, appear in the budget that is voted on each year in March by the People's Congress: foreign acquisitions, paramilitary expenditures (for the People's Armed Police), nuclear weapons and strategic missiles programs, state subsidies to the military-industrial complex, certain research expenditures, and extra-budgetary revenues.[15] On the basis of these items, American analysts estimate that China's real military expenditures are probably 40 to 70 percent higher than the official figures. But Beijing's possible dissimulation of part of its defense spending does not prove the existence of a Chinese threat. Several factors must be taken into account in order to make a more balanced assessment of the situation:

1. In 2012, American defense spending reached $729 billion, 41 percent of military spending worldwide—and almost seven times the official Chinese military budget ($106 billion).[16] Japan, which constantly criticizes China for its military spending, allocated $50 billion to defense in 2012, about 1 percent of its GDP.

2. Between 1978 and 1996, the Chinese military budget was relatively stagnant.[17] Regular increases began in 1996 and started accelerating in 2000. What caused the change by 1996? First, there was the Gulf War in 1991, which demonstrated American technological power and terrified the Chinese military and political leadership; then the dissolution of the Soviet Union at the end of the that same year, which left the United States in the dominant position militarily. In the previously mentioned speech on November 19, 1999, then-Texas Governor George W. Bush stigmatized China as an "enemy of religious freedom and a sponsor of forced abortions," and he designated it not as a

---

[15] RAND Corporation, *Modernizing China's Military: Opportunities and Constraints*, Project Air Force (Santa Monica, CA: 2005)

[16] "America's Staggering Defense Budget, in Charts," *Washington Post*, January 7, 2013.

[17] RAND Corporation, *Modernizing China's Military*, 105.

"strategic partner," as Bill Clinton had done, but as a "strategic competitor." He added that China's "regime must have no illusions about American power and purpose." Thus, China found itself raised to the rank of enemy number one of the United States, and had to accept the consequences.

## United States 2011 Defense Spending

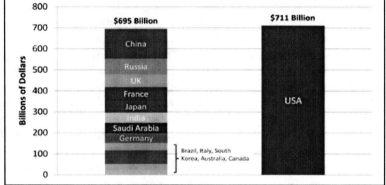

*Source: The Washington Post,* January 7, 2013.

3. The RAND Corporation's 2005 analysis of the Chinese military budget shows that the proportion of military spending relative to public spending had significantly decreased, from 15 percent in 1978 to 8 percent in 2002. Moreover, these expenditures represented between 8 and 10 percent of GDP in 1978, versus about 2 percent in 2012. In such circumstances it is difficult to speak of China's "militarization" when the United States spends $2,314 per inhabitant on its military power, compared to China's $79 per inhabitant.

4. China's geopolitical situation is particularly complex: it has land borders with 14 states (North Korea, Russia, Mongolia, Kazakhstan, Tajikistan, Kyrgyzstan, Afghanistan, Pakistan, Nepal, Bhutan, India, Myanmar, Laos, and Vietnam), three of which belong to the club of nuclear powers (Russia, India, and Pakistan), and undoubtedly a fourth, North Korea. Six others are faced with the presence of violent Islamist movements, while China itself must confront fundamentalist Islamist terrorism in Xinjiang, in the west.

5. In comparison, the United States borders on only two countries—one of which, Canada, is a parliamentary democracy, and the other, Mexico, is a developing country acutely dependent economically on it great neighbor to the north. Even more striking, Japan is an archipelago that since the Second World War has been protected by the American nuclear umbrella, and until recently it could claim to have only one credible military threat, and a very limited one at that: North Korea.

6. Thus, the legitimacy of extravagant American defense spending depends on foreign operations that are justified politically by the roles Washington has assigned itself as defender of the "free" world, policeman, and planetary promoter of the model of parliamentary democracy whose universalism is presented as revealed truth. But this forced "democratization" is perceived by developing countries, especially in the Islamic world, as "Westernization," and on that account provokes violent reactions of rejection.

7. As far as nuclear weapons are concerned, the Chinese nuclear program was initiated in 1954–1955, after the threats made in 1950 by the American President Truman and then in 1952 by his successor, Dwight Eisenhower, who both maintained that they would not hesitate to use nuclear weapons against China in the context of the Korean War. Currently, the Chinese nuclear program seems destined to pass from the stage of minimal deterrent to that of limited deterrent, which implies the ability to face a threat of conventional theater war, and of a strategic nuclear war, and to be able to control any escalation in the event of confrontation. This also implies China's ability to target not only the enemy's cities, but nuclear forces as well. In the last few years, the threat of nuclear power has become one of the coercive instruments of US foreign policy, as we saw prior to America's intervention in Iraq. This dangerous strategy was denounced by former Secretary of State Robert McNamara in May 2005. He stated in the journal *Foreign Policy*: "At the risk of appearing simplistic and provocative, I would characterize current US nuclear weapons policy as immoral, illegal, militarily unnecessary, and dreadfully dangerous."[18]

The modernization that began in the 1980s concerns, in particular, equipment and weapons that had become obsolete in all the sectors. The priority is on bringing the PLA's materials up to par in general, and this is supported by a rather tardy reform—only realized at the end of the 1990s—of the Chinese defense industry. This industry was paralyzed by bureaucracy, budgetary difficulties, and structural and organizational weaknesses. The military's influence over it had been especially reduced by the March 1998 dissolution of the Commission for Science, Technology, and Industry for National Defense, created in 1982. The agency that replaced it has the same name, but it is entirely civilian and under the control of the State Council.[19] Its decision-making power regarding acquisitions of military equipment for the PLA was considerably reduced, and it essentially became an administrative and regulatory entity for the Chinese defense industry. Similarly, a new department was created within the PLA in April 1998, the General Armaments Department, which was henceforth responsible for acquiring military materiel, and which consolidated the supply functions previously assigned to other PLA departments. After a new

---

[18] Robert McNamara, "Apocalypse Soon," *Foreign Policy*, May–June 2005.
[19] Evan S. Medeiros, *Analyzing China's Defense Industries and the Implications for Chinese Military Modernization* (Santa Monica, CA: RAND Corporation, 2004), 6.

reform of the PLA's supply system in October 2002, decreed by Jiang Zemin, the system was rationalized to achieve better overall management and a limitation of corruption.[20]

An examination of the reforms made since the beginning of the 1990s will clearly show that, although China is still heavily dependent on imports of weapons and military technology, its ambition is to gradually reduce this dependence in the most important sectors, such as aerospace science and naval construction. The sanctions imposed by the West on selling arms to China after the June 1989 events in Tiananmen Square, which persist despite all the efforts to have them lifted, are certainly connected to this quest for autonomy—even relative autonomy—when it comes to manufacturing the military equipment needed for modernization. We must also recall that the other major beneficiary of the arms embargo was Israel. The two countries only established diplomatic relations in 1992, following a secret visit to China by the Israeli defense minister, Moshe Arens, during which he negotiated the establishment of military and defense cooperation between the two countries.[21] During the decade following the embargo, Israel became China's second largest military supplier, which gave rise to violent pressure from Washington that, on at least two occasions (in 1999 and in 2005), resulted in Tel Aviv's canceling its military contracts with Beijing, obliging Israel to pay penalties of over $300 million to China.

## *Chinese military adventurism: a realistic hypothesis?*

The central question for Western leaders today is, therefore, to assess the possible consequences of the rise of a China with military capacities on a par with its weight in the international community. This analysis, if it is to be anything more than a flimsy attempt to conceal the expansionism of successive US administrations,[22] must be based on objective political, economic, and military factors. Many American observers, most often neoconservatives or the most conservative members of the right, systematically distort each new Chinese orientation into a demonstration of the Chinese regime's "natural" aggressiveness. Naturally, this approach also makes it possible to throw China at the mercy of Western strategic analysts, so as to divert the attention of the Chinese away from the true current objectives of the White House and to close the ranks of Western democracies around Washington's adventurist policies. Thus, in the United States it is considered good form to denounce China's efforts to modernize its military, and to present them as proof of its ambitions of global hegemony. For several years now, the United States has been the primary vec-

---

[20] Medeiros, *Analyzing China's Defense Industries*, 7.

[21] Jonathan Goldstein, ed., *China and Israel, 1948–1998: A Fifty Year Retrospective* (Westport, CT: Praeger, 1999).

[22] Philip S. Golub, *Power, Profit and Prestige, A History of American Imperial Expansion* (PlutoPress, 2010), 67.

tor of this anti-Chinese rhetoric, while at the same time maintaining a certain ambiguity regarding the concept of a Chinese "threat." The Republican administration that arrived in power in January 2001 stated the problem clearly by calling China a "competitor," and by condemning Bill Clinton's vision of China as a "strategic partner." Every year, the annual report to Congress on Chinese military power highlights the progress made in military modernization in order to instill a heightened vigilance in American leaders and, above all, to justify the constant expansion of the defense budget, which was previously justified by Soviet hostility, and then by "international terrorism." The gradual exhaustion of the image of Islamist terrorism as a major threat to the stability of Western societies has made it necessary to identify an "enemy" seen as more credible by public opinion due to its real capacities for economic, political, and military influence; and today only China has the right attributes to play this role of bogeyman-alibi. Such warnings are regularly repeated by members of Congress, and the US government finds itself caught between the need to reassure elected representatives and the importance of its economic relations with China. President Obama, however, since arriving in power, has tried to convince Americans of the need to gradually reduce the military budget in order to face the most serious economic crisis the United States has seen since 1929, and to place American foreign policy within a more multilateral framework in order to share the financial burden of foreign operations. But he has very little room for maneuver in this domain, which leads him to make ambiguous, vague, and often contradictory declarations. Thus, in May 2012 at Arlington National Cemetery, Barack Obama declared: "I can promise you I will never [send troops into harm's way] unless it's absolutely necessary, and that when we do, we must give our troops a clear mission and the full support of a grateful nation."[23]

Of course, the previous US policy of conquest justified its astronomical defense spending, to the financial benefit of a few corporations largely connected to the team in power in Washington during George W. Bush's two terms. The American military intervention in Iraq in April 2003 demonstrated the manifest collusion between the policies of the Bush administration and industrial groups connected to the war industry.

Although the United States is the primary promulgator of the theme of the Chinese military threat, its ally Japan has now joined in. Japan, whose relations with Beijing worsened considerably during Prime Minister Junichiro Koizumi's term (2001–2006), has officially considered China to be the main threat to its security since December 2004. Tokyo's rhetoric, which has become more and more aggressive toward Beijing, tends to justify the efforts made by conservatives to revise Article 9 of the Constitution, which forbids Japan from keeping a real army and carrying out military activities. This tendency appeared at the beginning of the 1990s and was confirmed in 1995, when the

---

[23] "Obama calls treatment of Vietnam War Veterans 'a disgrace,'" Reuters, May 28, 2012.

National Defense Program was revised for the first time to incorporate the "regions surrounding Japan" into the Japanese defense strategy. But domestic opposition to any hint of remilitarization hindered these developments, until Koizumi's accession to power. Today, Japanese authorities regularly reiterate their "concerns" about China's military modernization, and affirm with increasing clarity their desire to gradually reconstitute a "normal" military apparatus, with Washington's blessings.[24] On January 9, 2007, Japan even re-created a ministry of defense, for the first time since its defeat in 1945, and in January 2013 it announced the first budget increase for defense of the archipelago in 10 years.[25] The new prime minister, Shinzo Abe, has instructed the Japanese military chiefs to review the defense policies adopted in 2010 by the Democratic Party, which planned a gradual decrease in the defense budget and the development of a new five-year plan for military spending.

Thus, Tokyo's current strategy, like that of the United States, consists of grossly exaggerating the threat represented by the modernization of the Chinese military, and exaggerating the threat from North Korea, in order to justify its own remilitarization, with American complicity and military protection. The surge of nationalist fever in Japan these past few years—which has been very noticeable, not only in the powerful inner circles of Koizumi's government and then Abe's, but also among the ranks of the opposition and in public opinion—has broken the taboos inherited from the Second World War, and has opened the way for Japan to reestablish an autonomous defense structure, which in time will undoubtedly be independent from the United States.

Contrary to Japan, whose military adventurism during the first half of the 20th century left indelible traces in Asia, nothing in China's past indicates an inherent expansionist nature whose reemergence the current military modernization might encourage. As the Chinese leaders like to recall aptly, during the period when the empire's flotilla scoured the seas as far as the coasts of Africa, no attempt was ever made to establish trading posts or military bases. After a century-long phase of extreme weakness, China finally regained its unity and a strong central government with the founding of the People's Republic, in which millions of Chinese—finally delivered from Western contempt, the Japanese yoke, and the devastation of the Chinese Civil War—placed their hopes. But the People's Republic quickly stumbled into three decades of ideological turmoil that again generated a veritable civil war, the Cultural Revolution, and led it to the edge of the abyss. It was during this period that China organized its only three military expeditions beyond its borders (the Korean War, the Sino-Indian War in 1962, and the Sino-Vietnamese War of 1979), all of which were intended to loosen the stranglehold that was closing in due to the encirclement

---

[24] On February 10, 2005, in Tokyo, John Bolton stated that the growing assertiveness of Japan, which is seeking to increase its regional and international role and to reshape its defense policy, is a sign that it has become a "normal nation," one "with an interest in its own security." He added: "We are following very closely China's increase in military capacities, in particular its deployment capabilities in the Pacific." Press Roundtable with Japanese Media, U.S. Embassy, Tokyo, Japan, February 10, 2005.

[25] Martin Fackler, "Japan is Weighing Raising Military Spending," *New York Times*, January 7, 2013.

policies of the Soviet Union and the United States, and which were therefore aimed at defending its vital interests.

The military action of February 1979 against Vietnam, which had just overthrown the Khmer Rouge regime and occupied Cambodia, took place at a turning point in Sino-American strategic relations. The two countries had established diplomatic relations on January 1, 1979, a step that Beijing had clearly perceived as American support for its strategy of opposing the expansion of Soviet influence in Southeast Asia. In eastern Indochina, it was a matter of China's signaling to the leaders in Hanoi that their alignment with Moscow, which was obvious since the Socialist Republic of Vietnam joined COMECON in June 1978, had become a threat to China's security that could not be tolerated.

In 1991, two major events radically shifted the strategic landscape for China: the first Gulf War in January–February, and the dissolution of the USSR in December. With the first, Beijing discovered the incredible technological superiority of the United States military and measured the huge gap that separated its own military capacities from those of the country that would henceforth be its principal adversary. This observation would have decisive consequences for China's military modernization. The second event considerably reduced the external pressure on China, but served as a warning to the Chinese leaders. The obvious economic failure of the Soviet Communist Party had led to its total delegitimization in the eyes of the population and to its total collapse; and Chinese leaders had to learn from this failure of Soviet socialism. Finally, the American intervention in Iraq in 2003 and the long-term establishment of American forces at the heart of the planet's premier hydrocarbon-producing region—after the Americans had already established bases in Central Asia, also rich in hydrocarbons, in the aftermath of the military intervention in Afghanistan—represented a major threat to Chinese energy supplies from the Middle East. This last American move spurred Chinese diplomacy and crystallized the rapprochements underway with Russia and India.

The past 25 years have thus led the Chinese government to revise not only its economic policy, but also its strategic doctrine, in order to adapt it to the new international realities and to the emergence of a single superpower whose leaders maintain a hostility toward the Chinese political regime that is sometimes overt, but that is often hidden behind conciliatory discourse, the main objective of which is to avoid upsetting American economic interests vis-à-vis Beijing. This hostility leaves no doubt as to the long-term objectives of the United States: to bring about the disappearance of the Chinese socialist regime, in one way or another. Despite the alternately aggressive and conciliatory declarations from American leaders, this can only incite Chinese leadership to observe US movements attentively, to decode their long-term strategies, and to anticipate hostile American actions against them. With a certain naïveté, American military analysts express their surprise at the Chinese investments in national defense, and at a Chinese military modernization that will give

Beijing "a force capable of conducting a range of military operations in Asia, well beyond Taiwan," despite the fact that "China does not now face a direct threat from another nation."[26] The view from Washington is, of course, that the United States could not possibly be considered a military threat by China, and that China reveals its aggressiveness by "potentially posing a credible threat to the modern militaries operating in the region [Asia]," meaning the American forces deployed all the way from the Pacific Ocean to the Persian Gulf. What would the reaction of Washington be if, by chance, the Chinese navy decided to patrol the Caribbean Sea, on the pretext of maintaining the fragile balance in Latin America threatened by the tensions between the United States and the former president of Venezuela, Hugo Chavez? In reality, dialectical opposition is impossible for a very simple reason: this strategic analysis is based on a concept of "Good" and "Evil," with the world thus divided in an extremely Manichaean manner, which became even more obvious when neoconservatives took power in Washington after September 11, 2001. The United States has the imprescriptible right to crisscross the seas and oceans and to establish military bases the world over because it ensures the triumph of the "forces of Good." China, a Communist state, embodies "Evil," and must therefore remain in a defensive position in all areas. This extremely reductive view of the relations between nations serves as the guideline for American strategy, and consequently justifies US military—and, of course, economic—hegemony. Thus, American analysts candidly affirm that China could be "tempted to resort to force or coercion more quickly to press a diplomatic advantage, advance security interests, or resolve disputes."[27] Isn't this ascribing typically American methods to China? In fact, China is pursuing an economic ascent that requires it to ensure the protection of its vital interests in the medium and long terms, particularly through a parallel development of military power that could ensure a credible level of deterrence. But as we have seen, neither China's history over the past centuries nor its current investments in modernization are causes for any particular fears. Though the prospect of a declaration of independence by Taiwan would generate a crisis, Washington has the leverage to put pressure on the Taiwanese authorities and to impose a greater realism on them. Only a case of America's bungling on the Taiwanese question would really push Beijing into a military endeavor. This seems quite unlikely given the balance of power in the region and the willingness of the new Taiwanese authorities, following Ma Ying-jeou's election in March 2008, to resume negotiations on the details of an eventual reintegration of the island into the Chinese nation.

---

[26]Office of the Secretary of Defense, "The Military Power of the PRC – 2005," *Annual Report to Congress* (Washington, DC), 13.

[27]Ibid., p. 14.

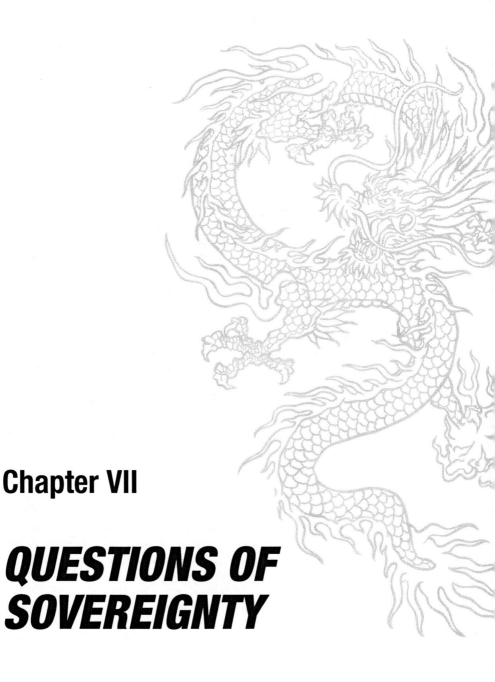

# Chapter VII

# *QUESTIONS OF SOVEREIGNTY*

T he globalized context in which China is emerging onto the international scene, where ideas and commodities spread at increasingly spectacular speeds across the artificial barriers that various actors can periodically erect to protect their economies, their security, or their political systems, is exerting greater and greater pressure on China as it inevitably opens itself. The Chinese nation as it appears today was formed gradually over the centuries out of an aggregate of very diverse peoples who were initially kept at a distance by a policy of containment based on ad hoc alliances and on a network of military strongholds tasked with controlling and stabilizing the borders of the empire, and who were then integrated into this same empire through the annexation of neighboring territories that were supposed to ensure the security of the Chinese whole. This process of forming the Chinese nation was based on a highly interwoven network of relations of subordination, submission, and alliance, which functioned according to very strict rules determined by the imperial court.

At the end of the 19th century, this process was almost complete, after the great Muslim rebellions of the mid-century, and the historic heart of China was surrounded by provinces often inhabited by native populations that had kept their cultural particularities but that, in general, recognized the sovereignty of the Qing court, which was itself Manchu. However, three peripheral regions posed major problems for the empire, each for a different reason. In the east, the island of Taiwan had been ceded to Japan in the Treaty of Shimonoseki (1895), and eluded Chinese sovereignty. In 1933, Xinjiang, which had officially become a Chinese province in 1884, was tempted by an Islamist secession that sought to take advantage of the confusion created by the Japanese invasion of China. As for Tibet, it had always oscillated between military confrontation with imperial troops and recognition of its ties of vassalage to the Qing court. It took advantage of China's weakness and British ambitions in the area to attempt to have its independence recognized. A century later, these three provinces remain problematic for China, and are strategic issues both for Beijing and for outside forces, either state-based or transnational, whose ambition is either to weaken the emerging Chinese power or to break the legal ties that unite these provinces with the People's Republic of China for either religious or ethnic reasons, but always within a highly politicized context.

These movements are taking place within a broader context of isolationism that has been noticeable for over a decade, and that is centered on various parameters (religion, culture, ethnicity, etc.), but fundamentally based on what Sigmund Freud, in *Civilization and Its Discontents*, called the "narcissism of small differences."[1] Real or imagined communities now tend to emerge within the international order and call into question the gains resulting from the formation—especially during the 19th century and the first half of the

---

[1] Sigmund Freud, *Civilization and Its Discontents*, trans. James Strachey (New York: W.W. Norton, 1962), 61.

20th—of economically and politically viable state entities. Those unitary states that had practiced cultural genocide in the process of nation-forming, such as France (which forced the effacement of Corsican, Basque, or Breton cultural specificities, for example, and did the same in Algeria[2]) or Spain (in the case of Basque country), have been for decades confronted with identity-based claims, often violent, which remain today and have not been entirely eradicated. Those countries that, like the United States and Australia, chose total genocide—that is, the physical extermination of native populations (the Native Americans in the United States,[3] the Aborigines in Australia, or the Herero in Namibia[4])— have escaped such claims, insofar as the survivors were too few and were totally subjugated. One must remember that criminal methods were used to this end, and that this history is very close to us. In the United States, the extermination of the Native Americans, for example, took the form of a veritable biological war, in addition to the massacres and deportations. In 1763, before the independence of the United States, the British General Jeffery Amherst, at Fort Pitt (Pennsylvania), for example, ordered his subordinate, Colonel Henry Bouquet, to "spread smallpox among the vermin [the Indians]," to which Bouquet responded that he had done so by means of contaminated blankets.[5] Until around 1890, the Native Americans were massacred in genocidal proportions. American citizenship was not granted to them until 1924, and forced cultural assimilation meant that young Native Americans were sent to boarding schools far from their families. In Australia, the extermination of the original inhabitants of this quasi-continent, the Aborigines, took place over two centuries— physical extermination in the first phase, quickly replaced by a veritable cultural genocide. Until 1970, the mixed-race children of Aborigines were taken from their families and sent to be educated with white families. The political, economic, and social system established in Australia could be compared to the apartheid system that prevailed in South Africa. In the case of Australia, the Aborigines still make claims, but the feeling of cultural inferiority that they had developed over these two centuries has led them to demand the right to be treated "like Whites," rather than the right to cultural difference.

In this context, the policy of the Chinese empire toward the native populations it gradually incorporated under its sovereignty was, it must be emphasized, generally very tolerant of cultural differences—the determining factor for the imperial court not being cultural assimilation but recognition of Chinese

[2]Olivier Le Cour Grandmaison, *Coloniser, exterminer: Sur la guerre et l'État colonial* (Paris: Editions Fayard, 2005). According to French sources from that time, the population of Algeria went from 3 million at the time of the conquest in 1830 to 2,125,051 in 1872, 40 years later; a million individuals thus died in the colonizing process during this period.
[3]Marc Ferro, *Le livre noir du colonialisme* (Paris: Editions Hachette-Pluriel, 2003), 71. The Native American population of the United States was only 250,000 in 1900, about 5 to 10 percent of the original population, which, according to the historian Marc Ferro represents "a demographic catastrophe on a scale probably unique in the history of humanity."
[4]Le Cour Grandmaison, *Coloniser, exterminer*, 89. In a single campaign lasting less than 10 years (1904–1911), the German colonizers brought the population of Herero from 80,000 to fewer than 15,000.
[5]Elizabeth A. Fenn, "Biological Warfare in Eighteenth-Century North America: Beyond Jeffery Amherst," *Journal of American History,* Vol. 86 (March 2000), 1552–1580.

territorial sovereignty. To be somewhat provocative, one could say that China is the victim of its great cultural tolerance, of not having thought of simply exterminating local populations and replacing them with a Han population. The current strength of identity-based demands from certain ethnic minorities in China—especially in Xinjiang and Tibet—demonstrates the problem posed by the nationalist myth, which is largely imported from abroad (the Islamic revival, on the one hand, and the Western spiritual crisis, on the other), and which forces Chinese leaders to search for the most appropriate methods to both preserve Chinese sovereignty over these peripheral regions and respond adequately to some of these cultural demands.

The March 2008 crisis in Tibet and the reactions it provoked abroad demonstrated not just the obvious political manipulations in the West, but also the impact that a certain religious romanticism and the tendency toward identitarian closure has on public opinion. Separatist movements have multiplied in the past two decades, even giving birth to state entities, like Kosovo, that are not economically viable, and that in reality obtain sovereignty but not independence. Their economic and sometimes political fragility forces them to put their destiny into the hands of more powerful nations or groupings of states—the United States or the Soviet Union, for example—and leads to the multiplication of state fictions. These small, artificial states make it possible for some great powers to strengthen their positions within the United Nations. This is the case of the American position when it comes to voting on Iraq, when it always receives the support of Pacific island states, such as the Solomon Islands or the Marshall Islands, that have a fictional sovereignty, but are actually territories under American control.

The growing confusion on the international level between nationalist thinking and the trend toward minority claims was forcefully illustrated in the Tibetan crisis by the gap between, on the one hand, the cultural claims of a portion of the Tibetan population, which hopes to see its cultural specificities recognized more broadly within the Chinese whole and, on the other hand, the deviations from this that have appeared in the discourse of a growing number of Tibetans in exile and their Western allies, who demand Tibetan independence in spite of the realities of contemporary history. Although the European Union has for many years clearly and officially recognized the sovereignty of the People's Republic of China over Tibet, some European leaders have allowed themselves to engage in declarations and commentary that are politically unacceptable with respect to their commitments as statesmen. The real difficulty, both in the case of Tibet and in the case of Uyghur demands, lies in thinking about the rights of cultural minorities according to a model other than the dominant nationalist model, and this can only lead to an increasing number of violent conflicts and a lack of understanding between peoples. Considerable efforts have already been made by the Chinese authorities since the beginning of reforms to give ethnic and religious minorities still greater autonomy, but now there should undoubtedly be a deeper scrutiny of these minorities' claims, in order to clearly identify the nature of these claims, the reasons for the minorities' discontent when it exists, and the solutions that can be found that would strictly respect Chinese national sovereignty. This is urgent because only such a policy can prevent minorities from sinking, as they have in many other countries, into this nationalist mythology, which is often revanchist and violent.

## *Native Muslim minorities*

The situation in Xinjiang involves many actors, both domestic and regional. The question of identity remains subject to various influences, and while the situation has been relatively stable since the end of the 1990s, China is encountering real difficulties in facing these problems and in defining a course of action for meeting the challenges posed by the coexistence of violent transnational movements, cultural demands, populations of very different ethnic origins that are nevertheless forced to live together, and the requirements of national security.

The problem of identity that China is facing today in Xinjiang is in a way rather similar to the problems of certain European countries, such as France or Spain. At its root are aspirations for independence that claim a historical and cultural legitimacy different from that of the annexing nation-state, and which are expressed through alternately peaceful and violent demonstrations for this right to be different. What distinguishes China's situation is precisely the constant concern of the Qing to respect or tolerate religious, cultural, and linguistic specificities within the empire, once the populations concerned had agreed to give allegiance to the central government. In the case of France, as soon as Brittany or Corsica was integrated into the national territory, the Jacobin state hastened to erase all traces of cultural particularism in favor of a single idea, the French nation. Not so long ago, the use of regional languages, including the patois of the Languedoc-Roussillon region, was forbidden in schools, and children were punished for breaking this rule. All the peripheral regions were subject to this policy, which did not really soften until the 1980s, when France's cultural diversity was finally recognized. In spite of these extremely authoritarian measures, and then of a greater openness to regional languages and cultures, autonomist claims still exist, and are sometimes expressed, as in the case of Corsica, with violence. It must also be noted that France, a signatory to the European Charter for Regional or Minority Languages in 1999, in 2008 refused to ratify it, thus going back on its agreement to this European policy of recognizing regional cultures at the very moment it was calling on the Chinese authorities to recognize the cultural specificities of Tibet.

In the 18th and 19th centuries, the Qing did not try to culturally integrate the Turkic-speaking peoples of Xinjiang, who were looked upon with indifference, and sometimes with a certain contempt, and toward whom imperial bureaucrats showed great tolerance, so long as they did not threaten regional stability. The unrest that has troubled Xinjiang since the end of the 1980s is in a way the result of this excessive tolerance toward ethnic and religious minorities on the part of the central Chinese government during the empire, and then later of the very mixed messages sent to these minorities by the Communist authorities. Since the Muslim populations of Xinjiang had not been culturally assimilated between the end of the 18th century and the founding of the People's Republic in 1949, the question of their autonomy within the new republic posed a dilemma for the Chinese leaders that was resolved with an ideological position. As the Soviet Union had done, the Chinese Communist Party decided to grant formal autonomy to the regions in which ethnic minorities formed a majority by creating "Autonomous Regions." Several factors then reinforced the feeling of particularism in Xinjiang, rather than encouraging integration into the Chinese nation, especially among the majority Uyghurs:[6]

- The creation of a "Xinjiang Uyghur Autonomous Region" with clearly demarcated borders, offered an ideal framework for Uyghur political fantasies.
- The institutionalization of minority identities, and the privileges accorded to them based on this criterion, greatly reinforced these identities.
- These legal and ethnic bases for recognizing the Uyghurs gave them an international audience, though it was only with the start of violent demonstrations in the 1990s that certain foreign groups mobilized in support of them, essentially out of religious solidarity.

There is, in addition to these criteria identified by Anglo-Saxon authors, another one that they refrain from pointing out: the considerable influence of transnational Islamist movements, beginning in the 1980s, on activists abroad, either through Wahhabi Islamist networks or through strategists determined to use the religious aspects of this identity-based malaise to weaken China, similar to the support once given to Afghani *jihadists* against Soviet troops. Indeed, China has a major strategic stake in Xinjiang, and the region's destabilization would have incalculable consequences on its long-term aspirations for power.

Xinjiang, which became the Xinjiang Uyghur Autonomous Region on September 13, 1955, has several specific characteristics that distinguish it from other provinces:

- its surface area (617,763 square miles, 16.6 percent of the national territory), with 3,355 miles of borders that place it in contact with

---

[6]Gardner Bovingdon, "Autonomy in Xinjiang: Han Nationalist Imperatives and Uyghur Discontent," *Policy Studies* 11 (Washington, DC: East-West Center, 2004), 4.

eight countries (Mongolia, Russia, Kazakhstan, Kyrgyzstan, Tajikistan, Afghanistan, Pakistan, and India);

- the significant native Muslim population (62 percent of the region's population, nearly 11 million people), which places Xinjiang first among the Chinese Muslim provinces;
- its energy resources, which represent about 25 percent of the nation's resources, particularly in oil and natural gas;
- its key location for Chinese energy supplies, because any imports of hydrocarbons from Central Asia must cross the region from west to east (this explains the extreme sensitivity of Xinjiang for Chinese authorities, and the interest other powers may have in maintaining, and even stirring up, tensions and chronic instability in this strategic zone); and
- its importance to the Chinese military, since nuclear tests have been carried out since the beginning of the 1960s at Lop Nur, in the west of Xinjiang.

Xinjiang is thus the most fragile zone in China's national territory, the one that poses the greatest number of challenges, which are also the most closely tied to the country's outer periphery. This region is situated at a strategic crossroads of Central Asia, on China's outer borders, and thus for centuries it has been subject to diverse and often antagonistic influences from the four corners of Asia.

# Xinjiang in the Chinese nation

Islam reached Xinjiang in the 10th century, under the Song dynasty, and gradually replaced Buddhism. By 552, the "Blue Turks" had overwhelmed the Mongolian and Indo-European peoples of Central Asia and extended their grip as far as Bactria and Sogdiana. Beginning in the 8th century, Islam conquered Central Asia, causing the disappearance of Zoroastrianism and the retreat of Buddhism from the region. With the disappearance of Buddhism from Xinjiang, a cultural break took place between the local populations and the Chinese. But it was only starting in 1513 that Islam definitively became the religion of the Uyghur and Kazakh populations, and of all the Turkish-speaking populations of the oases of the Tarim Basin. From the 17th century onward, Islam strengthened its hold over Xinjiang when a Sufism of Central Asian origin penetrated the region. Until the conquest of the region by the Qing dynasty, in the 18th century, Chinese influence over the native populations was very limited. The Chinese presence had until then been limited to the great oases of the east, in particular Turpan and Kumul (Hami). The relations between the local populations and Central Asia, and with the Turkish and Persian cultures, were much closer than those they maintained with China. The great Muslim capitals of that time, such as Baghdad, actually had closer relations with Beijing than did, for example, Urumqi.

It was not until the middle of the 18th century that Chinese sovereigns, at the height of their territorial expansion, decided to definitively place Xinjiang under their control. The military expansion of the Qing was unprecedented at the time: they embarked on conquests of the territories of the Mongol Dzungars,[7] the Turkestanis, the Miao (or Hmong), the Taiwanese, the Burmese, the Gorkhas, and the Annamese. In 1759, Emperor Qianlong conquered the region of the Tian Shan mountains, and named the section of the steppes extending north from this mountain range "Dzungaria," and the section to the south of these mountains "East Turkestan" (land of the Turks). The two zones were joined into one imperial dependency under the name of Xinjiang (新疆; Xīnjiāng, or "new frontier"), which was henceforth governed as a military colony under a military governor based in Ili (renamed "Ningyuan"; "Kulja" for the Russians, and today known as "Yining") who was assisted by deputy military governors, imperial agents, and over 20,000 troops stationed throughout the territory. With the definitive annexation of Turkestan and Ili, China expanded its empire by almost 579,153 square miles. Most of the high government officials and officers were Manchus and members of the Banners,[8] and they ruled over the population—for the most part Turkish-speaking Muslim Uyghurs—through the intermediary of local chiefs known as *begs*. The Manchu conquerors treated their Muslim subjects as uncivilized aborigines, levying very high taxes on them and demanding forced contributions to finance their extravagances. Ili was in reality no more than a large garrison, and the principal mission of the military governor was to maintain supervision over the peripheral regions of Kokand, Tashkent, Bukhara, Bolor (an ancient name for the Gilgit Valley now in Northern Pakistan), Badakhshan, Afghanistan, and Kanjut. The policy of the Qing was to interfere as little as possible in the lives of the local populations, but the Chinese officials in Xinjiang never made any effort to learn the languages and customs of the peoples they were governing.

In Xinjiang, the Qing carried out a policy of collaboration with the local religious establishment. Land and buildings belonging to the *waqfs*[9] benefited from a constant tax exemption; and the sheiks in charge of tombs and religious edifices, most of whom were Sufis or descended from saints, prospered. Even

---

[7] Dzungaria is situated to the north of the Tian Shan mountain range, and is part of the steppes.

[8] Surrounded by Chinese advisors, Nurhaci decided to distinguish the different regiments by the colors of their flags. This is the origin of the *qi*, the "Banners," military units with symbolic colors that were inaugurated in 1601 and that multiplied during the Manchu conquests. At the same time, the Banners incorporated foreign, especially Chinese, elements—whence the difference between the outer Banners, corresponding to auxiliary troops, and the inner Banners, formed of "authentic" Manchus. As a whole, it was one of the most efficient systems of military organization.

[9] In Islamic law, *waqfs* are assets that result from the donations of individuals to an institution for the benefit of the public, religious or charitable, and these assets become inalienable.

in the regions governed by autonomous hereditary sovereigns, such as Hami or Turpan, the princes had total freedom over the native populations, while the Chinese immigrants were under the direct control of the Chinese government.

But at the beginning of the 19th century, Jahangir, grandson of Burhan al-Din, a religious dignitary whom the Qing had chased into Badakhshan, led a rebellion. He declared *jihad* and assembled an army of several hundred men, mostly Kyrgyz. For several years, Jahangir led the struggle against the Chinese government before finally being led into a trap in 1828. The capture of the *Khoja* was presented by Beijing as a great victory, after seven years of fighting, the aid of 36,000 men, and over 10 million silver taels spent. But many thought that the Qing victory was in reality due to divisions among the East Turkestanis. The prisoners were exhibited in Beijing and executed. The Qing then sought to bring the rebellion to a definitive end.

In order to attempt to pacify the region, Beijing broke with the Manchu tradition of segregation in Central Asia and, in 1831, approved the immigration of Han civilians from China to Xinjiang and even to Altishahr, which until that time had been specially protected from migrations so as not to upset the religious leaders of this very sensitive region. An embryo of a Han population had begun to form. In the middle of the 1830s, 200 Han Chinese merchants were permanently established in Yarkand and many others came and went. Chinese became the dominant language, along with Turkic languages.

In the century that followed the Qing conquest, a dozen uprisings and invasions took place. In 1864, during a dynastic decline and a Muslim rebellion in the northwest of China, the Muslims of Xinjiang struck again. The local Qing administration was too weak to stop them, and the central government in Beijing was too busy with the Taiping, Nien, and other rebellions to take punitive actions. Yaqub Beg, a general from Kokand, entered Xinjiang in 1865 and declared himself ruler of Kashgaria, and of a part of northern Xinjiang in 1870. Xinjiang then became the prey of British and Russian imperialist designs: both empires sought from then on to weaken the Beijing court's authority over the region. The British in India encouraged the construction of Yaqub Beg's empire in order to curb Russian influence, and they sent missions to him to maintain cordial relations and supply him with weapons.

The Russians were disturbed by these developments, and saw the empire of Yaqub Beg (阿古柏; *Ā gǔ bǎi*) as an expansion of British influence. Furthermore, the troubles in Xinjiang had affected Russian trade and created instability among the Kazakhs, the Kyrgyz, and other minorities in Russia. The Russians then decided to occupy Ili until Chinese authority was reestablished over Xinjiang, and planned to return it in exchange for new commercial roads toward western China and for certain border rectifications. In July 1871, General Konstantin Petrovich von Kaufmann, the first governor-general of Russian Turkestan, occupied Ili with his troops. But it seems that St. Petersburg thought China would be unable to retake Xinjiang. In order to perpetuate the disorder and maintain their own occupation, the Russians signed a trade treaty with Yaqub (阿古柏) in 1872; the British followed suit one year later. By the end of 1877, all of Xinjiang had been reconquered, with the exception of Ili, which was still in the hands of the Russians. But the February 24, 1881, Treaty of St. Petersburg returned most of Ili to China. In 1884, Xinjiang was incorporated into the empire and became a full-fledged province of China.

It was in the 1930s that the challenge to Chinese power reappeared in Xinjiang. In November 1933 the first "East Turkestan Republic" was founded, in Kashgar. It brought together Uyghur, Uzbek, and Kyrgyz leaders. The new republic immediately adopted Islamic law, *shari'a*, and persecutions of Christian missionaries took place in Khotan. This new state drew the hostility of the Nationalist government in Nanjing and that of the Soviet Union, which feared that the Japanese, after having annexed Manchuria and invaded Inner Mongolia, would extend their influence to Xinjiang and annex it, too. The East Turkestan experiment came to an end in 1934 thanks to a convergence of interests between the Dungans (Chinese Muslims) and the Soviets. Until 1941, due to the weakness of the Nanjing government and the civil war raging in China, Xinjiang remained a satellite of the Soviet Union. The Kuomintang only regained control over the region in September 1944. A second anti-Chinese rebellion then took place, this time in Yining, in October of the same year. A Muslim religious leader, Elihan, proclaimed the "Islamic Government of Turkestan." This entity was quickly forced into negotiations by a collaboration between China and Russia, which signed a Treaty of Friendship and Co-operation in August 1945, thus depriving the rebels of Soviet support against the Chinese government. Stalin acknowledged that the issue of Xinjiang was part of China's "internal affairs." The situation remained complicated until the Communists' complete victory in October 1949—the Kuomintang and the leaders of the Yining rebellion had formed a heterogeneous coalition government that could not survive the fundamental antagonism between the Nanjing government's ambitions and those of the rebels.

## The populating of Xinjiang

In reality, Central Asia, at the crossroads of Turkish, Mongolian, and Chinese influences, was referred to as "Turkestan," or "land of the Turks," beginning in the 12th and 13th centuries, without this denomination ever corresponding to any state or real cultural identity. Although Chinese influence had been very weak until the Qing conquest, the peoples of the region had never constituted a coherent cultural, linguistic, or religious entity in relation to external influences.[10] At the end of the 18th century, the region called "East Turkestan" was inhabited by mainly by Turkish-speaking populations, with the exception of a

---

[10]S. Frederick Starr, *Xinjiang: China's Muslim Borderland* (Armonk, NY: M.E. Sharpe, 2004), 327.

small minority that spoke Tajik, a language derived from Persian. The population at the time was less than 300,000. All accounts from that period indicate that these populations of East Turkestan had no particular name by which to designate themselves as an identifiable ethnic group. They all simply used the names of their oases of origin. It was the British and Russians who, extending their imperial ambitions to Central Asia in the 18th century, used the term "Turkestan" again.

## Population of Xinjiang

|          | 1941 | 1964 | 1990 | 2000 |
|----------|------|------|------|------|
| Uyghurs | 2,984,000 | 4,021,200 | 7,195,000 | 8,345,622 |
| Han | 187,000 | 2,445,000 | 5,696,000 | 7,489,919 |
| Kazakhs | 326,000 | 501,400 | 1,106,000 | 1,245,023 |
| Hui | 92,000 | 271,100 | 682,000 | 839,837 |
| Kyrgyz | 65,000 | 69,200 | 140,000 | 158,775 |
| Other | 76,000 | 133,500 | 337,900 | 383,424 |
| *Total* | *3,730,000* | *7,441,800* | *15,156,900* | *18,462,600* |

At the beginning of the 19th century, Xinjiang already had several hundred thousand Chinese inhabitants. There were, on the one hand, the troops of various garrisons and their families. These garrisons represented a heavy financial burden for the imperial government, which the taxes levied lightened in only a very symbolic way. But the Qing court had decided to encourage the settlement in the region of Tian Shan of several hundred thousand Chinese from the inner provinces, as well as Chinese Muslims, called "Dungans" by the Turkestanis, who were Sunnis divided between Hanafism and Shafi'ism.[11] The authorities converted vast regions of pastureland into civil colonies (户屯; *hù tún*), particularly in the districts of Barköl, Turpan, and Ürümqi.

In western Xinjiang, where the Chinese presence was weaker than in the east, the Qing pursued a strict policy of segregation by isolating the populations of Altishahr from the Han Chinese in order to prevent the latter from taking economic control of the region and thus provoking anger and rebellions on the part of the Turkestanis. On the cultural and religious levels, the authorities avoided interfering and, after the conquest, allowed the Turkestanis

---

[11]The Shafi'i school originated in the 9th century with Muhammad ibn Idris al-Shafi'i, who had acquired his religious learning through his travels before settling in Cairo.

to keep their Islamic calendar and to wear their traditional clothing, and they did not require the Turkestanis to wear a queue (braid), with the exception of the *begs*. The conflicts that arose between Chinese and Muslims were settled according to Islamic law. The first great wave of Han Chinese immigrants came in 1832 and established settlements in Qara Qoy, near Barchuk, in the district of Kashgar. In 1834, Beijing changed its policy and ordered the Chinese settlements to be taken down. But the next year, before the decision was carried out, the government changed its mind once again, and reinstated the colonies. From then on, Beijing encouraged poor populations to emigrate to Xinjiang, in particular to Altishahr.

## The particular case of the Bingtuan (生产建设兵团; shēngchǎn jiànshè bīngtuán), the Xinjiang Production and Construction Corps

The *Bingtuan* system has given rise to many polemics, and today it is one of the major subjects of dispute concerning the presence of Han Chinese in Xinjiang, so it is important to mention it here. The *Bingtuan* originated with the Maoist vision of the role of the people's army, one of whose main missions is to actively participate in production. It was for this reason that, in October 1954, the Communist Party of China (CPC) decided to form the Xinjiang Production and Construction Corps by bringing together elements of the First, Second, Fifth, and Sixth armies, which had participated in the liberation of the region in 1949.[12] The *Bingtuan* were entrusted with the development of several hundred thousand hectares of land in order to accelerate the economic development of the region, while at the same time maintaining a predominant role in defending the territories' borders and maintaining public order. According to Chinese sources, 20 percent of these troops would remain responsible for public order and 80 percent would devote themselves to economic tasks. In fact, the settlements were a continuation of the pioneer farms, which had been established in the peripheral regions of China during the Han dynasty (206 BC–220 AD) and the Tang dynasty (618–907), and reinforced under the Qing dynasty, beginning in the 18th century.

The *Bingtuan* were also touched by the troubled periods of the Great Leap Forward and the Cultural Revolution, the consequences of which were undoubtedly determining factors in the emergence of separatist claims. Beginning in 1964, the government organized massive population movements from the overpopulated provinces of the east, in particular the region of Shanghai, to Xinjiang. Hundreds of thousands of young people moved to the region, and the *Bingtuan*, while remaining auxiliaries of the People's Liberation Army,

---

[12] 德洙 [De Wei], 新疆知识简明读本 [*Concise Guide to Knowing Xinjiang*] (Beijing: Wenhua, 2003), 105. It was 193,000 according to Chinese sources; Starr, *Xinjiang: China's Muslim Borderland*, 90. It was 100,000 according to Starr.

gradually became more civilian in nature. Their settlements were used as detention camps, thus becoming a part of the larger system of *laogai*: forced labor. The statistics regarding this point are, however, untrustworthy and most often contradictory. According to certain authors, the incarcerated population was 144,000 in 1954 and 120,000 in 1965,[13] while many other sources estimate that the total population of the *Bingtuan* was about 200,000 in 1954.[14] Whatever the case may be, the *Bingtuan* evolved over the years and gradually ceased to serve as prisons. In March 1975, as the Cultural Revolution was coming to a close, the authorities decided to end the system, and the *Bingtuan* were disbanded. Today, official sources cite their disappearance as the main reason for the economic difficulties the autonomous region encountered in the 1970s.[15] Their reestablishment in December 1981 by Deng Xiaoping gave a new momentum to the system, and the *Bingtuan* quickly took a central place in the economic development of Xinjiang. According to the *People's Daily*, beginning in 1984 they have been responsible for 25 percent of Xinjiang's agricultural and industrial production and today employ 2.5 million people, occupying 7,433,000 hectares, of which 1,600,000 hectares are under cultivation.

The *Bingtuan* are criticized for the overwhelming predominance of Han in their ranks (85.5 percent of the *Bingtuan* population in 2011), and they are accused of representing a veritable instrument for populating non-Chinese regions with Han. Indeed, the growth of the Han population, which went from 200,000 in 1954 to 2,680,000 in 2011—12.3 percent of the total population of the autonomous region[16]—took place almost exclusively through the settlement of hundreds of thousands of Han Chinese from the interior of the country during various periods. Thanks to this system, a Han population has settled in the oases of the southern Tarim Basin, for the first time in the history of western China. Of particular importance for the Chinese authorities, the *Bingtuan* guarantee the defense of Xinjiang's 1,253 miles of borders, which gives them a capital role in the current context. Confiding the task of defending the borders to these corps, which are overwhelmingly made up of Han, is an implicit sign of distrust of native populations, including, of course, the Uyghurs, who represent the majority of the natives in Xinjiang. But this situation, which corresponds to a stage in the country's development and to a specific security context—and which has been tense since the former Soviet republics of Central Asia gained independence, on account of the rise of Islamist fervor—could evolve in the years to come if mutual trust is finally established between the minority nationalities population of Xinjiang and the central government thanks to economic development and its impact on the standard of living of native populations.

---

[13] Jean-Luc Domenach, *Chine: l'archipel oublié* (Paris: Editions Fayard, 1992), 466.
[14] Starr, *Xinjiang: China's Muslim Borderland*, 90.
[15] *Concise Guide to Knowing Xinjiang*, 107.
[16] 兵团第六次全国人口普查暨兵团人口统计主要数据公报 [*Sixth National Census of the Bingtuan and Report on the Main Statistical Data on the Bingtuan Population*], Bureau of Statistics of the 3rd Division Bingtuan, July 14, 2012.

## Outside influences

On the religious level, though all the peoples of this region were converted to Islam and belong to the Hanafi[17] Sunni branch of Islam—with the exception of the Kyrgyz, who adopted Shiism—there nevertheless remain important differences among religious factions and the Sufi brotherhoods. The latter have always played an essential role in the Islam of Central Asia, and have long been considered by the Communist authorities, Soviet and Chinese alike, as dangerous breeding grounds of Islamist and nationalist resistance. The most important among these, the Naqshbandi order, established itself solidly in Xinjiang, where, in the 16th century, Kashgar became the second Naqshbandi center after Bukhara, its spiritual center.[18] The order particularly distinguished itself by leading "holy wars" against Buddhists in Turkestan in the 17th and 18th centuries, and then against the Russians in the Caucasus at the beginning of the 20th century. However, today it is impossible to assess the activities and real influence of the Sufis of Xinjiang.[19]

Two factors came together at the end of the 1980s to give a new impetus to religious demands in Xinjiang. With the end of the Cultural Revolution and its excesses, the native Muslim populations entered a new era, not only economically, with the beginning of Deng Xiaoping's reforms, but also culturally and religiously. Ethnic minorities regained a cultural and religious freedom that suddenly allowed them to express their particularities with respect to the Han population. In Xinjiang, hundreds of mosques were built, religious dignitaries returned to teaching, and minority languages regained their place under the terms of the Constitution. In this context of near-euphoria, certain groups began to claim even greater autonomy from the central government and, behind closed doors, to denounce the difference in standards of living in Xinjiang between the Han population and the ethnic minorities.

This identity-based movement, following a traditional pattern, resulted in part from Uyghurs' discontentment at the discrimination they faced in employment, notably in the public sector and, on the political level, from their weak representation in the regional government and especially within the Party. This situation indeed testified to the lack of confidence the Chinese authorities had in these minorities, who were always kept at a distance from political power—the power of the Party, not of the State. On an economic level, the relatively poor employment situation of the non-Han populations of the region was, and remains, not only the result of a certain distrust of Muslims, but also of a linguistic divide produced by the proclaimed will to respect

---

[17] This legal school was founded in the 8th century by Abū Hanīfa, member of the Kûfa school, which served the Caliph Harun al-Rashid. The school was adopted by the Seljuq Turks and spread throughout Central Asia, South Asia, and China.

[18] Alexandre Bennigsen and Chantal Lemercier-Quelquejay, *Le soufi et le commissaire: les confréries musulmanes en URSS* (Paris: Editions du Seuil, 1986), 65.

[19] Starr, *Xinjiang: China's Muslim Borderland*, 336.

local, non-Han cultures. In fact, primary school and high school were taught in minority languages, and Chinese was relegated to a second language. In spite of the autonomy officially granted to minority regions—which is manifested symbolically at the central level by the multitude of interpreters providing translations of all the Popular Assembly debates in Beijing—administrative relations between the provinces and the center are carried out in Chinese, and so it is difficult to imagine any non-Chinese-speaking government official in a position of power beyond the strictly local level. This is, incidentally, exactly the problem raised by the French government in its refusal to ratify the European Charter for Regional or Minority Languages. This obstacle can only be removed by expanding the teaching of Chinese as a first language to the entirety of the population, as is the practice in the United States and in European countries that have integrated linguistically diverse populations into their national space—but this policy raises accusations of *sinicization* and of cultural integration of minority populations. However, it would seem rational that all citizens of a state—whether it is a unitary state with strong autonomous regions, or a federal state—be capable of expressing themselves in the national language: both out of a long-term concern for reducing conflicts among different groups and out of a concern for giving everyone the same chances in terms of education. Higher education in China takes place in Mandarin.

This identity malaise was reinforced by the regional geopolitical context. In effect, the Soviet intervention in Afghanistan in 1979 was a wake-up call to radical Sunni Islamism in Central Asia. The US support for Afghan *jihadist* fighters and their ultimate victory over the Soviet Union strengthened radical Islamist movements in the Middle East and in Central Asia. The Islamists' rise to power in Afghanistan, the disintegration of the Soviet Union in 1991, the birth of the new republics in Central Asia, and the Taliban's taking power in Kabul all contributed to generating Islamist separatist currents in Xinjiang that benefited from powerful outside support.

The first violent expressions of this new trend appeared at the end of the 1980s in the interior of the country. Certain identity-based movements began to express themselves openly, and hundreds of Uyghur students took to the streets in Beijing to demand greater autonomy. Unsettled by the information concerning radical Islamists coming from Central Asia, in March 1990 the central government launched a campaign against Islamic fundamentalism, to which the Islamic Party of Eastern Turkestan, a predominantly Uyghur Islamist movement, responded a month later with a call to *jihad* aimed at obtaining Xinjiang's independence. On April 5, the first major riot took place near Kashgar and led to the death of some 50 Uyghur protesters and police. The Chinese authorities later accused Osama Bin Laden of having inspired this riot. Beginning in 1991, the attacks in Xinjiang multiplied, and reached a high point in 1997 and 1998. A number of these attacks targeted local religious leaders who were accused of collaborating with the Chinese authorities. In fact,

Islamist radicalism seems mainly to have touched young Uyghurs, who have challenged their elders' wisdom and their refusal to adopt the Wahhabi version of Islam that the younger Uyghurs had discovered in Afghanistan. Thus, the Uyghur population was confronted with a veritable generational conflict.

The undeniable infiltration of Islamist ideas into Xinjiang seems to have come mostly from young Uyghurs who fought in Afghanistan or received paramilitary training there or in Pakistan. The armed movement known as ETIM (East Turkestan Islamic Movement) was effectively established in Kabul during the Taliban regime, and was even incorporated into the Taliban "Ministry of Defense." The demands expressed on multiple occasions during public demonstrations in Xinjiang in the 1980s and 1990s included not only slogans against the Han population and the Communist Party, but also calls for "the establishment of an Islamic caliphate,"[20] the creation of an "Islamic Republic of East Turkestan," and *jihad* against the Communist regime.[21]

Faced with this increasingly active opposition, as much within the country as abroad, the Chinese authorities were forced to react to preserve China's strategic interests and to guarantee its security. At first, its reaction was conditioned by security concerns, and it demonstrated China's complete lack of anticipation and analysis of the phenomena developing in its western regions. China was taken by surprise by the appearance of radical Islamism. Priority was given to reestablishing order, and the repression fell heavily on the Uyghur population, apparently in a rather disorganized fashion, with the forces of order unable to distinguish between Islamist and separatist activists and demonstrators simply expressing their discontent. These events created tension in interethnic relations in Xinjiang, and led to a rapid polarization over cultural and religious claims. Some authors see greater cultural autonomy as the solution to the problems of Muslim fundamentalism in China, as they judge that Salafi Islam "has been and will continue to be largely unwelcome in Uyghur society. The young will only become radicalized if they sense that their language and religion are under threat."[22] The Chinese, for their part, tend to reduce the antagonism of native Muslims to an economic problem, and think that they have found the solution in the implementation of the Great Development of the West policy (西部大开发; *xībùdàkāifā*), which they think will make it possible to drive back this Islamist threat and, combined with an unrelenting repression of troublemakers, to eliminate it.

Although there is undoubtedly some truth to these two approaches, they are too quick to discount external factors, which in many countries play a fundamental role in the penetration of Salafi Islam. In open societies such as France, where there is complete freedom of religion, Islamist preachers have

[20]Michael Dillon, *Xinjiang: China's Far Northwest* (New York: RoutledgeCurzon, 2004), 60.
[21]Bovingdon, "Autonomy in Xinjiang," 8.
[22]Arienne M. Dwyer, "The Xinjiang Conflict: Uyghur Identity, Language, Policy, and Political Discourse," *Policy Studies* 15 (Washington, DC: East-West Center, 2005), 3.

multiplied in the past few years, and they find an attentive audience, especially among youths craving a sense of identity. Among the bourgeois and intellectual classes of most Muslim countries, this same Islam has been propagated and now defies the framework long used to classify people as sympathizers or fundamentalist activists. In both cases, the success of Salafi Islam is based neither on economic inequalities nor on a lack of religious freedom, but rather on the power of transnational networks that have found fertile grounds. Without these networks and their financial power, this malaise would be expressed sporadically but would not be able to spread or bring people together.

Over the past 20 years, these outside influences have varied in nature but have come together to contribute to the emergence of a latent challenge to Beijing's authority in Xinjiang and of some major identity-based claims. Certain external factors have played a determining role in the rise of identity fervor among native Chinese Muslims.

• *The role of Turkey*: The independence of Turkic-speaking peoples in what was formerly Soviet Central Asia has led Turkey to believe that it could unite these peoples around a concept of Turkishness, which would have justified Ankara's dominant position in Central Asia. Naturally, this Pan-Turkism applied to all the Turkic-speaking populations of Central Asia, even though linguistic, cultural, and historical differences between them and Turkey would seem to make such an alliance highly improbable. This Turkish offensive translated into a significant cultural activism around Turkic-origin languages and elements of cultural convergence among these peoples. Because Turkey never formally recognized Chinese sovereignty over Xinjiang, relations between Peking and Ankara became tense. Uyghur groups living in Turkey and supported by Turkish nationalists organized demonstrations demanding the independence of Xinjiang and respect for the rights of the Uyghur Chinese population. Some sources even maintain that former Turkish militants directed Uyghur training camps in the east of Turkey. In Xinjiang, Pan-Turkism was represented by two armed groups, the East Turkestan Radical Youth Group, whose members trained in Afghanistan and allied themselves with the Uyghur Liberation Organization, which was established in Uzbekistan and Kyrgyzstan; and the United National Revolutionary Front of East Turkestan, particularly known for its assassinations of Muslim religious figures favorable toward Chinese policies. Abroad, this Pan-Turkish vision is spread by the East Turkestan Information Group, whose headquarters are in Germany.

But since the end of Süleyman Demirel's presidency in May 1999, the foreign policy of Turkey in Central Asia has regained some realism in the face of the weak results obtained after a decade of activism in Central Asia. On October 22, 2003, the Chinese and Turkish interior ministers signed a "Document of Consensus" concerning Xinjiang and terrorism in which

Turkey officially recognized Xinjiang as an "inalienable part of Chinese territory" and committed to fighting against activities aiming to divide China's
territory. However, the Turkish government, torn between the Islamism of
the AKP, the party in power, and the increasing nationalism of a growing
part of Turkish society and of political circles, has a very ambiguous policy
on this issue, alternating between economic engagement with Beijing and
undiplomatic declarations, such as the call by the Turkish minister of industry and commerce in July 2009 for a boycott of Chinese products following
incidents in Xinjiang,[23] or the declaration by Prime Minister Recep Tayyip
Erdoğan that same month describing these events as "a kind of genocide."[24]
Consequently, mutual suspicion continues to define the relations between
the two countries, and only the economic aspect of this partnership can, at
this stage, keep tensions at an acceptable level. Nevertheless, following the
rapid degradation of Turkey's relations with Israel after the December 2008
invasion of the Gaza Strip, Ankara has attempted a rapprochement with
China, which led to China's participation in October 2010 in the annual
"Anatolian Eagle" exercises, which, since they began in 2001, have been
dedicated to strengthening Turkey's ties to NATO. This was the first time
that China participated in joint exercises with a member state of NATO.
In the context of the Turkish AKP's current strategy of gradually turning
its back on Europe and, more prudently, on the United States in order to
position itself as the leading partner of the Arab world (particularly after
the start of the Arab revolts in 2011), a move toward Asia is likely, but this
would probably mean that Ankara would have to abandon all its support
for separatist Uyghur movements and cooperate with Beijing on security in
this matter.

• *Islamist movements*: Islamist ambitions, supported by Pakistan and the
Taliban, have aimed at creating an Islamic state in Central Asia that would
include Xinjiang and would allow Muslims to throw off Chinese, Russian,
and Indian tutelage. This goal is supported by several Islamist organizations, in particular the Free Turkestan Movement.

• *The American strategy of containment*: Contrary to the hopes of the
Uyghur movements, especially after NATO's intervention in Kosovo, the
United States has refused to give them logistical support in their struggle
against the Chinese presence in Xinjiang. In the current economic and strategic context, the US government cannot provoke China on this matter,
let alone at a time when the fight against terrorism still dominates official
discourse. But the United States does apply indirect pressure through the

---

[23] "Turks Call for Boycott of Chinese Products," Associated Press, July 9, 2009.
[24] "Turkish PM Erdogan likens Xinjiang violence to 'genocide,'" AFP, July 10, 2009.

positions it takes on the human rights situation in Xinjiang and by the accusations it regularly makes against Beijing regarding religious freedoms. The matter of Uyghur prisoners in Guantanamo is particularly illuminating in this regard. Although dozens of prisoners, upon leaving Guantanamo, were deported to their countries of origin—oftentimes countries that are not exactly known for the democratic nature of their legal systems (Iran, Yemen, or Saudi Arabia, for example)—Washington categorically refused to send the Uyghur Islamists detained at Guantanamo back to China on the grounds that their lives would be in danger if they were to return. The cynicism of the American government is all the more flagrant in this case because Washington also categorically refused to allow these same prisoners onto American soil, though they were officially considered "enemy non-combatants." The United States spent months looking for a country to take them in before finally obtaining the agreement of the Albanian government, which no doubt came at a high price.

The Uyghur question is the main identity-based geopolitical challenge that Chinese authorities will have to face in the years to come, due to the international implications and strategic significance of the matter. Solving it will depend on a certain number of options over which China would just have partial control or no control at all, but which would put it in a very uncomfortable situation internationally:

- granting greater religious freedom to Muslims, which would mean the risk of sliding toward a less "sinicized" Islam than the Party would like;
- relaxing controls over religious activities, which could encourage the expansion of radical Salafi Islam;
- in the short term, establishing real autonomy for the Xinjiang Uyghur Autonomous Region, with the nomination of minorities to positions of real authority, which would risk leading to a loss of authority and control by the central government over local affairs and could endanger the current system of energy security as well as military security; and
- accelerating economic and social development of the region to the benefit of native populations—however, this process will be slow, and it will be a while before its full effects reach the remotest regions. It is crucial that stability be maintained during this transition phase, which could last between 15 and 20 years, and new tensions are likely to arise between now and then. They already exist in other regions of the country due to inequalities in development, but they could take on an inter-ethnic dimension in Xinjiang that would threaten the stability of western China.

The stability of Xinjiang thus remains a priority, but the central Chinese authorities still appear to be searching for an effective policy to manage the identity-based challenge that native Islam represents in China. The indispensable opening of the region to the markets of Central Asia, which would mean a greater freedom of movement of goods and persons, would also increase the risk that ideas and weapons will be imported, and would therefore justify the development of security cooperation with Russia and the ex-Soviet republics.

## *Tibetan identity*

Tibetan identity is based on a religious and cultural specificity that goes back to the very first centuries of our era. In the 7th century, the nomadic tribes of the Lake Kokonor region, which had been turbulent for centuries but had never been a major problem for the Chinese empire, became a powerful Tibetan kingdom that set out to conquer the region of Pamir in the west, Yunnan in the east, and Tarim Basin in the north. After conquering what is today the province of Qinghai, they went up as far as Gansu, which they occupied after the An Lushan rebellion, thus cutting off the Chinese military establishments in Tarim and Dzungaria from their eastern bases. But this expansion was short-lived, and starting in 842, the Tibetan kingdom crumbled and abandoned the territories it had conquered, ceasing to be a strategic threat to China.

The culture of Tibetans was entirely different from that of their Chinese neighbors. Possessing a script and language derived from those of India, their theocratic model was profoundly different from the Chinese administrative system, and the two seemed incompatible. Efforts at rapprochement were made between 750 and 850, a period when the Tibetan aristocracy attempted to adapt to Chinese culture by sending its children to study in China and favoring marriages with members of the Tang aristocracy, but in vain. Tibet never regained its former power, in spite of the attempts made in the 14th century by a priest, Byang-chub-rGyal-mtshan, to rebuild Tibetan nationalism without Mongolian influences—the Mongolian dynasty of the Yuan having ruled Tibet from 1271 to 1368. Shaken by internal political rivalries among various religious schools, Tibet remained for centuries a peripheral kingdom that could be a nuisance to the Chinese empire, but incapable of opposing it in a sustained manner. During the Ming dynasty, the Chinese empire maintained a constant relationship of suzerainty with Lhasa. Tibet's distance from the political center of China and its inaccessibility allowed it to preserve a great degree of independence and strong cultural particularities.

Divided among three religions—Tibetan Lamaism, a native religion called *Bon*, and Islam—the small Tibetan population (no more than 6 million at the beginning of the 19th century) was essentially agricultural and was spread across several sovereign territories. Some of these territories—like Baltistan, also known as "Little Tibet," a Muslim kingdom practicing Twelver Shia Islam, or Lahaul, which was under the control of Indian rajas from Kullu—escaped the authority of the Dalai Lama, the political-religious Tibetan sovereign based in Lhasa. The other territories were vassals of Lhasa: Ladakh, Sikkim, Bhutan, and various districts of the region of Kham (which was called the province of "Xikang" between 1911 and 1949, and was then split among the provinces of Sichuan, Qinghai, and Yunnan, and the Tibet Autonomous Region) and Amdo (today the province of Qinghai).

A spiritual and temporal leader, the Dalai Lama relied on a bureaucratic aristocracy to govern a kingdom comprised of fiefdoms that were gradually united under his control but were often in conflict with each other. During the Dalai Lama's childhood, management of the country's affairs was entrusted to a regent, and for most of the 19th century the country was effectively governed by regents. After centuries of adjustment, the Tibetan political system had, by the 19th century, taken a definitively theocratic and feudal form. The country was run by a government equally divided between religious figures and laypeople, and it possessed an army—or, more precisely, a local militia—that could be mobilized if necessary.

At the end of the 18th century, Chinese influence had attained its apogee, following the intervention of Qing armies in the war between Nepal and Tibet in 1792. However, a certain ambiguity hovered over Sino-Tibetan relations. For the Qing court, the Dalai Lama was merely a cleric placed under the tutelage of the emperor of China. In the Tibetan system, however, laypeople could only occupy posts subordinate to those of religious figures, and so the emperor was merely a secular sovereign in an inferior position to that of the Dalai Lama. The year after he had integrated Tibet into the empire in 1792, Emperor Qianlong imposed his authority on the Tibetans by requiring that the Dalai Lama's successor be designated by drawing lots out of a golden urn, violating the traditional method, which relied on a long process of studying signs indicating that a child might be a reincarnation of the Dalai Lama. The Chinese policy alienated the Tibetan population, and revolt was in the air. But Great Britain's eruption onto the regional scene caused the Tibetans to draw nearer to the Qing. When the British conquered Nepal, the Dalai Lama asked the Chinese emperor for a military intervention to protect the small Nepalese kingdom, but the imperial government judged that the war fell outside of its jurisdiction, and abandoned the Nepalese to the British. The Qing did not grasp the threat to their strategic interests represented by Britain's break into China's periphery from its bases in the Indian Empire. Great Britain displayed a growing interest in commerce with Tibet and tightened its grip on the region, while at the same time remaining careful not to make China nervous with a too openly offensive attitude. In 1844, at the request of a part of the Tibetan government, China intervened to overthrow the regent Tshe-smongling—who had seized power in 1819 and assassinated several reincarnations of the Dalai Lama— and exiled him to Manchuria. But the Tibetans primarily affirmed their submission to Beijing in order to keep British and Nepalese threats at bay, in particular after the 1855–1856 war with Nepal and the invasion of Sikkim by British troops in 1861. However, the weakening of the Chinese empire in the face of increasing pressure from colonial powers—particularly from Britain and Russia in Central Asia—led to the gradual effacement of the Manchu court's influence in Tibet, which Russia and Great Britain both coveted and saw as a major strategic stake. Still, in 1886 Great Britain recognized Beijing's suzerainty over Tibet by signing the "Convention Relating to Burma and Tibet" with China. It was at the beginning of the 20th century that the situation dramatically shifted to Beijing's detriment. Whereas Tibetan aspirations for independence from China were clear, once again the British, hoping to keep the Russians away, recognized Chinese control over Tibet through the Anglo-Chinese agreement of 1906. However, Lhasa also accepted the semi-tutelage of Great Britain since Tibet could no longer develop its relations with other countries without obtaining authorization from the British first. In order to seize the initiative against a burgeoning independence movement, imperial troops entered Lhasa in 1910 to impose a Chinese government, for the first time in the history of Sino-Tibetan relations. The 13th Dalai Lama fled to India, and then returned in 1913 to proclaim Tibet's independence after the collapse of the Manchu dynasty and the abolition of the empire. The young Chinese republic was too weak to reestablish its authority, but it refused to recognize Tibet's independence, which Great Britain was trying to establish through negotiations in Simla (in India), so as to affirm its own hegemony in the region.

Throughout the 19th century, Tibet's closure to foreigners encouraged an endogamous cultural evolution, bereft of all innovation, in both literature and philosophy, and in religion. But Chinese influence grew among the dominant social classes, influencing various areas such as painting, decoration, and cuisine. The constant arrival of Chinese migrants heading to Central Asia, particularly merchants, contributed to the development of anti-Chinese sentiment and to the crystallization of a national identity. The Tibetans took advantage of the civil war in China to maintain a relative sovereignty, but the young age of the 14th Dalai Lama—who had ascended to the throne in 1940 at the age of four—was a hindrance to their demands for independence. In 1946, the Tibetans participated in the drafting of the new republican Chinese Constitution in Nanking.

With the independence of India in 1947, the founding of the People's Republic of China in October 1949, and the beginning of the Cold War with the start of the Korean War in June 1950, Tibet became a major strategic stake for China, India, and the United States. The Tibetan plateau is located at an average altitude of 16,404 feet, and stretches over 386,102 square miles in the Tibet Autonomous Region alone. Control over it would have given the United States an ideal observation point of China's borders, and would have given India a definite strategic advantage in its rivalry with the new China. Beginning in 1950, the People's Liberation Army entered Tibet in order to organize its integration into the new republic and to definitively eliminate any tendencies toward independence. In reality, the new Chinese leaders were only continuing the discourse used by republican Chinese leaders since 1911—including Washington's faithful ally, Chiang Kai-shek—when they affirmed that Tibet would remain under Chinese sovereignty. But in addition to this historical approach to the Tibetan question, there was now a strategic dimension, which the CIA's clandestine operations in the region beginning in 1951 confirmed for Beijing. Indeed, the Dalai Lama had sent envoys to meet with American representatives in India to obtain their support in resisting the Chinese. From that moment forward, the CIA contributed material support to the Tibetan resistance and trained hundreds of its members at a base in Colorado who were then brought back to India and infiltrated into Tibet to organize an anti-Chinese guerrilla war. Several tens of thousands of Tibetan combatants participated in these operations, and the Dalai Lama's brother, Gyalo Thondup, played a key role as an agent of the CIA.[25]

During the 1950s, the policy of the Chinese Communist authorities toward a theocratic system they described as "feudal" naturally alienated the clergy. Tibetan society was essentially divided between an omnipotent clergy and a large majority comprised of serfs (about 700,000 out of 1.2 million inhabitants) who most often belonged to the monks and lived in particularly terrible conditions. The implementation of agricultural reform and the fight against what the Chinese considered backward and barbaric beliefs provoked resistance by the monasteries and bitter discontent among a poorly educated population that for centuries had been imbued with respect for religious figures and could not accept their power being called into question. In March 1959 a general insurrection took place in Tibet, thanks to subversive operations carried out by the Americans and by exiled Tibetans who entered from India, and thanks to errors made by the Chinese troops. The repression was violent and the Dalai Lama fled to India with the aid of the CIA. Thousands of Tibetans were killed in the fighting, and China definitively consolidated its hold over the region, which in 1965 became the Tibet Autonomous Region. As for the Dalai Lama, who settled in Dharamsala, in India, he began a long career of lobbying the international community to put pressure on Beijing in the hope of one day obtaining independence. China installed the 10th Panchen Lama in Lhasa to replace the Dalai Lama in exile, and for years refused to have any contact with the Tibetan opposition in exile. Western leaders had all understood that Tibet's administrative integration into the People's Republic of China was a fait accompli, and that it was useless to contest it beyond the usual standard formulas.

In 1989, the 10th Panchen Lama died and his replacement set off a crisis between Beijing and the Tibetan ecclesiastical hierarchy. In 1995, the Dalai Lama recognized the reincarnation of the Panchen Lama in a young boy,

---

[25] Patrick French, *Tibet, Tibet* (New York: Vintage Books, 2004), 254.

Gendun Choeki Nyima, who was living several hundred miles from Lhasa. The Chinese authorities invoked the tradition of drawing lots from a golden urn initiated in 1793 by Emperor Qianlong to contest this choice, provoking a revolt in the Shigatse region. The 11th Panchen Lama has since been living outside of Tibet. The Tibetan opposition and human rights organizations accuse China of kidnapping him, while Beijing regularly maintains that the boy was placed under their protection so that he would not be kidnapped by the Tibetans in exile. Today it is Bainqen Erdini Qoigyijabu, the Panchen Lama selected by the golden urn method, who holds office in Lhasa, and in December 2005 he celebrated the 10th anniversary of his enthronement.

Since 2004, the 14th Dalai Lama, Tenzin Gyatso, seems to have adopted a new strategy toward Beijing. His death will pose a major problem for Tibetans in exile. He anticipated his succession in a curious way by announcing in 1997 that he would reincarnate himself abroad if the dispute with China were not settled by then.[26] But the aura that surrounds the current spiritual leader of Tibet, and which gives him international stature, may well disappear with him. By ruling out the possibility of reincarnation within Chinese territory, he is from the outset de-legitimizing any successor that China would designate.

Nevertheless, beginning in 2003, there was some movement toward negotiations over the future of Tibet. India's recognition of China's sovereignty over Tibet in 2003 was a significant gesture. The Tibetan government in exile, which no state recognizes, not even India, then found itself in a new situation that required it to revise its strategy toward the international community and toward China. The visit to Beijing in September 2004 of two envoys of the Dalai Lama to resume discussions after a 10-year interruption was an indication that the negotiation process had indeed been revived, and China was glad for this visit, which made it possible to envisage an eventual settlement of the issue. That same month, during a visit to Costa Rica, the Dalai Lama affirmed that if he were to return to Tibet, he would cede his power to a democratically elected government, "in the hope that it would be democratically elected."[27] In December, he declared in Johannesburg that he still hoped to return to China and that he was not demanding independence. In an interview with *Time* magazine several days later, he affirmed that it would be preferable for Tibet to remain under Chinese sovereignty as long as "its culture and environment" were respected. But China, while keeping the channels of dialogue open, increased pressure on him by disapproving of his travels abroad, saying that "he is not an ordinary religious figure but a separatist who engages in separatist activities,"[28] an accusation the Dalai Lama denied in a March 2005 interview with the *South China Morning Post*, saying that Tibetans were "ready to be

---

[26]World Tibet Network News, June 3, 1997.
[27]AFP, September 25, 2004.
[28]Declaration by Li Zhaoxing, Minister of Foreign Affairs, AFP, November 27, 2004.

part of the PRC,[29] to accept that the People's Republic of China governs and ensures the preservation of the culture, spirituality, and environment of Tibet," adding "I am not in favor of separation." He recognized the status of Tibet as an Autonomous Region of China, and said he was glad about China's material progress, which extended to Tibet, citing as an example the construction of the railroad connecting the province of Qinghai to Lhasa, which has been so often decried by the Western media and by Tibetans in exile. "If we had a separate state, it would be very difficult and we would not be able to benefit from it," he declared. The Tibetan "prime minister" in exile, Samdhong Rinpoche, re-iterated this several months later, displaying optimism regarding the contacts with China and affirming that international mediation was not necessary, as the Tibetans recognize China's sovereignty, and the conflict was an internal one that had to be resolved "between ourselves."

In the spring of 2008, the Tibetan opposition in exile, with the strong back-ing of Western so-called nongovernmental organizations and small groups of self-proclaimed human rights defenders, seized the opportunity presented by the approaching Olympic Games in Beijing to launch a new campaign of accu-sations against China. There were riots in Lhasa and several other places within Chinese territory. These events, which were clearly planned, gave the Tibetans timely media visibility and increased the political pressure on China that had begun in early 2007 with the matter of Sudan. For several years, China's de-tractors have painted a picture of the Dalai Lama and of the Tibetan opposi-tion that perfectly fits the Western public's expectations, particularly those of a European public craving religiosity. The portrait of an affable spiritual leader, always smiling, and preaching nonviolence in the face of what is presented as an autocratic regime, seduced public opinion and succeeded in convincing it of the Tibetan people's inherent nonviolence under Chinese oppression. The images of riots broadcast in March and April 2008 had a twofold effect. On the one hand, embellished with aggressive and often deceitful commentary, they touched Westerners, who were often convinced they were witnessing a "cultural genocide," as it was described in many media sources. But on the other hand, they also made another part of the public aware of the fact that the Tibetans are a people like any other, and that they, too, could be hooligans and display violent racism toward all non-Tibetans, enough to assassinate Han Chinese and Muslims in the streets and to set the Muslim neighborhood in Lhasa on fire. Confronted with this surge of criticism and accusations by the West, a growing part of the general public felt manipulated, and so sought to learn more about the history of Tibet and about the current situation, and discovered that a large part of the information given to them by the media had been mendacious or simply inaccurate. The general public thus gradu-ally discovered what had been hidden from it: the preservation of the Tibetan

---

[29]People's Republic of China.

language and the free practice of Buddhism in China, the freedom of movement Tibetans enjoyed domestically, and the considerable investments the central government had agreed to for the preservation of Tibet's cultural patrimony and the development of its infrastructure. But in general, although European political systems are considered democratic, they are free of neither disinformation nor political manipulation, as has been demonstrated by the role played by the French association Reporters Without Borders—which is particularly militant against China and is also very close to certain American political milieus, from which it receives funds.

After decades of paying insufficient attention to the development of peripheral regions populated by native minorities, in 1999 Beijing launched the Great Development of the West Program, intended to allow these inland provinces (Gansu, Guizhou, Ningxia, Qinghai, Shaanxi, Sichuan, Tibet, Xinjiang, Yunnan, and the municipality of Chongqing), which make up 56 percent of the Chinese territory, to catch up to the eastern provinces. A very significant program of infrastructure construction has been implemented, notably including the construction of the Chengdu–Lhasa railroad, the highest railroad in the world, and of a third airport in the Nyingchi district, the first to be built in 30 years. There is a special focus on the development of the regions bordering on India, in order to eventually facilitate the development of cross-border trade. But this policy displeases the partisans of the Tibetan opposition, who see it as a way for Beijing to encourage mass immigration of Han to Tibet—after, however, decades of accusing China of intentionally keeping Tibetans in a state of underdevelopment to facilitate Chinese control over the territory. Indeed, Tibetans are little by little entering the modern world, and DVD stores and karaoke bars are sprouting up in Lhasa, where they are frequented not only by Chinese but also by the Tibetan middle class, which is increasingly detached from the model of society imposed by the clergy.

But can a noticeable improvement of the Tibetan population's standard of living really counteract the separatist tendencies that subsist among certain fringe groups? The wide dispersion of the Tibetan population across a territory that is vast and difficult to access undoubtedly limits the spread of technological progress. The Chinese immigrants apparently bring with them their spirit of enterprise, and they contribute to the opening up of Tibet to the rest of China, but the confrontation between two cultures so different from one another can also generate tensions, which certain anti-Chinese groups could stir up. The Chinese authorities remain very vigilant regarding this possibility, as the regular arrests of religious figures accused of spreading anti-Chinese propaganda testify. The proliferation since 2009 of self-immolations by fire committed by Tibetans in China—there have been about 100 to this day—poses a real problem for Chinese authorities, who have made incitation to immolation by fire a crime, and who accuse the Dalai Lama's partisans in exile of being behind these spectacular actions.

However, the influence of monasteries can only diminish with time, as a result of the population's increasing level of education and its openness to economic realities. Until recently, the fact that primary education took place in the Tibetan language, in conformity with Beijing's policy toward all native minorities, contributed to maintaining cultural differentiation, as in Xinjiang. The increasing spread of Chinese as the national language, which goes along with easier access to higher education, should eventually favor integration into the Chinese nation, even if Tibetans keep their religious particularity, which would then be limited to the private sphere. The debate over the teaching of both languages nevertheless continues to rage, with opponents within the Chinese government justifying their position by the extra cost an entirely bilingual education would represent and by the work it would require from the students, and opponents on the Tibetan side arguing that teaching Chinese beginning in primary school would gradually dissolve Tibetan identity. The dilemma is serious. One of the major reasons for the lag in the development of the Tibet Autonomous Regions is the difficulty young Tibetans have in accessing higher education, which is in Chinese, due to their linguistic inadequacies. But the stalwart defenders of Tibetan identity, who accuse the Chinese authorities of having deliberately kept Tibet in a state of general underdevelopment, also oppose the teaching of Chinese from a young age. This policy would make sense, however, for the economic and social development of the region within the Chinese state. The contradictions remain insurmountable, for they are driven by an ideological, not rational, approach to the debate.

****

Whether it is a matter of the populations of Xinjiang or Tibet or of other ethnic minorities less prone to protest, the Chinese authorities are confronted with a challenge to their way of dealing with minority identities that they have serious difficulties analyzing objectively. In a country the size of China, an administrative and political model based on a strong, unitary state with some established "autonomous regions" within the framework of a unitarian state was undoubtedly inappropriate for a federal government structure, which is more flexible when it comes to governing peripheral regions. The ethnic minorities who protest the most—mainly for religious reasons—have felt insufficiently represented and deprived of any real power to manage their affairs. It is nevertheless true that the federal model used in the USSR did not prevent the disintegration of the Soviet empire. In China's case, the external pressures and centrifugal tensions that have troubled peripheral regions these past few years should have caused the government to rethink its administrative system for these regions. But the Han Chinese still have a very reductive and very "folkloric" perception of these minorities—what Mao Zedong used to call "great Han chauvinism" (大汉沙文主义; *Dàhàn shāwén zhǔyì*)—the traditions of which are regularly praised in the media. Chinese analysts and economists, for example, consider that "conservatism and cultural backwardness" (思想观念保守落后; *sīxiǎng guānniàn bǎoshǒu luòhòu*) are major factors in the inner provinces' lagging behind the provinces of the east.[30] But these populations have remained isolated from Chinese development for 25 years due to the marked indifference toward them on the part of the central government, and the linguistic policy mentioned above is a manifestation of this. Only the complete integration of these minority populations into the national Chinese framework could allow them to seize the opportunity represented by the country's current economic development, and to allow this development to spread as if through capillaries. But this would require Beijing to break the taboo on the sinicization of minorities that haunts the discourse of the Chinese regime's detractors, and to adopt a policy similar to that of various European countries—France in particular—in order to form a national melting pot based on a common national language and culture that relegates regionalisms to localized expressions of identity that cannot threaten national unity. The effort to spread wealth to these regions, and these regions' greater openness to the eastern provinces (thanks to the infrastructure projects undertaken to open the western regions to the outside world), must incite minorities to learn Chinese in order to be able to benefit from development and to intensify their commercial relations with the coastal economic centers.

## *The issue of Taiwan*

Taiwan, of course, is a special case, because the island officially belongs to the People's Republic of China but has been in a situation of political rupture with China since 1949, with a status quite close to independence. In contrast to the cases of Tibet and Xinjiang, in Taiwan it is not a matter of strictly identity-based claims in the religious or cultural sense, but of a form of political dissidence.

The question of identity in Taiwan is rather complex. In order to grasp the depth of the antagonism that some Taiwanese feel toward mainland Chinese, it is necessary to take into account the past three centuries of the island's history.

The history of China's presence in Taiwan—which was called "Ilha Formosa" (the "Beautiful Island") by the first European travelers, who arrived in 1590—began in the 17th century when a partisan of the fallen Ming dynasty, Zheng Chenggong,[31] decided in 1661 to retreat to the island, which was still wild and had been partially occupied by the Dutch East India Company since 1624. Several hundred Chinese immigrants were already settled in the south and gravitated toward the Dutch colony. Zheng Chenggong founded

---

[30] 汉文化多元文化与西部大开发  揣振宇-杨荆楚 [Chuai Zhenning], [*Han Multicultural Culture and the Great Development of the West*], 民族出版社 (Beijing: Nationalities Editions, 2003), 33.
[31] Zheng Chenggong was also called Koxinga (国姓爷), or "Lord of the Imperial Surname."

his capital city, named the Eastern Capital (of the Ming [东部明京; Dōngbù Míng jīng]), before dying in isolation in 1662. He was idealized after 1949 by Taiwanese with deep roots on the island, as he both embodied their ethnic Chinese identity and symbolized their resistance to forced domination by the mainland. In 1683, the Manchu dynasty of the Qing reconquered the island from Zheng Chenggong's descendants and integrated it into the southern province of Fujian. For two centuries, waves of Chinese immigrants, often groups of rebels who used the island as a rear base for armed operations against the continent, settled there. Two populations thus cohabited on the island: the aborigines, who were of Malay-Polynesian origin and had been living on the island for centuries, and Chinese emigrants, mostly from the provinces of Fujian (70 percent) and Guangdong (10 percent), who were always more numerous than the aborigines. There were about 200,000 Han in 1680 and 2 million in 1810, whereas the aborigines were fewer than 1 million at the end of the 17th century. Beginning in 1876, immigration to Taiwan was authorized—it had been forbidden for two centuries for political reasons, although this was not really enforced—and thousands of Chinese from Fujian and Guangdong settled there. Nevertheless, in 1895, when the island was ceded to Japan, between 200,000 and 300,000 of them returned to the mainland. The Fujian-origin majority spoke the Minnan language (閩南語; *mǐnnán yǔ*), which today is commonly referred to as Taiwanese, whereas the Chinese from Guangdong spoke Hakka (客家; *kèjiā*). Conflicts between the aborigines and the Chinese over land were inevitable given the scarcity of usable land. Fierce fighting took place between the two communities in the mountainous regions of the center, for the aborigines had also acquired firearms. Chinese troops suffered heavy losses until Japanese colonization.

The Sino-French War of 1884–1885 and the French military operations led by Admiral Amédée Courbet incited the Qing court to reinforce the defense of the island, which had already undergone British occupation of Keelung during the First Opium War and a Japanese invasion in 1874. On October 12, 1885, Taiwan was detached from the province of Fujian by imperial decree and became the 20th province of the empire. The new governor of the Province, Liu Mingchuan, had already been appointed in 1884 as governor of Fujian with residence on Taiwan.[32] He had organized the island's defense during the French invasion, and immediately launched a development policy aimed at fortifying the island's defenses and modernizing its infrastructure (railroads, roads, communications). The capital, Tainan, formerly a Dutch fort, was replaced by Taipei. Liu Mingchuan ordered cannons from Europe to equip both the main island and the Penghu Islands. But this defensive effort was in vain. The defeat of the Chinese army by the Japanese in February 1895 drastically altered the destiny of the Taiwanese. During the Shimonoseki peace negotiations, the

---

[32] *Cambridge History of China*, Vol. 11, Late Ch'ing 1800–1911, Part 2, 258–260.

Japanese navy demanded that China cede the island, as it wanted a base for operations in Southeast Asia. When the Treaty of Shimonoseki was signed, on April 17, 1895, Taiwan left the bosom of China for half a century. In reaction, the Chinese leaders in Taiwan proclaimed the island's independence on May 25, 1895, and founded a republic, offering the presidency to the governor then in office. But their efforts amounted to nothing in the face of pressures from the imperial court and the Japanese troops. In October 1895, the adventure of independence came to an end and Japan took control of the island.

Taiwan remained under Japanese administration until 1945. The retrocession of the island to the Republic of China on October 1945 should have reconciled the Taiwanese and mainland Chinese. Indeed, the Taiwanese welcomed the departure of the Japanese and reattachment to China with enthusiasm. Although colonization had brought undeniable development to the island, allowing its inhabitants to enjoy a standard of living much higher than that of the mainlanders, the Taiwanese had always been treated as second-class citizens. The territorial government had been completely dominated by the Japanese, and they monopolized all the positions of power. Taiwanese activists had struggled for recognition of their rights during the colonial period, with little success. The Japanese capitulation and the liberation of the island allowed them to recuperate property confiscated by the Japanese authorities and to fill the administrative posts abandoned by the Japanese. However, the rapid reestablishment of Chinese authority brought immediate disappointment. Under the leadership of the new governor, General Chen Yi, the Kuomintang Nationalists monopolized all the centers of power on the island and pushed the Taiwanese away from them. The endemic corruption that immediately appeared and the errors in management made by the new authorities quickly turned the population against them. A growing number of Taiwanese came to miss the Japanese era, which had at least ensured a high standard of living, whereas the Nationalist authorities immediately plunged the island into a grave economic crisis.

On February 28, 1947, revolt broke out following a relatively benign police incident that turned into a confrontation between the Taiwanese and mainlanders. The Nationalist regime engaged in extremely violent repression, and in several weeks massacred between 10,000 and 20,000 Taiwanese. In an appeal to General George C. Marshall, the American Secretary of State, in February 1947, just before the massacre, Formosan intellectuals invoked the need to "reconstitute our democratic organizations" and their own deep "anti-tyranny" convictions. The Taiwanese Youth Movement demanded to be placed under the administration of the United Nations, even temporarily. In the first issue of *Formosan Magazine*, published in March 1947, these youths asserted the "historic separatism" of Taiwan in relation to the mainland. But the majority of Taiwanese demanded recognition of their particularities while at the same time acknowledging that they belonged to China. On March 6, 1947, at the height of the crisis, the daily newspaper *Ming Pao* of Taipei affirmed:

*However excited the Formosans become, their conception that they are a part
of the Chinese race will not change. Since we belong to the same race, we
should behave like brothers to one another.*[33]

The United States, whose intervention was sought by the independence
movement, limited itself to recalling the principle of Chinese sovereignty over
the island. As the main actor in the region, it intended to support the reestablishment of Nationalist authority over the island. Thus, it armed the troops
who disembarked by the thousands on March 8 at the Port of Keelung (基
隆).[34] During the next two weeks, the island witnessed an unleashing of violence under the indifferent eye of the American consular staff.

In 1948, Washington was seriously contemplating the establishment of
military bases on the island to complete the Japan–Okinawa–Philippines
arc. The American press and lobbies started a campaign in favor of Chiang
Kai-shek and his wife, who were on the point of leaving the continent under
Communist pressure and who were entirely devoted to converting China to
Christianity—religion was already all the rage in the United States as a basis
for supporting foreign policy—and had to be protected from the barbarian,
atheist, Communist hordes who had swept across China.[35] After the Kuomintang regime fled the mainland in 1949 and settled on the island, it disowned
all local identity, forbidding the use of the Taiwanese dialect and references to
a non-Chinese past. A number of "historical" Taiwanese—those who had put
down roots on the island but who had come from the mainland, and thus were
also Chinese—felt a certain bitterness toward this policy, especially due to the
monopolizing of all posts of responsibility by the Chinese refugees of 1949. As
for the natives—the aborigines—they were restricted to mountain reservations
and were scarcely more than a tourist attraction. In 1949, over 10,000 people
were arrested in Taiwan, accused of Communist or independentist sympathies,
and many of them were summarily executed.

In December 1949, Chiang Kai-shek took refuge in Taiwan with 2 million supporters, including 500,000 Nationalist troops. They had previously
transferred $300 million in gold, silver, and currency to the island. Initially,
the American President Harry Truman refused to give the Kuomintang the
military support that Pentagon chiefs were proposing on the grounds that the
Nationalists' performance against the Communists on the mainland had been
so mediocre, there was no point in fighting alongside them against the new
People's Republic of China. The year 1950 was a decisive turning point. The
invasion of South Korea by North Korean forces in June 1950 changed the
perspective of the Americans, who were henceforth convinced of the existence
of a Soviet expansionist strategy in East Asia. In this context, accepting the

---

[33]George H. Kerr, *Formosa Betrayed* (Boston: Houghton Mifflin, 1965), 289.
[34]Ibid., 291.
[35]Ibid., 360.

occupation of Taiwan by Chinese Communist troops amounted to letting another domino fall into Soviet hands, and would have seriously harmed American strategy in the region. Thus, Washington agreed to extend its protection to Taiwan and to supply it with significant military and economic assistance. This policy lasted until the beginning of the 1970s.

In 1949, 6 million Taiwanese originally from the mainland were living on the island, but their identity had been significantly altered by Japanese colonization. Most of them spoke Japanese and had grown accustomed to Japanese culture (e.g., music, film), and hundreds of them had studied in Japan. Awareness of their Chinese roots, in spite of the fact that their linguistic traditions had been preserved, had gradually weakened. Beginning in 1950, the Nationalist regime endeavored, with undeniable success, to eradicate these Taiwanese particularities and to establish classical Chinese culture, the use of Mandarin as the national language, and references to the glorious past of Chinese civilization. Japanese music and literature were even forbidden. This process of re-sinicization was also based on the development of a strong anti-Communist identity. The struggle against Communism, which was the main threat to the survival of the Nationalist regime, was used as an excuse to also repress any hint of movements in support of autonomy or independence, as these would have called into question the Kuomintang's official goal of reconquering the mainland. Chiang Kai-shek imposed a one-party system dominated by a familial clan that systematically plundered the island. Fundamental freedoms, which Washington accused the People's Republic of China of violating, were denied on the pretext of a state of emergency. For nearly four decades, what the Taiwanese called the "White Terror" reigned on the island. The military courts heard between 30,000 and 70,000 cases, each one usually involving several defendants. The number of victims rose to over 200,000. The two last political prisoners were freed in 1984. The Kuomintang had established a penal colony on the Green Island (綠島; *lù dǎo*) where over 20,000 prisoners were held and over a thousand executed. A group of prisoners who were freed when martial law was abrogated in 1987 joined together to form the Democratic Progressive Party. When this party ended the Kuomintang's monopoly in 1995 through elections, former political prisoners and activists entered the new government.

Separatist discourse was violently repressed until the end of the 1980s. It was secretly supported by the many American evangelist churches on the island. When martial law was lifted, this discourse—which is based on both identity and anti-communism—reemerged, and accounted for Chen Shuibian's narrow victory in the 2000 elections on a platform strongly oriented toward independence. For five years, Taiwanese leaders flirted with the idea of independence, blowing hot and cold in their relations with Beijing and were regularly put back in place by Washington. In the People's Republic of China, without a real model to propose, the discourse of reunification seemed to run out of steam. The principle of "one country, two systems" in place in Hong

Kong and initially envisaged for Taiwan no longer functioned, in the eyes of the Taiwanese, on account of the political difficulties Hong Kong had encountered. Chen Shui-bian's government had also continued the policy begun by Lee Teng-hui in 1995 of giving a specifically Taiwanese orientation to educational and cultural policy in order to encourage the expression of a properly Taiwanese identity, freed from traces of Chinese culture. This Taiwanese "nationalism" suffers, however, from the relative opposition that still exits between "historic" Taiwanese and mainlander Taiwanese. In 2005, the reconciliation between the Kuomintang and the Communist Party of China, consecrated by the visit of the Kuomintang's leader to Beijing, underscored this antagonism and gave Taiwanese public opinion cause for reflection. When Beijing signaled its opposition to independence by enacting the anti-secession law, it sent a warning to the Taiwanese, which seems to have been quickly understood, judging by the poor showing Chen Shui-bian's party made in the December 2005 local elections and his ultimate defeat in the March 2008 elections. A majority of Taiwanese still believe in a negotiated reunification that would respect their specific characteristics—above all political—although the model for integration still remains to be invented. Political exchanges have continued and have deepened. Over the past decade, the two parties have displayed their willingness to maintain the status quo until a definitive solution can be found, without upsetting the situation. In March 2012, Lien Chan, the "honorary president" of the Kuomintang, made an official visit to Beijing, presumably to meet China's new leader, Xi Jinping. When asked about the meaning of his visit, Lien Chan very significantly responded that the goal was to "explore the framework of a single China, peace between the two shores of the strait, mutual interests, integration, and *the glorious revitalization of the Chinese nation*" (中华民族伟大复兴; *Zhōnghuá mínzú wěidà fùxīng*).[36] This declaration confirms the Kuomintang's desire to negotiate the reintegration of the island of Taiwan into the Chinese national whole as best as possible and to settle the political dispute with Beijing once and for all. No doubt, the nationalist leaders have in mind the possibility that Beijing might open the political landscape to the Kuomintang as a Chinese political party—China is dominated by the Communist Party but is formally a multi-party system (eight other parties officially exist)—which would open the way for the renegade province's definitive integration into the People's Republic of China.

Economically, integration is already well advanced. In 2011, Taiwan was the second largest outside investor in China; over 65,000 Taiwanese companies have investments on the mainland, and over a million Taiwanese live there. Taiwanese business milieus are today more in favor of rapprochement with Beijing than confrontation.

---

[36] "习近平总书记会见连战一行" ["General Secretary Xi Jinping Meets with Lian Zhan's Group"], Xinhuanet, Beijing, February, 25, 2012.

As I have already mentioned, there is a major strategic dimension to the relation between the People's Republic of China and Taiwan. For Beijing, the island is the key to the Pacific Ocean, to which its navy must absolutely have smooth access in the years to come in order to counter American pressures in the region. Chinese military presence on the island would make it possible to neutralize the Strait of Taiwan, and the American fleet would be pushed away, to Guam—the level of the second insular barrier (第二岛链; *dì'èr liàndǎo*). Thus, one main consequence of reunification would be to loosen the vice around China that compels it to pay excessive attention to this area. Japan would naturally remain the other threatening element in East Asia, but its position would be weakened by Chinese territorial expansion. The possibility of the American-Japanese anti-missile shield being extended to Taiwan—though this is far from taking shape on a technological level—would thus be a cause for war for Beijing, because, as in Japan, it would encourage Taiwan to develop, with American assistance, military power that would make the island a sanctuary. Overall, in its strategy for the medium term, Beijing must create conditions favorable to strengthening its eastern side against American threats, and integrating Taiwan into its strategic apparatus is essential. Thus, Chinese authorities must continue their efforts to seduce the Kuomintang. They must also, however, develop a proposal that takes into account both Taiwanese desire to keep the existing democratic model and also the political situation on the mainland. The political question is thus key to resolving this critical matter, and Beijing must try to avoid military conflict with Taiwan in order not to seriously endanger its own economic development.

The results of a Chinese military operation against Taiwan would depend in large part on the attitude taken by the United States. It is obvious that such an action would be widely condemned by the international community and would lead to sanctions against Beijing. But what states would really be ready to commit to militarily supporting Taiwan, with its 23 million inhabitants, compared to China's market of over a billion? Would even the United States be able to conceive of an armed engagement against a nuclear power such as China, and would American public opinion accept the necessary sacrifices? In reality, it seems unlikely that Washington would be able to retaliate directly against China, despite the presence of the 7th Fleet in the Far East. Maritime incidents between American and Chinese naval forces are conceivable, but an American intervention on Chinese soil seems remote, given the nuclear consequences this could have—China's nuclear potential is certainly still limited, but it is nevertheless effective. This is clearly the objective Beijing is pursuing with the strategy the Americans call "Anti-Access"[37]—a term, however, which

---

[37] Roger Cliff, "Anti-Access Measures in Chinese Defense Strategy," Santa Monica, CA: RAND Corporation, January 2011).

never appears in Chinese military literature—which aims to neutralize American reaction capacity in the event of an open conflict over Taiwan.

An armed confrontation over Taiwan would have a very negative impact on American interests in China. Washington is capable of putting enough pressure on Taiwanese authorities to dissuade them from crossing the red line drawn by Beijing—a unilateral declaration of independence—in particular if the party of former chairman Chen Shui-bian, who is today in prison in Taiwan for corruption, returns to power. For the United States, Taiwan is essentially an issue used to maintain soreness on China's eastern side, a strategy whose limits have however been clearly identified. The Kuomintang's rise to power in Taipei and the first gesture made by Taiwan, only nine days after Ma Yin-reou took office—sending the chairman of the Kuomintang, Wu Poh-hsiung, on a visit to Beijing in May 2009—seems a clear indication of a shared desire to make up for time lost under Chen Shui-bian and to return to the path toward economic and political rapprochement, without, however, predetermining the date and terms of an eventual reunification. The process of rapprochement now seems well underway, and this old dispute must be resolved through patience and pragmatic development, following the Chinese method.

# CONCLUSION

C hina entered the 21st century in desperate need of economic and social successes. In the 19th century and the first half of the 20th, the lag accumulated over two centuries due both to foreign interferences and the poor performances of their leaders led the Chinese to doubt themselves, to look to foreign models, and to be tempted to deny their cultural heritage. This complex is gradually disappearing today thanks to the prodigious economic development of the past 30 years, which must first and foremost be attributed to the perseverance of Chinese leaders and the formidable resilience of the Chinese people, their sense of effort, and to the strength of tradition. The Chinese have patiently and doggedly worked to build a stronger and richer nation, with a success that now worries other nations, in particular in the West. They are not ready to risk losing these real but still fragile gains in order to satisfy the sometimes excessive demands of their foreign partners. Within the new phase of reforms that will raise the country to the status of a superpower within the next three centuries, the threat that now weighs on the Chinese people is the threat of nationalism, which some—both in China and abroad—will attempt to justify as fair revenge for past humiliations. The 20th century—the century of the triumph of nationalism and its attendant wars, mass graves, deportation and reeducation camps, and conquests in the name of a concept of *nation* invented by the French Revolution—should have definitively delegitimized the idea of an indestructible bond between individuals and the ideal of *nation*. This temptation to nationalism—which most often is nothing more than a negation of the Other—unfortunately seems to be on the rise again today, and China is not spared from this pathology. In the face of the outside pressures put on Beijing in the name of democracy, human rights, or beneficent liberalism, Chinese public opinion is expressing itself with increasing violence—occasionally in the streets but daily on the Internet—to show its anger and indignation over relations that, as in the 19th century, are all too often unequal. The Chinese system that has been in place since 1978 resembles none other today. Its detractors have tried to ascribe ideological labels to it, in order to classify it among known political regimes: fascism, dictatorship, autocracy, and other avatars of the excesses of the human spirit. It is necessary to recognize that this attempt has not been convincing.

From the beginning of the 1978 reforms, Chinese leaders adopted an attitude inspired by the philosopher Xunzi (3rd century BC) who gave priority to order in managing affairs of the state. For him, "better to preserve the status quo, even if you know perfectly well that it is arbitrary and conventional, than to risk toppling into anarchy by wanting to call things into question."[1] For the critics of the Chinese political regime, this philosophy corresponds to the Party's concern to maintain an order it continues to dominate absolutely. It is nevertheless true that the current political and economic stability, the longest in

---

[1] Anne Cheng, *Histoire de la pensée chinoise* (Paris: Editions du Seuil, 1997), 228.

the history of contemporary China, also corresponds to the interests of the vast majority of Chinese, who aspire to an ever better future. Since 1978, China has renounced the totalitarian Maoist order that denied the individual in favor of the abstract concept of "mass." But it has not yet fallen into a liberalism that denies the group to the sole benefit of the individual, even if certain current tendencies sometimes give reason to fear this. The political system that is very slowly emerging in China seems to belong to the age-old tradition of Chinese syncretism and to be gradually shaping a new order that is the outcome of borrowings from not only Chinese tradition but also from foreign experiences.

But this process is taking place within a globalized context, in spite of the political control currently exerted, which has however considerably softened in the past 30 years. The spread of modern communication technologies and the opening of the country to the world—in particular through travel and hundreds of thousands of Chinese citizens studying abroad—makes the policy of controlling information more and more obsolete, even though it can sometimes seem necessary to preserve stability in a country whose demographic scale allows for no political deviation. The gradual opening up of the country has created a phenomenon of historically unprecedented economic development, the corollary of which is now reform of the political framework. This reform must offer the Chinese greater room to participate in political life, even if such an opening, which will no doubt contribute to calming certain domestic tensions, can also favor interference by foreign actors. Pursuit of economic growth remains Chinese leaders' priority and the growing interdependence of economies on a global scale compels them to stress their country's integration into the international community, no matter what the cost.

*The Spaniards met Chinese, both resident traders and sea-farers; but the contact was not a happy one. Finding that the Chinese by their numbers and trading ability were likely to hinder their own success, the Government cleared them out of the islands by a wholesale massacre in which 20,000 people were killed.*[2]

This is the missionary Hughes' description of the Spanish conquest of the Philippines in the 16th century. Anxiety about China's potential power is not a new phenomenon. Since 1978, the concept of transformation—which has deep roots in traditional Chinese thought as the only concept capable of bringing ultimate harmony—has won out over the concept of permanent revolution, a synonym for rupture and destabilization. But this development is as terrifying to the West as the former possibility of revolutionary cataclysm. In the eyes of the West, the gradual elevation of the Chinese standard of living carries the long-term potential for clashes over control of the planet's resources. The

---

[2] Ernest Richard Hughes, *The Invasion of China by the Western World* (New York: MacMillan, 1938), 9.

Chinese "American dream" is a nightmare for Westerners. In order to reassure its partners, China—although it is still a developing country—is already working to implement measures in the areas of the environment or energy savings that developed countries themselves—including the United States, which is far behind the others—still do not apply to themselves. Whereas Europe and the United States based their development in the 18th and 19th centuries on practices that are condemned today (exploitation of workers, plundering of natural resources of colonized countries, destruction of the environment, etc.), China must take into account the requirements of a new international environment, even if in certain sectors it still tries to resist this. Its eventual success will only be all the more meritorious.

Confronted with the ongoing campaign to denigrate its successes, which, given the international context, will continue for many years, China—and above all, the Chinese people—must absolutely avoid sinking into a nationalist reaction of defiance that will only accentuate the gap of incomprehension between it and the world and give ammunition to its enemies. It seems essential to me that the concept of "harmonious society" (和谐社会; *héxié shèhuì*), which former President Hu Jintao placed at the center of the Chinese project, be maintained and deepened as a guideline for Chinese leaders both domestically and internationally—even if, as a concept inspired by Confucianism, it is difficult for the outside world to understand and accept. It is just as essential that significant efforts be made to communicate the substance and interest of this idea to China's partners, using a mode of communication intelligible to Westerners, which requires considerable effort by Beijing to find the appropriate channels and register for communication. The major cultural differences between China and its partners force it to sometimes abandon overly *Chinese* formulations of its ideas, especially those that have a major impact abroad, so as to privilege the content of the message over its form. The Tibetan crisis clearly showed the limits of "Chinese-style" communication and China's difficulty in transmitting messages if they are not adapted to the cultural context of the intended audience.

Both observers of China like myself and those members of the public who have an interest in the country—whether based on curiosity or anxiety—must keep in mind the antiquity and richness of Chinese civilization and ponder both the teachings of Chinese philosophers and the analyses of our predecessors who knew China during the blackest periods of the past two centuries. Claude Farrère, a member of the French Academy, a great traveler, and a friend of Victor Segalen, wrote in 1924, when China was embroiled in the turmoil of imperialism and its own cultural introspection:

> *The Chinese people is not at all in a phase of decadence, for its population is increasing rather than decreasing, its capacity for work has never weakened, its curiosity for learning is constantly growing, and its formidable activity*

*continues to have no conception of lassitude. Let us not be struck by the anarchy that has plagued the Chinese nation for so many years: for forty or fifty centuries, fifteen or thirty times, China has already experienced the most terrible troubles and the worst upheavals. China will not fall to pieces for so little.... There is a reserve of strength there of a kind that exists nowhere else. What can happen to a nation that is so robust, so hard working, so tenacious, so tireless in every task; to a nation whose political activity manifests itself in an incredible number of secret societies; a nation constantly bubbling with life? Everything can happen! And I continue to expect from China the greatest, most fabulous things. At a time when we in Europe and America rather childishly multiply our chatter and conferences, exacerbate our internal rivalries, and push our arrogance so far as to dispute the very oceans—the Pacific, the Atlantic, and the others—it is not inconceivable that one day a nation more populous, more industrious, more wise as well, in spite of appearances, will suddenly stand up alongside our nations.... above them, perhaps! ... In fact, if the advent of this nation were for the purpose of imposing greater peace on the world, based on mandatory labor and equitable justice, I, for my part, would not be sorry if this nation were named China!*[3]

How can we fail to be fascinated by this premonition of what China would be, once it emerged from the enslavement to which it had been condemned since the Opium Wars? Several years later, another French traveler, Elie Faure—author of the monumental work *History of Art*, first published in 1909—brought back the following, equally premonitory observations from his journey to the Far East:

*They must begin everything again, but they will, for they represent, by their slow and subtle virtues a positive core, toughness against fatigue and misfortune, sobriety, honesty, gentleness, a so to speak active resignation, an incommensurable force. Morally reduced to dust as their hieratic and ritual gangue comes apart in slabs and crumbs, they fall back on their land, which awaits only the rain and the plowshare ....Who believes this people to be dead? The Chinese are waiting. They are fallow. They are never in a hurry. Aphrodite will be born again out of the mire of the yellow rivers, I tell you truthfully.*[4]

The rain has indeed fallen since 1978, as Elie Faure predicted, and China no longer lies fallow. Confronted with China, it appears that Westerners will bear a large share of the responsibility for the ultimate form its emergence will take in the decades to come. Between containment and engagement, asymmetric

---

[3] Claude Farrère, *Extrême Orient* (Paris: Flammarion, 1924), 97–98.
[4] Elie Faure, *Mon périple: Tour du monde, 1931–1932* (Paris: Société française d'éditions littéraires et techniques, 1932), 108, 114.

war and cooperation, Europeans and Americans must choose the policies that will best serve their long-term interests. If isolationism is no longer an option in the 21st century as it might have been in the 18th or 19th, protectionism remains a weapon that politicians lacking imagination—either Chinese or Western—may be tempted to use. The polemics that today oppose Chinese and American political leaders resemble those of the end of the 18th so closely that they could be confused:

> *As to trade with foreigners, the Empire had all that it required within its own borders and felt no need of the goods they offered. Europe, however, increasingly demanded Chinese silk, porcelain, lacquer and, above all, tea. As the foreigners had nothing China wanted with which to barter in exchange, payment had to be made in silver. This was a serious problem until it was found that the Chinese could be induced to buy [Indian] opium.*[5]

History has shown us how the opium policy ended. In the 21st century, will the West look for a new opium, or will it finally agree to treat China on an equal footing?

---

[5] Hughes, *The Invasion of China by the Western World*, 15.

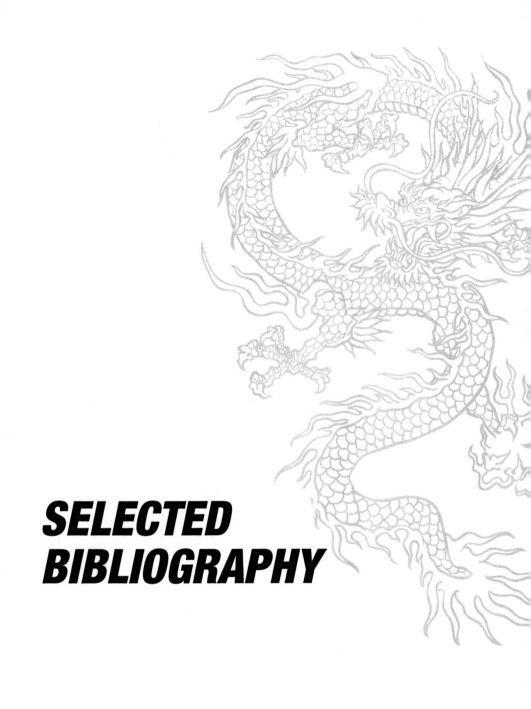

# SELECTED
# BIBLIOGRAPHY

## *Works in French*

Balci, Bayram. *Missionnaires de l'Islam en Asie centrale: Les écoles turques de Fethullah Gülen.* Paris: Maisonneuve & Larose, 2003.

Balci, Bayram, Bertrand Buchwalter, Ahmet Salih Biçakçi, Habiba Fathi, Alexandre Huet, Arnaud Ruffier, and Johann Uhres. *La Turquie en Asie centrale: La conversion au réalisme (1991–2000).* Istanbul: Institute Français d'Etudes Anatoliennes, 2001.

Balme, Stéphanie. *Entre soi: l'élite du pouvoir dans la Chine contemporaine.* Paris: Editions Fayard, 2004.

Béja, Jean-Philippe. *A la recherche d'une ombre chinoise: le mouvement pour la démocratie en Chine, 1919-2004.* Paris: Editions du Seuil, 2004.

Bennigsen, Alexandre, and Chantal Lemercier-Quelquejay. *Le soufi et le commissaire: les confréries musulmanes en URSS.* Paris: Editions du Seuil, 1986.

Bergère, Marie-Claude. *La République populaire de Chine de 1949 à nos jours.* Paris: Armand Colin, 1987.

Chaigne, Christine, and Charles Zorgbibe. *La reconnaissance des gouvernements chinois par la France: contribution à l'étude du principe d'effectivité en droit international public.* Aix-en-Provence: Presses Universitaires d'Aix-Marseille, 1996.

Dieckhoff, Alain. *La nation dans tous ses États: Les identités nationales en mouvement.* Paris: Flammarion, 2000.

Domenach, Jean-Luc. *Chine: l'archipel oublié.* Paris: Editions Fayard, 1992.

Elisseeff, Danielle, and Vadime Elisseeff, *La civilisation japonaise.* 211 héliogravures, 9 planches en couleurs, 64 cartes, dessins et plans. Paris: Arthaud, 1974.

Étiemble, René. *L'Europe chinoise.* Paris: Gallimard, 1988.

Gentelle, Pierre. *Economie de la Chine.* Paris: Armand Colin, 1994.

Izraelwicz, Erik. *Quand la Chine change le monde.* Paris: Grasset, 2005.

Joyaux, François. *La tentation impériale: politique extérieure de la Chine depuis 1949.* Paris: Imprimerie Nationale, 1994.

Jullien, François. *Procès ou Création: Une introduction à la pensée des lettrés chinois.* Paris: Editions du Seuil, 1989.

———. *Dialogue sur la morale.* Paris: Grasset, 1995.

Mervin, Sabrina. *Histoire de l'islam: Doctrines et fondements.* Paris: Flammarion, 2000.

Thiesse, Anne-Marie. *La création des identités nationales: Europe, XVIIIe-XXe siècle.* Paris: Editions du Seuil, 2001.

Yingxiang, Cheng. *Dégel de l'intelligence en Chine 1976-1989: quatorze témoignages.* Paris: Gallimard, 2004.

## Works in Chinese

陈丹：《美国的安全战略与东亚》，世界知识出版社，北京市，2002.

揣振宇：《汉文化多元文化与西部大开发》，民族出版社，北京市，2005.

郭万超：《中国崛起：一个东方大国的成长之道》，江西人民出版社，
南昌市，2004.

马洪 、王梦奎：《中国发展研究》，中国发展出版社，北京市，2004.

胡鞍钢：《中国 ：新发展观 》，浙江人民出版社，杭州市，2004.

李德洙：《新疆知识简明读本》，华文出版社，北京市，2003.

李德洙：《西藏知识简明读本》，华文出版社，北京市，2003.

丁松泉：《中国崛起与中美关系》，中国社会科学出版社，北市，2005.

倪健民、陈子舜：《中国国际战略》， 人民出版社，北京市，2003.

潘志平：《中南亚的民族宗教冲突》，新疆人民出版社，乌鲁木市，2002.

王树增：《1901：一个帝国的背影》，海南出版社，海口市，2004.

肖迎：《维吾尔族》，云南大学出版社，昆明市，2004.

阎学通 、孙学峰:《中国崛起及其战略》，北京大学出版社，北京市，2005.

张蕴岭：《未来10-15年中国在亚太地区面临的国际环境》，中国社会科学
出版社，北京市，2003.

张西明：《新美利坚帝国》，中国社会科学出版社，北京市，2003.

周伟洲：《西北民族论丛》，中国社会科学出版社，北京市，2002.

铁木尔、毛公宁：《新疆研究文论选》，民族出版社，北京市，2003.

## Works in English

Bernstein, Richard, and Ross H. Munro. *The Coming Conflict with China*. New York: Vintage, 1998.

Bovingdon, Gardner. "Autonomy in Xinjiang: Han Nationalist Imperatives and Uyghur Discontent." Policy Studies 11. Washington, DC: East-West Center, 2004.

Brzezinski, Zbigniew. *The Grand Chessboard: American Primacy and its Geostrategic Imperatives*. New York: Basic Books, 1997.

Dietrich, William S. *In the Shadow of the Rising Sun: The Political Roots of American Economic Decline*. University Park, PA: Pennsylvania State University Press, 1991.

Dillon, Michael. *Xinjiang: China's Muslim Far Northwest*. New York: RoutledgeCurzon, 2004.

Dwyer, Arienne M. *The Xinjiang Conflict: Uyghur Identity, Language, Policy, and Political Discourse*. Policy Studies 15. Washington, DC: East-West Center, 2005.

Flanagan, Stephen J., and Michael E. Marti (eds.). *The People's Liberation Army and China in Transition*. Washington, DC: National Defense University Press, 2003.

Frum, David, and Richard Perle. *An End to Evil: How to Win the War on Terror*. New York: Ballantine, 2004.

Gellner, Ernest. *Nations and Nationalism*. Ithaca, NY: Cornell University Press, 1983.

Guillermaz, Jacques. *The Chinese Communist Party in Power, 1949–1976*. Translated by Anne Destenay. Boulder, CO: Westview Press, 1976.

Gurtov, Mel, and Byong-Moo Hwang. *China's Security: The New Roles of the Military*. Boulder, CO: Lynne Rienner Publishers, 1998.

Huntington, Samuel P. *The Clash of Civilizations and the Remaking of World Order*. New York: Simon & Schuster, 1997.

Jacques, Martin. *When China Rules the World: The End of the Western World and the Birth of a New Global Order*. New York: Penguin Press, 2009.

Johnson, Chalmers. *Blowback: The Costs and Consequences of American Empire*. New York: Metropolitan Books, 2001.

Kagan, Robert. *Of Paradise and Power: America and Europe in the New World Order*. New York: Vintage Books, 2004.

Kissinger, Henry. *Does America Need a Foreign Policy: Toward a Diplomacy for the 21st Century*. New York: Simon & Schuster, 2002.

———. *On China*. New York: Penguin Press, 2011.

Liu, Alan P. L. *Mass Politics in the People's Republic: State and Society in Contemporary China*. Boulder, CO: Westview Press, 1996.

Massonnet, Philippe. *The New China: Money, Sex, and Power*. Translated by Hannah Taïeb. Boston: Tuttle Publishers, 2000.

Millward, James A. "Violent Separatism in Xinjiang: A Critical Assessment." *Policy Studies* 6. Washington, DC: East-West Center, 2004.

Needham, Joseph, Ling Wang, Gwei-Djen Lu, and Ping-Yu Ho. *Clerks and Craftsmen in China and the West: Lectures and Addresses on the History of Science and Technology*. Cambridge, England: Cambridge University Press, 1970.

Reischauer, Edwin O. *Japan, Past and Present*. New York: Knopf, 1964.

Rosenbaum, Arthur Lewis. *State and Society in China: The Consequences of Reform*. Boulder, CO: Westview Press, 1992.

Shenkar, Oded. *The Chinese Century: The Rising Chinese Economy and its Impact on the Global Economy, the Balance of Power, and Your Job*. Upper Saddle River, NJ: Pearson Education, Inc.—publishing as Wharton School Publishing, 2006.

Starr, S. Frederick. *Xinjiang: China's Muslim Borderland*. Armonk, NY: M.E. Sharpe, 2004.

Swaine, Michael D. *The Military and Political Succession in China: Leadership, Institutions, Beliefs*. Santa Monica, CA: RAND Corporation, 1992.

Williams, William Appleman. *The Tragedy of American Diplomacy*. New York: Norton Paperback, 1972.

# INDEX

Dr. Lionel Vairon, CEO of CEC Consulting, holds a PhD degree in Vietnamese Studies (Mention Political Science) from the Institut National des Langues et Civilisations Orientales (INALCO) in Paris, and master's degrees in Chinese language and culture and in Political Science. He was a journalist with the Groupe Jeune Afrique (1985–1989), an official with the French Ministry of Foreign Affairs, and a diplomat stationed in Asia and the Middle East (1985–1989, 1991–2002). He worked in the Arab Office of the Delegation on Strategic Affairs of the French Ministry of Defense (2003–2008), and has taught at the Université Paris 7, INALCO, at the Collège Interarmées de Défense, and at Hautes Études Commerciales de Paris (HEC Paris). He has been a lecturer at many institutions in France, China, and throughout the Arab world. He is currently a lecturer in the Institut des Hautes Études de Défense Nationale (France).

Today, Lionel Vairon heads his own consulting company, CEC Consulting, which specializes in strategy, geopolitics, intercultural exchanges, and prospective analysis for China, East Asia, the Middle East, and Sub-Saharan Africa. He is a regular guest speaker at China Executive Leadership Academy Pudong (CELAP) and in various Chinese and Arab think tanks.

The company also trains leading officials in the public and private sectors in Europe and in China, in particular.

He has published numerous research articles on international relations, and, in 2009 published this book entitled *China Threat?* (中国的威胁) in Chinese with the People's Daily Press.

CPSIA information can be obtained at www.ICGtesting.com
Printed in the USA
BVOW03s1039130914

366179BV00007B/17/P

9 781627 740890